AF378290

Heimskringla:
An Interpretation

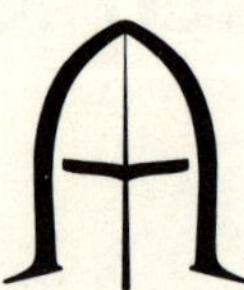

MEDIEVAL AND RENAISSANCE
TEXTS AND STUDIES

VOLUME 483

Heimskringla:
An Interpretation

by Birgit Sawyer

ARIZONA CENTER FOR MEDIEVAL

ACMRS

AND RENAISSANCE STUDIES

Tempe, Arizona
2015

THE ARIZONA CENTER FOR
MEDIEVAL &
RENAISSANCE
STUDIES

Published by ACMRS (Arizona Center for Medieval and Renaissance Studies)
Tempe, Arizona
© 2015 Arizona Board of Regents for Arizona State University.
All Rights Reserved.

Library of Congress Cataloging-in-Publication Data

Names: Sawyer, Birgit, author.
Title: Heimskringla : an interpretation / by Birgit Sawyer.
Description: Tempe, AZ : ACMRS Arizona Center for Medieval and
Renaissance
   Studies, 2015. | Series: Medieval and Renaissance texts and studies ;
   Volume 483 | Includes bibliographical references.
Identifiers: LCCN 2015040026 | ISBN 9780866985383 (alk. paper)
Subjects: LCSH: Snorri Sturluson, 1179?-1241. Heimskringla. | Sagas--History
   and criticism. | Iceland--History--To 1262.
Classification: LCC PT7278 .S39 2015 | DDC 839/.61--dc23
LC record available at http://lccn.loc.gov/2015040026

Cover Art:
Kringlublaðið (c. 1258–1264)
Lbs fragm 82
National and University Library of Iceland
Public domain

∞
This book is made to last. It is set in Adobe Caslon Pro,
smyth-sewn and printed on acid-free paper to library specifications.
Printed in the United States of America

Jakob Benediktsson in memoriam

TABLE OF CONTENTS

Preface

Much has been written about Snorri Sturluson's *Heimskringla*, why yet another book about it? When I wrote my doctoral thesis on Saxo Grammaticus, the same question was put to me about *his* work: *Gesta Danorum*. The answer was and is: if one does not agree with earlier interpretations and is convinced that they are deficient—even misleading—new analyses are needed.

According to most earlier interpretations of *Gesta Danorum*, Saxo, commissioned by Archbishop Absalon, was a propagandist for policies on which King Valdemar I and Absalon were agreed. Further, Saxo has been thought to glorify kings, especially Valdemar I and his son Knud, and to faithfully have fulfilled his patron's intentions, expressing the "official values" of his time. My own analysis of Saxo's work led to quite contrary results: in *Gesta Danorum* we often witness how the interests of Valdemar and Absalon clash; there is no glorification of kings, ancient or contemporary, and, even if Absalon often overshadows Valdemar, Saxo also raises serious questions about his patron. Far from forwarding the "official values" of his time, Saxo is actually *opposing* them in subtle ways:[1] Instead of official values we should rather talk about *issues of conflict;* for Valdemar I it was important not only to legitimize his rule and line, but also to unify Denmark, establish hereditary kingship and strengthen royal power. For Absalon ecclesiastical aims were a priority, above all to establish the right of women to inherit and to consent to marriage.

How are such contrary interpretations of a work possible? The answer is that Saxo mastered the art of ambiguity; while he explicitly says one thing, he can imply another (even contrary) thing. The tension between these two levels in his text had not been properly studied, but once discovered, it cried out for closer study. The question whether Saxo was expressing the views of a specific social group is impossible to answer; we ought rather to see him as a man of independent ideas who needed support and protection. His work had to be acceptable to both secular and ecclesiastical powers, and in a rapidly changing world he had to ride several horses at the same time. His situation was, indeed, similar to that

---

[1] Birgit Sawyer, "Valdemar, Absalon and Saxo. Historiography and Politics in Medieval Denmark," *Revue Belge de Philologie et d'Histoire,* 63 (1985), 685–705.

of his hero, Hamlet, who was forced by circumstances, to dissemble.[2] In order to escape suspicion and to survive, Saxo—like Hamlet—had to conceal his own thoughts and opinions, and in doing so elevated ambiguity to a fine art.

After reading my thesis on Saxo, the Icelandic scholar Jakob Benediktsson urged me to "do the same thing with Snorri Sturluson." I have at last done so and here offer my interpretation of *Heimskringla*. Already when studying Saxo, I wondered whether Snorri Sturluson was as sophisticated. They were almost contemporaries; Snorri created his history only shortly after Saxo, and both had access to the same sources.

According to received opinion, *Heimskringla* is a compilation of Sagas of Norwegian kings from their mythical origin to Magnus Erlingsson. Snorri's "impartiality" is often emphasized, with some allowance for bias in favour of Icelandic heroes. Although all kings are not favourably portrayed, Snorri is nevertheless thought by many to have been a loyal supporter of Norwegian kingship, all the more so, since he was King Håkon Håkonsson's man and had promised to forward Norwegian interests in Iceland.—My analysis suggests a very different interpretation.

For many years I have been able to try my ideas in teaching, especially in Trondheim (NTNU), and in discussions with the many graduate students and colleagues, whose judgements I sincerely trust. Here in Uppsala I have been invited to give lectures on my ongoing work with *Heimskringla* for university seminars, run by e.g., "ENES" (Early Northern European Seminar) and "Isländska Sällskapet." For valuable comments and help in preparing my various articles on the topic (see References, below) I especially want to thank Theodore M. Andersson, Heimir Pálsson, and above all, Claus Krag and Sveinbjörn Rafnsson, both of whom have read and commented on earlier versions of the manuscript for this book. Without their constructive criticism and support, I would not have managed to complete this project, the aim of which is to encourage a lively discussion. Last, but not least, I want to thank my husband Peter, who has had to share me with Snorri for a long time, contributed with many useful ideas and never failed to ecourage me!

---

[2] Cf. Kurt Johannesson, *Saxo Grammaticus; komposition och världsbild i* Gesta Danorum (Stockholm, Almqvist & Wiksell, 1978).

Explanatory Notes

Icelandic name forms are used for prehistoric times; thereafter Scandinavian (mostly Norwegian, sometimes Swedish and Danish), and British equivalents are used for both people and places, see "Concordances". Other deviations from Hollander's translation are:

1. *Trøndelag* instead of "Trondheim", which today refers not to the district but to the city, earlier called *Nidaros*.
2. *Bóndi* (*bændr*) instead of "farmer/s", referring to yeoman/yeomen. The Old Norse *bóndi* signifies not only an agriculturist but an independent landowner, i.e. an important and influential man.

The chapter divisions in all editions and translations of *Heimskringla* are due to editors/translators, most probably not to Snorri himself (see ch. 1, section 4 and Conclusion). I use those adopted by Hollander:

The sagas in Heimskringla[1]	Abbreviations used here
1. Ynglinga saga	S. Ynglings
2. Hálfdanar saga svarta	S. Halvdan the Black
3. Harald's saga ins hárfagra	S. Harald Fairhair
4. Hákonar saga góða	S. Håkon the Good
5. Haralds saga gráfeldar	S. Harald Greycloak
6. Óláfs saga Tryggvasonar	S. Olav Tryggvason
7. Óláfs sasga Helga	S. Saint Olav
8. Magnúss saga ins góða	S. Magnus the Good
9. Haralds saga Sigurðarsonar	S. Harald Hardrade
10. Óláfs sasga kyrra	S. Olav the Gentle
11. Magnúss saga berfœtts	S. Magnus Barelegs
12. Magnússona saga	S. Magnus's sons
13. Magnúss saga blinda ok Haralds gilla	S. Magnus the Blind & Harald Gille
14. Haraldssona saga	S. Harald's sons
15. Hákonar saga herðibreiðs	S. Håkon the Broadshouldered
16. Magnúss saga Erlingssonar	S. Magnus Erlingsson

---

[1] Titles according to Íslenzk fornrit: *Heimskringla* I–III (Reykjavík, 2002).

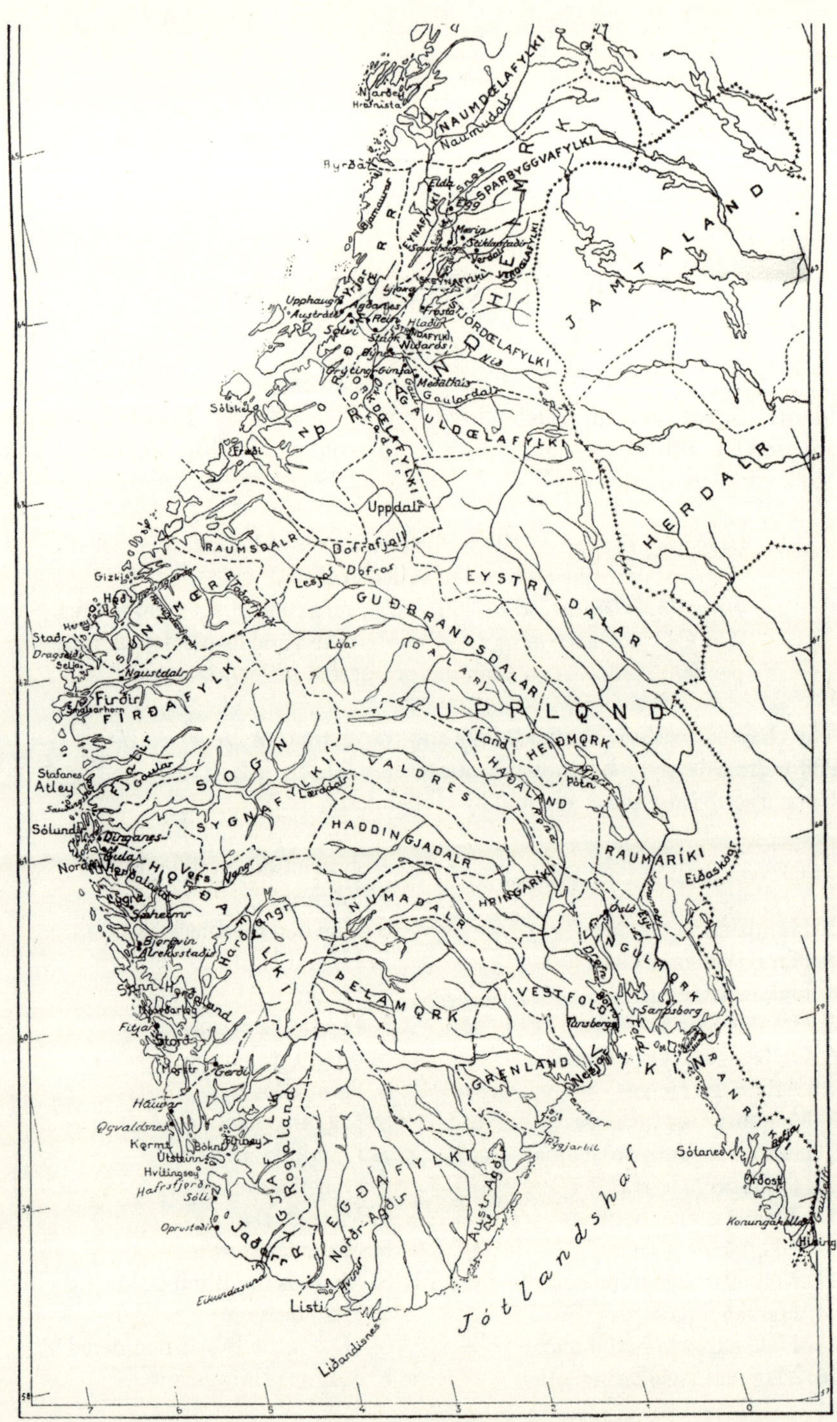

Southern Norway. Reproduced with permission from Hið íslenzka fornritafélag. *Heimskringla*.

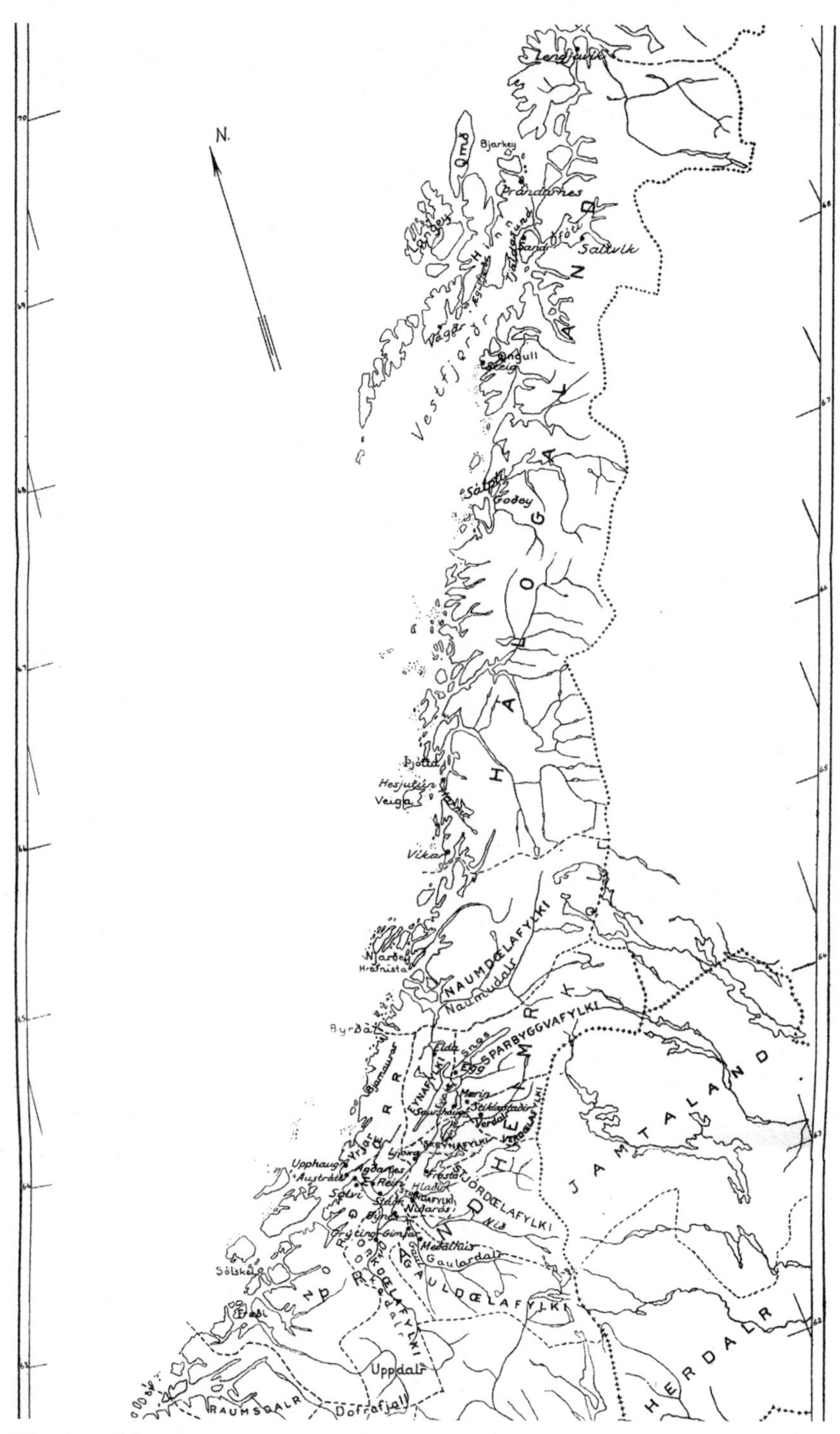

Northern Norway. Reproduced with permission from Hið íslenzka fornritafélag. *Heimskringla.*

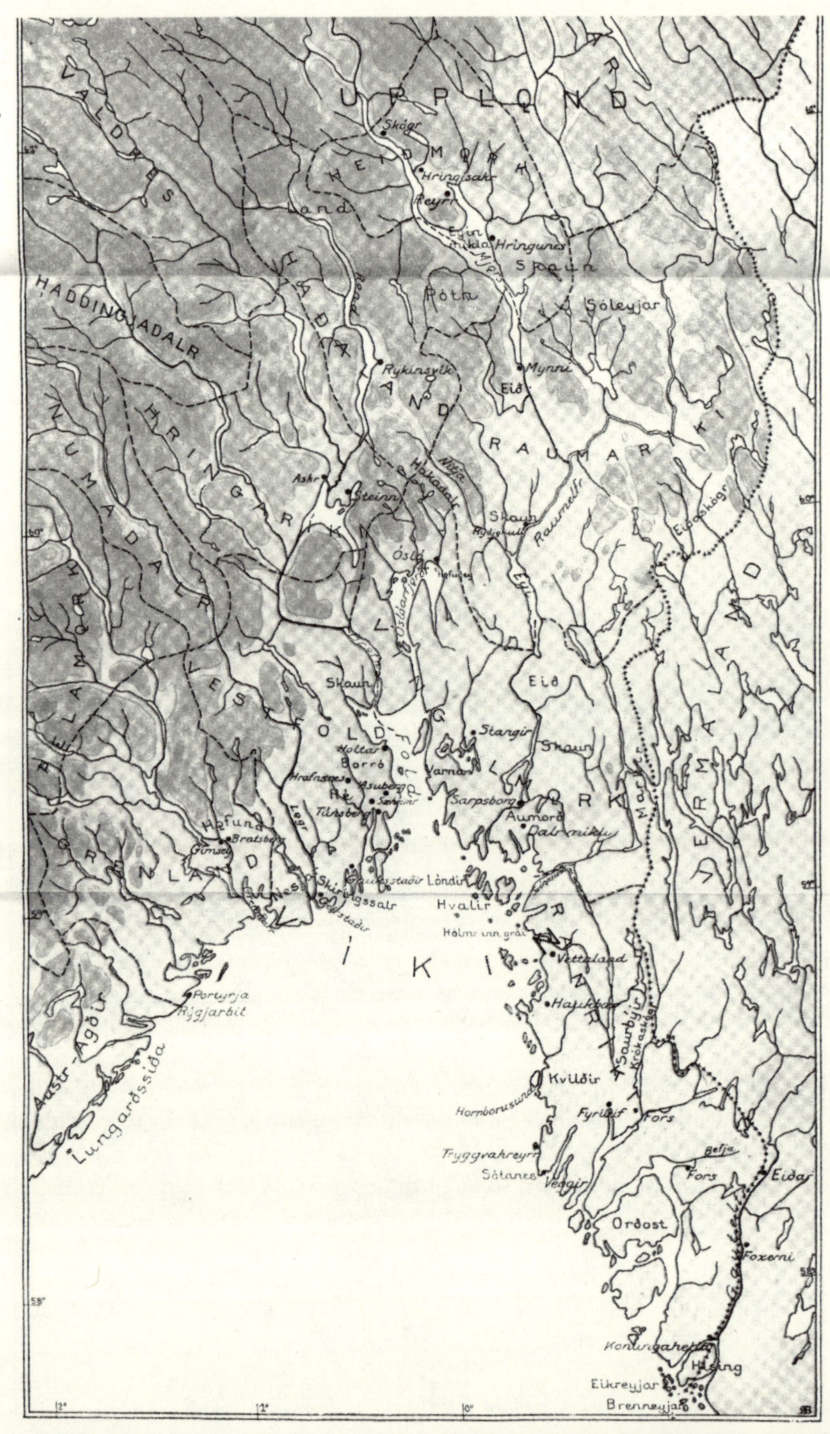

Viken and Opland. Reproduced with permission from Hið íslenzka fornritafélag. *Heimskringla*.

Chapter 1
Introduction

The aim of this book is to present a new interpretation of Snorri Sturluson's *Heimskringla*, based on its historical context and the way the author dealt with his material. In this chapter I will discuss the authorship and title of the work, its contents, relationship with contemporary accounts of the same period, and whether it is possible to discover the author's intentions. No survey of earlier research will be attempted, but relevant references will be given.[1] As a historian I use the critique of ideology, i.e., the analytical method that takes account of the historical, social, and cultural structures current when a text was written in order to discover their influence in shaping it.

All episodes in *Heimskringla* involve at least two people, and some involve many more. Discussions of Snorri's attitude to the leading characters in his narrative, and to many minor ones, require a review of his comments, explicit and implied, on each one. Repetition is, therefore, unavoidable, but rewarding.

Heimskringla, regarded as a masterpiece of medieval historiography, was written during the 1230s and is the last of several works dealing with Norwegian history before King Sverri's time (i.e., before 1177). Apart from the twelfth century works by Sæmund (now lost) and Ári's *Íslendingabók*, the oldest are Theodoricus Monachus's *Historia de antiquitate regum Norwagiensium* (ca. 1180), *Historia Norwegiae* (ca. 1180) and a brief collection in Old Norse: *Ágrip af Nóregs Konungasögum* (ca. 1190). Closer to *Heimskringla* in time are the other "synoptics," *Morkinskinna* (before 1220?) and *Fagrskinna* (1220s), which—like *Heimskringla*—deal with the whole period from King Halvdan the Black (ninth century) to 1177.

It is clear that Snorri used some of these works, as well as ca. 600 verses by more than seventy skalds. He refers to Ári in his prologue, and other works that can be identified as his sources include the now-lost *Hryggjarstykki* by Eirikr Oddsson, *Ágrip*, *Morkinskinna*, and *Fagrskinna*. Insofar as he copied from these

---

[1] In the following discussion, some readers may miss references to both older and more recent works on the subject, but my aim has not been to present yet another comprehensive research survey. For that I refer to Diana Whaley, *Heimskringla: An Introduction* (Viking Society for Northern Research, London 1991).

texts, he is not likely to have done so passively but—as other authors—used only what he could accept and what served his own interests and intentions.[2] An important question is why so many authors—within such a short period—dealt with the same period, if they had not intended to give *their own interpretations* of it. As Halvdan Koht expressed it "We know that the period when saga-writing flourished, was a time of dramatic changes, and I think it could be said that the changes themselves were an important reason why they were written at all." ("Vi veit jo at den tid da sagaskrivningen blomstret, det var en tidsalder med voldsomme samfundsbrytninger, og jeg tror ennog det tør sies, at selve brytningene hadde en vesentlig del i at sagaene i det hele blev skrevet."[3]

It has repeatedly been shown how important it is to have detailed knowledge of the historical background of literary works, in particular the situation when they were produced.[4] Historians in the past were not uncritical compilers who tried to preserve as much as possible for posterity but active debaters with their own purposes who—above all—wrote to influence their contemporaries. Their zeal was not to *preserve* but to *create* a memory of the past, a memory in accord with their own intentions.[5]

A historical work should be studied in its own context; indeed, the very existence—or lack of—history writing is in itself evidence. In Scandinavia it began in Denmark (c. 1100), to provide king and Church with a native saint. It flourished later, not only in Denmark but also in Norway and Iceland, a significant development, for it was then that royal power was consolidated in both Denmark and Norway after several years of civil war. The production of royal chronicles can thus be seen as a crisis symptom, a response to political reorganization and a reaction to the social and economic upheavals that followed. The authors present their own views on contemporary conflicts. In Denmark, Sven Aggesen served royal power and its adherents, while Saxo Grammaticus expressed the reaction of the Church and aristocracy.[6] In Norway, King Sverre himself and

---

[2] Cf. Gustav Indrebø, *Fagerskinna* (Oslo: Grøndahl, 1917), 124. Cf. also Hanne Monclair, "Snorre som historiker," *Dagbladet* 27/11 (2003).

[3] Halvdan Koht, "Sagaenes opfatning av vår gamle historie," *Innhogg og utsyn* (Kristiania: Aschehoug & Co., 1921), 77.

[4] E.g., Walter Goffart, *The Narrators of Barbarian History* (Princeton, N.J.: Princeton University Press, 1988); Ian Wood, "Christians and Pagans in Ninth-Century Scandinavia," *The Christianization of Scandinavia*, ed. Birgit & Peter Sawyer and Ian Wood (Alingsås: Viktoria Bokförlag, 1987); Ian Wood, *The Merovingian Kingdoms 450–751* (London & New York: Longman, 1994).

[5] Cf. Sverre Bagge, who maintains that Snorri wrote his sagas simply to mediate knowledge about the deeds of great men. See Sverre Bagge, *Society and Politics in Snorri Sturluson's* Heimskringla (Berkeley & Los Angeles: University of California Press, 1991), 202.

[6] Birgit Sawyer, "Valdemar, Absalon and Saxo. Historiography and Politics in Medieval Denmark," *Revue Belge de Philologie et d'Histoire*, 63 (1985): 685–705.

Ágrip give a royal view of the development, while Theodoricus presents the view of the Church, and the author of *Historia Norwegiae* the view of both Church and aristocracy. Snorri's immediate predecessors, the authors of *Morkinskinna* and *Fagrskinna*, present opposite views; *Morkinskinna* is characterized by Icelandic self-assertion and a predilection for an earlier period, free from the threat of Norwegian interference, while, in contrast, *Fagrskinna*, commissioned by King Håkon Håkonsson, clearly sides with kings, praising especially those who were strong and warlike—unlike *Morkinskinna* which praises peaceful kings.[7]

Thus, it must be expected that Snorri also took sides in contemporary conflicts. Of course, we will never know what he actually *meant*, but we can study the *effects* he achieves and so discover what his views probably were.

1. Authorship and the authorial point of view

The question whether it really was Snorri Sturluson who wrote *Heimskringla* has been hotly debated; in the nineteenth and early twentieth centuries, most scholars regarded Snorri as the author, working independently and critically,[8] but there were also those who who regarded him as merely a compiler.[9] In the second half of the twentieth century, the latter opinion was revived,[10] and in 1973 Michail Steblin-Kamensky denied that the concept of authorship existed in the medieval North. Thus—and in contrast to Halvdan Koht—he regarded it as pointless to look for a consistent authorial view of history in a work such as *Heimskringla*.[11] The role of individual authors has been toned down by the "new traditionalists" who emphasize the importance of oral tradition in the Icelandic sagas. The problem however, is how to discern between orally transmitted material and authorial use of it (evaluating, ordering, formulating). Different methods are be-

---

[7] See Theodore M. Andersson, "The Politics of Snorri Sturluson," *Journal of English and Germanic Philology* (1994): 55–78.

[8] E.g., P. A. Munch, *Det Norske Folks Historie* (Oslo: Chr. Tønsbergs Forlag, 1852–1859), 1032, 1040 ff.; Gustav Storm, *Snorre Sturlassons Historieskrivning* (Copenhagen: Luno, 1873), 1 ff., 77 ff. Halvdan Koht went even further, maintaining that Snorri gave his personal interpretation of the history he presented; see Koht, "Sagaenes opfatning," 76ff.

[9] P. E. Müller, *Undersøgelse om Kilderne til Snorres Heimskringla og disses Troværdighed* (Copenhagen; Det Kongelige Danske Videnskabernes Selskabs philosophiske og historiske Afhandlinger, 1823); Konrad Maurer, Über die Ausdrücke altnordische, altnorwegische und isländische Sprache (Munich: Verlag der K. Akademie, 1867), 51ff.

[10] Lars Lönnroth, "Tesen om de två kulturerna," *Scripta Islandica* 15 (1964): 83 ff.; Thorkil Damsgaard Olsen, "Kongekrøniker og kongesagaer," *Norrøn Fortællekunst*, ed. H. Bekker-Nielsen et al. (København: Akademisk Forlag, 1965), 68.

[11] Michail Steblin-Kamensky, *The Saga Mind* (Odense: Odense University Press, 1973), 61–62.

ing used to discover traces of orality in the texts, but they are far from reliable.[12] The Swedish scholar Tommy Danielsson traces it in the "objectivity" in the sagas, where quite often opposite views and opinions are expressed. [13]

What Danielsson interprets as objectivity is, however, a characteristic of the saga style, whose neutrality is very deceptive; already in the 1970s Lars Lönnroth argued that even if saga authors often give both sides of a story and seem to avoid expressing their own views, they still make their opinions evident *in less obvious ways*. These can be traced in their use of loaded adjectives, description of characters, and alleged judgments of the "people" or leaders, representing collective morality. [14] And, as Theodore Andersson puts it, "The contents of the stories was no doubt agreed on by many people, but the selection and ordering of the stories was left to the individual teller or writer who shaped them."[15]

The role of the author is still much debated (cf. the earlier combat between the doctrines of free-prose and book-prose!), but nowadays most scholars agree that if we bear the nature of medieval authorship in mind, we are fully justified to treat each text as stamped by its author's personal views. One characteristic of medieval authors is that they often worked in collaboration not only with their scribes but also with lay patrons and/or clergy, and another is that they were unlikely to express their opinions directly. Further, as Diana Whaley points out, "The individual text is not so much a fixed entity as a stage in a process, for in an age before printing every manuscript can be anything from a near-exact copy to a brand-new work, with all kinds of revised editions in between."[16] In my opinion the first characteristic could actually give more weight to the tendencies found in a work, since they are likely to have been shared by others, but the second makes the original author somewhat elusive. Since we seldom can analyze the original texts but have to deal with—sometimes much younger—copies, our conclusions about authorial intentions can never be anything but tentative.

Nowadays most scholars agree that Snorri Sturluson is the author of *Heimskringla*, but it is still hotly debated what role Snorri had in its creation.[17] There is no consensus about this; some regard him as both author and editor, others as

---

[12] Carol Clover, "Icelandic Family Sagas," *Old Norse-Icelandic Literature; A Critical Guide* (Ithaca & London: Cornell University Press, 1985), 279–94. See also Gísli Sigurdsson, *The Medieval Icelandic Saga and Oral Tradition: A Discourse on Method* (Cambridge, Mass.: The Milman Parry Collection of Oral Literature, 2004).

[13] Tommy Danielsson, *Sagorna om Norges kungar; från Magnús godi till Magnús Erlingsson* (Uppsala: Gidlunds förlag, 2002).

[14] Lars Lönnroth, "Rhetorical Persuasion in the Sagas," *Scandinavian Studies* 42 (1970): 157–89.

[15] Theodore Andersson, *The Growth of the Medieval Icelandic Sagas (1180–1280)* (Ithaca & London: Cornell University Press, 2006), 19.

[16] Whaley, *Heimskringla: An Introduction*, 19.

[17] See, e.g., Whaley, *Heimskringla: An Introduction*, 13–19.

merely editor, and still others, including Jonna Louis-Jensen, as author but not final editor.[18] Sverre Bagge regards Snorri as "an author with definite ideas as to what to include and what not, and both able and willing to make bold reconstructions and rearrangements in his sources in order to create a coherent history."[19]

We will probably never know for certain what the true answer is, but I agree with Louis-Jensen and Jon Gunnar Jørgensen that Snorri is most probably *not* responsible for the final form of *Heimskringla*[20] and with Sverre Bagge that he worked as a modern author in reconstructing and rearranging his sources.[21] I find it difficult, however, to accept his claim that Snorri did not think of the past as qualitatively different from the present.[22] On the contrary: there can be no doubt that Snorri was fully aware that conditions were changing; he drew a sharp line between pagan and Christian times, and the fact that social and political rules are presented as very much the same in the past and in his own time cannot be taken as evidence that he viewed society as 'static'.[23] Here it will be argued that he had his own good reasons for depicting society in this way.[24]

Snorri´s own text is not preserved, but we have some more or less complete fourteenth-century manuscripts, and—fortunately—a fragment of *Kringla* from *c.* 1260, which contained the whole work (the rest was destroyed by fire in Copenhagen University Library 1728).[25] Thanks to Ásgeir Jónssons careful transcript (made between 1688 and 1704), we can come close to the original. The justified criticism[26] against conflating manuscripts of disparate dates in order to represent a single "original" text does not really apply to *Heimskringla*, since the transcript of *Kringla* is the main basis for most editions.[27] Scholars also agree that the disagreements between the manuscripts are mainly of a minor and predict-

---

[18] Jonna Louis-Jensen argues that there is more to indicate that it was not Snorri who wrote *Heimskringla* in its final form. She does not deny that Snorri may have written the text but questions that he put it together into a chronological work of history. See *Senter for høyere studier; informasjonsblad nr. 2, (2002) 6–7.*

[19] Bagge, *Society and Politics in Snorri Sturluson´s Heimskringla*, 57.

[20] Jon Gunnar Jørgensen, *Ynglingasaga etter Kringla* (Oslo: Unipub Forlag, 2000), iv.

[21] Bagge, *Society and Politics*, 61.

[22] Bagge, *Society and Politics*, 6.

[23] As Bagge does; ibid., 230–231.

[24] A clear indication that Snorri did not see human nature and society as static is the fact that in *Hkr*, most strong and independent women as well as all magic and sorcery disappear after the Christianization of Norway—which was how it *should* be but was, of course, not really the case!

[25] The fragment consists of a leaf that was stolen by the Swedish agent Jón Eggertsson before the fire in Copenhagen. See *KHL* IX (1964), cols. 287–288.

[26] See Patricia Pires Boulhosa, *Icelanders and the Kings of Norway: Medieval Sagas and Legal Texts* (Leiden & Boston: Brill, 2005), 21–31.

[27] Diana Edwards Whaley, "Heimskringla," *Medieval Scandinavia: An Encyclopedia,* ed. Philip Pulsiano (New York & London: Garland), 276.

able kind.[28] We must, however, keep in mind that all manuscripts have their own value, as they were intended for specific audiences. It is particularly important to take account of the situation when *Kringla* was written, ca. 1260.[29]

The authorial point of view

The saga style is apparently "objective" in the sense that the authors remain in the background and seldom comment on what they relate. For a long time, this hindered attempts to look for biases and tendencies in sagas, but the conviction that there are subjective points of view in them was first presented by Halvdan Koht in his *Innhogg og Utsyn* (1921). Though at first resisted, this view was widely accepted by the mid-1960s. The question now is how to discover the author's own opinions.

One answer has been given by Sverre Bagge, who divides the contents of the sagas in *Heimskringla* into three categories: (1) "scenes" and narrative; (2) short summaries and Snorri's comments; and (3) speeches and dialogues. He considers categories 2 and 3 more likely to contain value judgments and personal opinions than category 1, but emphasizes that the narrative (with its "scenes") does not contain "neutral" information; it contains only a small selection of all that took place, arranged and reworked. Nevertheless, Sverre Bagge regards the narrative as "a test case" for the conclusions drawn from the rest.[30]

This method, however, does pose problems that can be illustrated by Bagge's own analysis of the reasons for St. Olav´s fall, in which categories 2 and 3 are represented by

(2) Olav as the *rex iustus,* who met strong opposition from the magnates, and King Knud's gold that tempted magnates to join him.

(3) The Danish bishop Sigurd´s speech that, according to Bagge, gave a "fairly adequate summary of Olav´s career as already told by Snorri, though he evidently intends the speech to present it from a distorted perspective."[31]

Even though Bagge has stated that he considers categories 2 and 3 most likely to reveal Snorri´s personal opinions, he now dismisses them by stating that Snorri´s explicit explanations (cat. 2) are "conventional phrases with scant importance for the work as a whole,"[32] and (cat. 3) that Snorri here allows the adversary of his hero to present his case.[33] Instead, he now puts more trust in the narrative (cat.1),

---

[28] Ibid., 277.

[29] Cf. Andersson, "The Politics of Snorri Sturluson," 78.

[30] Ibid., 63.

[31] Ibid., 67.

[32] Ibid., 66.

[33] Ibid., 67.

which, he claims, makes it "clear that the opposition to Olav is not the expression of a fundamental conflict of interest between monarchy and aristocracy, but the result of a series of conflicts between the man Olav and individual members of the aristocracy."[34]

Bagge here undermines his own method. In the first place, his interpretation is highly questionable. The description of Olav as a *rex iustus* is not a "conventional" phrase "with scant importance for the work as a whole"; on the contrary, Snorri elsewhere shows his appreciation of rulers who distinguish between high and low status, as well as his opposition to those who treat everyone in the same way. Nor can Knud´s gold be explained away so lightly; in *Heimskringla* we encounter other rulers who buy adherents in this way. As far as cat. 3 ("speeches") is concerned, Bishop Sigurd´s speech against Olav is not necessarily due to Snorri´s greatmindedness in letting an enemy have his say; it is more than likely that Snorri sympathizes with Sigurd and has put his *own* words in the bishop´s mouth.[35] Finally, the *narrative* itself (cat. 1) can be interpreted in different ways; Snorri's explanation of Olav's fall as the result of conflicts between the *man* Olav and *individual members* of the aristocracy does not necessarily mean that he *regards* the conflicts as personal. It could reflect his refusal to accept the king as essentially different from other magnates. This was an ideological opposition to contemporary royal claims. As we shall see, Snorri´s description of most kings in *Heimskringla* reflects his opposition to strong royal power.

A more reliable method of finding the authorial point of view is to compare what Snorri says explicitly with what he implies. Throughout *Heimskringla,* we find a contrast between these two levels, which makes the text highly ambiguous and open to different interpretations. Personal views, be they appreciation or criticism, were best conveyed by implication, and analyses of the tensions between direct and indirect meaning can guide us to Snorri´s own opinions.

2. Title and contents

We do not know what Snorri himself called his work; the manuscript *Kringla* takes its name from the opening words: *Kringla heimsins* ("the circle of the world"), but the title *Heimskringla* is later.[36] Other medieval texts have such titles as *Konunga bók, Ævi, Sogur,* or *Bók Nóregskonunga.*[37] Most modern translations of *Heimskringla* use equivalents to the English "Kings Sagas" in the title or sub-

---

[34] Ibid., 67.

[35] See Chapter 4 below.

[36] This title was first used in Johann Peringskiöld's edition (Stockholm, 1697). See more in Bjarni Adalbjarnarson's editions, Íslenzk fornrit 26 (1941), V and Íslenzk Fornrit 28 (1951), 468.

[37] Íslenzk Fornrit 28, 276.

title and thereby lead the reader to expect exactly that. As will be shown, however, it is much more.

It is important to be cautious about the titles of medieval texts, for they are often misleading. Despite its title *Historia ecclesiastica gentis Anglorum* Bede's history does not deal with the English people and their church but about the *Northumbrian church and its leaders*. It is especially dangerous when a work has become known under a title which its author did not intend; so, for example, *Historia Francorum* by Gregory of Tours is not a history of the Franks but a manual on the Christian faith—the title is a later invention.[38] We do not know what Saxo Grammaticus called his work; the title *Gesta Danorum* is a later invention; judging from its contents, it is a "King's mirror," a manual of statecraft, not a history of the deeds of the Danes.[39]

What is Heimskringla *about?*

Norwegian kings do have a prominent role in *Heimskringla*, but so do others, not least magnates (secular and ecclesiastical), land-owning *bœndr*, and their wives and female relatives.[40] In his preface, Snorri says that he has written down "old accounts about the chieftains (*höfðingjar*) who had dominion in the North," among whom we find not only the kings of Norway but also other rulers: local/regional kings, earls, landed men, and military leaders; and throughout *Heimskringla* the focus is on *the relationship between them*. Some of the magnates overshadow contemporary kings, notably Earl Håkon, Erling Skjalgsson, Einar Tambarskjelve, Gregorius Dagsson, and Erling Skakke. More attention is paid to them than to some Norwegian kings. Although we also meet magnates and usurpers who are anything but virtuous, the conclusion that can be drawn is that Snorri did not write a royal panegyric but measured the morality of kings and their subjects on the same scale.

Thus, in *Heimskringla*, kings are not essentially different from magnates; neither they nor their opponents seem to fight for special ideas, and the conflicts seem to be between individuals who seek personal gain. So far I agree with Sverre Bagge, but *not* with his conclusion that the picture Snorri gives of society and politics contributes to our knowledge of Snorri´s society "as it actually

---

[38] Goffart, *The Narrators of Barbarian History*, 112–234. See also Ian Wood, *The Merovingian Kingdoms 450–751*, 24–32. The original title of Gregory's work is *Decem Libri Historiarum*.

[39] Kurt Johannesson, *Saxo Grammaticus; Komposition och världsbild i Gesta Danorum* (Stockholm: Almqvist & Wiksell, 1978; B. Sawyer, "Valdemar, Absalon and Saxo," 685–705.

[40] And—to a lesser degree—sorcerers and sorceresses (in the first part of the work).

was."[41] Why then did Snorri represent society and politics as he did? This raises the question of why he wrote *Heimskringla*, a question that has been answered in different ways.

3. Why did Snorri write Heimskringla?

It was probably the first king's saga, *Sverri's Saga* (written c. 1185–1200), that triggered the production of history works, first the Norwegian and then the Icelandic synoptics *Morkinskinna*, *Fagrskinna*, and *Heimskringla*, the two latter ending with the year Sverri became king (1177).

For many generations of scholars, *Heimskringla* was the most important source of knowledge about early Norwegian history. For centuries the information Snorri gave was regarded as historical truth, but since the early twentieth century source criticism has abandoned this view. According to Halvdan Koht, the struggle between monarchy and aristocracy that earlier scholars had seen throughout *Heimskringla* was invented by Snorri, interpreting the past in the light of contemporary developments, above all the conflict between King Sverre and the aristocracy.[42] Koht´s reinterpretation of both Snorri and other saga writers has had a great impact on historians but met with opposition from some philologists and literary historians.[43] Most scholars, however, accept Sture Bolin's judgment that in medieval histories "contemporary conditions are seen in the light of those in the past and past conditions in the light of contemporary ones."[44]

Sverre Bagge thinks that Koht went too far and regards him guilty of anachronism in transferring modern ideas of historical development and political conflicts to the Middle Ages: "The idea of the aristocracy as a class fighting the monarchy as an institution may therefore very well turn out to be the result of Koht´s and other modern historians´ reading of Snorre."[45] Instead, Bagge argues that Snorri wrote his sagas to record and make known the achievements of great men in order to equip future politicians with instructive examples.[46] If so, one wonders what use Snorri´s contemporaries made of these *exempla* in a society where the rules of the political game were changing so radically. It is Bagge, not

---

[41] See Bagge, *Society and Politics*, 1 and passim. See also Birgit Sawyer, "Samhällsbeskrivningen i Heimskringla," (Norwegian) *Historisk Tidsskrift* (1993): 223–37; and Sverre Bagge, "Samfunnsbeskrivningen i Heimskringla; svar til Birgit Sawyer," (Norwegian) *Historisk Tidsskrift* (1994): 205–15.

[42] Koht, "Sagaenes opfatning."

[43] E.g., Hallvard Lie, *Studier i Heimskringlas stil* (Oslo: Skrifter utgitt av Det norske vitenskapsakademi i Oslo, II. Historisk-filosofisk klasse 1936, no. 5,1937), 120–1.

[44] Sture Bolin, *Om Nordens äldsta historieskrivning* (Lund: Lunds universitets årsskrift, 1931), 229.

[45] Bagge *Society and Politics*, 65.

[46] Ibid., 202, 231.

Koht, who is guilty of anachronism, underestimating medieval authors and their audience.

In his interpretation of *Heimskringla*, Theodore Andersson compares *Heimskringla* with *Morkinskinna*, which he thinks is different from other kings sagas thanks to its Icelandic assertiveness. He suggests that *Morkinskinna* may have been intended to counteract the new danger posed by King Sverre's dynasty, by recalling an earlier era of cordial relations between the Icelanders and Norwegian kings without the threat of Norwegian intervention.[47] To Andersson, *Heimskringla* represents "a royalist readjustment" in comparison with *Morkinskinna*; while in the latter, peaceful monarchs dedicated to domestic policy are set against warrior kings "of more questionable character" engaged in foreign exploits. Andersson does not find that contrast in *Heimskringla* and concludes that it seems clear that "Snorri set about neutralizing the opposition and softening the original critique of the foreign adventures."[48]

I cannot agree with Andersson; instead of neutralizing the opposition and critique in *Morkinskinna*, Snorri is even more critical. While Andersson emphasizes the Icelandic assertiveness in *Morkinskinna*, Ármann Jakobsson focuses on other features, above all its courtliness: "it is a saga about a society in which court plays no less a role than the kings and [. . .] its stage is vast, colourful and civilized."[49] In its lively descriptions of towns, great houses, castles, feasts, and games, however, we also hear about assaults and fights. The author is interested not only in exotic stories about distant countries but also in private life, and Jakobsson characterizes *Morkinskinna* as a "harbinger of a new age."[50] Jakobsson's analysis complicates the traditional contrast made between *Morkinskinna* and *Fagrskinna* by suggesting that they were both intended to suit the taste of Håkon Håkonsson, who, in the 1220s, had several works of courtly literature translated into Norwegian.

Comparisons between the kings' sagas composed between the 1190s and the 1230s are indeed very fruitful, and in this field much more needs to be done. Why, in the first place, were so many versions of the same stories written in Latin and Old Norse after *c.* 1170? And why were three different compilations, dealing mainly with the same period, written in Iceland within such a brief period (10–15 years)? More detailed analyses are needed, but it may reasonably be suggested that they were all, in some measure, written in response to the many fundamental changes that were occurring then, in particular to express approval

---

[47] *Morkinskinna: The Earliest Icelandic Chronicle of the Norwegian Kings (1030–1157)*, translated with Introduction and Notes by Theodore M. Andersson and Kari Gade (Ithaca & London: Cornell University Press, 2000), 58, 71.

[48] Andersson, "The Politics of Snorri Sturluson," 71.

[49] Ármann Jakobsson, "En plats i en ny värld. Bilden av riddarsamhället i Morkinskinna," *Scripta Islandica; isländska sällskapets årsbok* 59 (2008): 27–46.

[50] Ibid., 46.

or disapproval of growing royal power. This hypothesis explains why they were no longer written in Denmark and Norway when royal power was firmly established and why historical writing began so much later in Sweden, where royal power continued to be weak and disputed throughout the Middle Ages. It also explains why the main production was in Iceland, where the new order meant submission to the Norwegian king, a development that was vigorously resisted by some Icelanders.[51]

While *Fagrskinna*, written for Håkon Håkonsson and his court,[52] praises strong and warlike kings, *Morkinskinna* praises peaceful kings, the "builders" and "lawmakers." According to Theodore Andersson, the author of *Morkinskinna*, "displays a thematic nervousness about Norwegian kings," infusing the sagas with "undertones of impending loss."[53] In light of this, it might be tempting to interpret *Heimskringla* as simply a compromise between the two earlier compilations and their tendencies, but *Morkinskinna*'s interest in Norwegian courtly life casts doubts on its "Icelandic assertiveness," and I agree with Patricia Pires Boulhosa, who argues against Andersson's view of the Norwegian king as a haunting threat to the Icelanders and their submission as a catastrophe:

> . . . Icelandic submission—for all that it shocked Icelandic scholars from the seventeenth to the nineteenth century—was not a sudden, radical change which was brought about by the Icelanders' political ineptitude and poverty (and therefore an isolated, lamentable fact). On the contrary, the Icelanders' decision to submit to the power of the Norwegian king was part of a process comprising negotiations between them.[54]

Snorri was, after all, not the only person to pay homage to a Norwegian king; *Heimskringla* has many examples of other Icelanders having done so earlier, and in his own time an increasing number of chieftains did the same.

Thanks to his own writings (most probably including *Egils saga*) we know that Snorri had his own agenda, and he was less concerned with the relationship between Iceland and Norway than that between the "aristocracy" (in both countries) and the central power, King and Church. In order to learn about Snorri's purposes, we have to consider the political situation during his lifetime (see Chapter 3).

---

[51] Birgit and Peter Sawyer, "Adam and the Eve of Scandinavian History," *The Perception of the Past in Twelfth-Century Europe*, ed. Paul Magdalino (London & Rio Grande: Hambledon Press, 1992), 37–51.

[52] Indrebø, *Fagerskinna*, 280.

[53] Theodore M. Andersson, "The King of Iceland," *Speculum* 74 (1999): 923–34. Quotations from pp. 927, 934.

[54] Boulhosa, *Icelanders and the Kings of Norway*, 212.

4. Composition

The invented title *Kings' Sagas* not only distracts attention from other important protagonists in Snorri's history, but it also tends to reinforce the conviction *that the division into separate kings' sagas* is original. We do not know, however, how Snorri divided his text; the division in later manuscripts and modern editions raises many questions.[55] Only the saga about Saint Olav forms a natural unity. In other sagas, less attention is paid to kings than to others, most obviously in Olav Tryggvason's saga, where Earl Håkon as well as his sons, the earls Eirik and Svein, figure prominently. We meet Einar Tambarskjelve already in Harald Greycloak's saga, and then he figures prominently in both Olav Tryggvason's and Saint Olav's sagas, in which Erling Skjalgsson is also an important actor. In the sagas about the sons of Harald and Håkon the Broadshouldered, Erling Skakke and Gregorius Dagsson are key figures, and in Magnus Erlingsson's saga, the real main figure is his father Erling Skakke. The fact that the same king is sometimes described in two or more sagas confirms the suspicion that the saga-division and the saga-titles were made by someone other than Snorri.[56] There is much to indicate that Snorri did not intend to write separate biographies but—like the author of *Morkinskinna*—episodic narratives, into which he wove different strands (*Þættir*). Intertwined with other stories we find comprehensive stories about some kings' opponents, for example, Earl Håkon, Sigurd Slembedjakn, Erling Skjalgsson and Einar Tambarskjelve. Snorri's fascinating portrait of Gunnhild (Eirik Bloodaxe's widow) is spread over no fewer than five sagas, and there are several other portraits of important people, not least Icelandic heroes, who oppose the kings' wishes.

The way an author begins his work is also revealing, because it strikes the tone for what follows. Saxo Grammaticus begins his history emphasizing how the first Danish king was *chosen*, while his contemporary Sven Aggesen begins his by stressing how the Danish kingdom was originally *hereditary*. By beginning his history with a long description of the Amazons, allegedly of Gothic origin, Jordanes sets the tone for his work: in his—ironic—perspective all Goths are on equal footing with the Amazons, i.e., in their generation of power they have behaved in an unnatural way, and in relation to the—manly—Romans they represent female submission and dependence, which is accentuated at the end of the work, where a Gothic woman and a Roman man are united in marriage.[57]

---

[55] See ch. 8: "The division into chapters."

[56] So, for example, we meet Magnus the Blind in three different sagas, Harald Gille in two, and Håkon the Broadshouldered in three.

[57] Walter Goffart, "Jordanes and His Three Histories," in Goffart, *The Narrators of Barbarian History*, 20–111.

Thus, the fact that Snorri begins his work with *Ynglingasaga* is significant (see Chapter 3).

A basic rule of narratology is to pay close attention not only to the beginning of texts but also to their *middle* and *end*, but if we want to trace an author's intentions, this is not possible if we do not have the original or a full copy of it. Since it is highly probable that Snorri was not responsible for the version of *Heimskringla* that has been preserved, we can only discover the intentions of later editor(s). Snorri undoubtedly meant *The Saga of the Ynglings* to begin his work, and the year 1177 to be the end, as did his predecessors. What Snorri meant to be the middle, however, we do not know, although the saga about Saint Olav seems to be the oldest (based on Snorri's earlier "Separate Saga") and constitutes in many ways a climax. In Chapter 3 the beginning and end of *Heimskringla* (*The Saga of the Ynglings* and *Magnus Erlingsson's Saga*) will be discussed in more detail. The next chapter is devoted to the historical background of *Heimskringla* and its main contents.

5. Principles used in the analysis

Snorri — like Saxo and many other classical and medieval authors — had learned the paradigmatic technique of using *exempla*, i.e., using scenes to illustrate an ideal or its opposite.[58] According to Livy, what made the study of history salutary and fruitful was that one could learn from all kinds of examples and choose what was worth imitating — and what ought to be avoided. Collections of *exempla* were translated in both Norway and Iceland early; Gregory's *Dialogues* into Norwegian already in 1150 (preserved in an Icelandic manuscript from *c.* 1200), and Sveinbjörn Rafnsson has shown that *Disciplina Clericalis* by Petrus Alfonsi was used, e.g., in *Egils saga*.[59]

How, then, can we know what standard(s) Snorri used? In dealing with older texts there is always the risk of being anachronistic; the values of a medieval author are, of course, not the same as ours. It is necessary, therefore, to declare my principles in analyzing Snorri's narrative. Like most late antique and medieval authors, he must have been familiar with the classical and Christian teaching of cardinal virtues,[60] the heavenly virtues, and the deadly vices.[61] At the same time, he must also have been influenced by Old Norse ideals, most of which in fact correspond to classical and Christian ones. There are, however, some significant differences.

---

[58] Johannesson, *Saxo Grammaticus.*

[59] *Saga* 30 (1992), pp. 81–121. I am grateful to Sveinbjörn Rafnsson, who has drawn my attention to the use of *exempla* in Icelandic literature.

[60] presented already by Plato and Aristotle. See also *KHL* IV (1959), cols. 97–8.

[61] Used by the early Church Fathers.

The four cardinal virtues[62]
Prudentia   (prudence, wisdom, eloquence)
Justitia   (justice, honesty, generosity)
Temperantia   (temperance, "the golden mean," moderation)
Fortitudo   (strength, both physical and psychological, courage)

The seven heavenly virtues		*The seven deadly sins/vices*	
Castitas	(chastity)	Luxuria	(lust, desire)
Temperantia	(temperance)	Gula	(gluttony)
Caritas	(charity)	Avaritia	(greed)
Industria	(diligence)	Tristitia	(sloth)
Patientia	(patience)	Ira	(wrath)
Humanitas	(kindness, friendliness)	Invidia	(envy, selfishness)
Humilitas	(humility, reverence)	Superbia	(pride, irreverence)

Old Norse ideals[63]

Many of the Old Norse ideals correspond to the classical/Christian ones, not least the principle of "the golden mean" (*aurea mediocritas, temperantia*). *Fortitude* is illustrated by people who are described as courageous and strong (including athletic strength), *prudence* by people who are wise and/or eloquent, and *iustitia* by those who are law-abiding, generous and honest. The opposites of these cardinal virtues also figure prominently in *Heimskringla*, where we find strong people using their strength in the wrong way, imprudent people, being undecided or ignoring good advice, unjust and deceitful people breaking laws, and uncontrolled people being wrathful and cruel.

Most of the seven heavenly virtues are also praised by Snorri, even though chastity, charity, and humility are seldom illustrated. Conversely, he is critical of people who show the opposite characteristics, i.e., people who are proud, unruly, ruthless, and imperious. It is impossible to know what Snorri himself thought about chastity, but it is worth noting that—in contrast to the kings—the magnates he respects are described as having had only one wife.

Some of the ideals Snorri admires, however, do *not* correspond to the classical/Christian ones; so, for example, *honour* plays a very important role in his world, as something to be defended and fought for. He also admires people who are handsome and—in accordance with advice given in the *Poetic Edda*—show *distrust*, are *cautious, cunning*, and *untruthful* when necessary. My conclusion is

---

[62] Discussed by Plato and Aristotle, later included in Christian teaching.

[63] Described in the *Poetic Edda* (*Sæmundar Edda*); see Peter Hallberg, "Eddic Poetry," *Medieval Scandinavia: An Encyclopedia*, ed. Philip Pulsiano (New York & London: Garland, 1993), 149–52.

that Snorri's standards were a mixture of Old Norse and classic/Christian traditions, and I will use them in the following analysis of his work.

How are kings measured?

According to Snorri, *good kings are those who cooperate with the people, i.e., the magnates.* In *Heimskringla* we meet only a few: Håkon the Good, Magnus the Good (after Sigvat the Skald's warnings!), Øystein Magnusson, Harald Gille, and — to a certain degree — Inge Haraldsson. As will be shown in Chapters 4 and 5, Snorri gives several examples of magnates and skalds giving advice to kings — more or less successfully. Two examples of successful advisers, however, that are not dealt with in these chapters are, therefore presented here:

In the first, Asbjørn of Medalhus made King Håkon the Good yield to his advice; on behalf of the Frostathing Assembly he opposed King Håkon's request that all should let themselves be baptized. Asbjørn refers to the pagan faith of their forefathers, which — he says — had served them very well, and he threatens to abandon King Håkon, if he does not "observe moderation and ask only that of us which we can give you and which is within reason." After that, King Håkon was persuaded by Earl Sigurd to give up his attempts to force Christianity on the *bœndr*.[64]

Another example of a king yielding to a magnate is the Swedish king Olof Eriksson, who had serious conflicts with the Norwegian king Olav Haraldsson. In a Swedish assembly, the Norwegian messenger Bjørn the Marshal told the Swedish king that he had been sent to Sweden for the purpose of offering him peace "and that boundary which has from of old been between Norway and Sweden." The Swedish king refused to listen to Bjørn, and when his own earl, Ragnvald, also advised him to make peace with the Norwegian king, he was furious. He reproached the earl bitterly and called him guilty of high treason against himself, but then Torgny the Lawspeaker arose, and all the *bœndr* with him. Torgny reminded the Swedish king of his predecessors, first Erik Emundsson, who had subjected many lands in the east and always took advice from important men, then King Bjørn and King Erik the Victorious, who increased the Swedish dominion and were both easy to approach with advice. In contrast to those kings, Torgny accused King Olof as a king who:

> lets no one presume to talk to him except about what he himself wants done; and on that alone he is intent, but lets lands tributary to him defect from him through his lack of energy and enterprise. He has the ambition to keep the dominion of Norway in his power which no other Swedish king

---

[64] S. of Håkon the Good, chaps. 15–16; *Heimskringla, History of the Kings of Norway by Snorri Sturluson*, translated with Introduction and Notes by Lee M. Hollander (Austin: University of Texas Press, 1977), 109. Hereafter: Hollander.

ever coveted before, and that causes trouble to many. Now it is the will of us farmers that you make peace with Olav the Stout, the king of Norway, and give him your daughter Ingigerth in marriage. Now if you intend to regain those lands in the east which your kinsmen and forbears have possessed there, then we shall all follow your leadership to do so. But if you will not do as we say, we shall set upon you and kill you, and not tolerate from you lawlessness and hostility. That is what our forbears did: at the [Mórathing][65] they plunged five kings into a well because they were swelled up with the same arrogance as you show against us. Say now right quickly what you decide to do.

Clashing their weapons together and making a great din, the people showed their approval of Torgny's speech. Then the king arose and promised to follow their will in all matters.[66]

It is clear that Asbjørn and Torgny—as well as Sigvat the Skald—have Snorri's sympathy; they express the conditions under which the magnates are prepared to obey their kings. As will be shown (in Chapters 4 and 5), other magnates tried to advise kings, sometimes with success, sometimes in vain. Those kings who do not take advice are negatively described, and, in contrast to them, the earls of Lade are always presented in a very positive way. Why? Since the earls were the agents of Danish kings, this is remarkable; Snorri is, after all, pro-Norwegian and anti-Danish. The explanation seems to be that the earls, deeply rooted in the class of Norwegian magnates, kept Danish royal power at a distance (before 1030). This obviously echoes the relationship that Icelandic magnates wished to have with the Norwegian kings, a system with internal control, distanced from, but in cooperation with, royal power in Norway.[67]

---

[65] In Snorri's text it is "Múlathing," which has been interpreted as "Mórathing," the assembly near Uppsala (in Sweden).

[66] S. Olav's Saga, ch. 80; Hollander, 318–21.

[67] I am grateful to Claus Krag, who has drawn my attention to the roles of Asbjørn of Medalhus and Torgny the Lawspeaker, and to the relevance of Snorri's positive attitude towards the earls of Lade.

CHAPTER 2
HISTORICAL BACKGROUND[1]

In the 1220s Snorri set out to write *his* version of what had led to the political situation in his own time. This was a major task, starting with the formation of Norway, Norwegian expansion, the building of the Icelandic "state," Christianization and establishment of church organization, development of towns and trade, and the growth of central power, both royal and ecclesiastical. What does he emphasize, what does he pass over quickly, and what does he ignore? What does he explicitly say he intends to do?

In his preface Snorri declares that he has written about "the chieftains who had dominion in the North," and with "chieftains" we are to understand not only kings (native and foreign) of different kinds but also *hersir* (regional leaders), earls, and magnates of various importance. Thus, whatever Snorri wanted his history to be called, it is clear that he did not write only about the Norwegian kings.

Reading both Snorri and his contemporaries often leaves us confused by what is meant with the different titles they use. Authors writing in Latin use such titles as *rex*, *regulus* ("petty king"), or *dux*, which makes it difficult to know what reality lies behind them. Snorri seems to give us *some* help in his *Skáldská-parmál*, where he says (ch. 50):

> It is also normal for a king who has tributary kings under him to be called king of kings. An emperor is highest of kings, but after him any king who rules over a nation is indistinguishable in all kennings from any other king in poetry. Next are the people that are called earls or tributary kings, and they are indistinguishable in kennings from a king, except that those that are tributary kings must not be called national kings.[2]

---

[1] See *The Cambridge History of Scandinavia*, vol. I: *Prehistory to 1520*, ed. Knut Helle, (Cambridge: Cambridge University Press, 2003): Claus Krag, "The early unification of Norway," 184–201; Knut Helle, "Towards Nationally Organised Systems of Government," 345–352. See also Birgit Sawyer & Peter Sawyer, "The Making of the Scandinavian Kingdoms," *Die Suche nach den Ursprüngen; von der Bedeutung des frühen Mittelalters*, ed. Walter Pohl (Wien: Verlag der Österreichischen Akademie der Wissenschaften, 2004), 261–70.

[2] *Snorri Sturluson Edda: New Complete Translation by Anthony Faulkes* (London & Melbourne: Everyman's Classic Library, 1987), 128. From "Skáldskaparmál" in *Edda*

The period c. 870–1177

Thus, in *Heimskringla* we encounter both "overkings" (kings of "nations") and "underkings" (tributary kings/earls). The English word *nation*, however, is misleading; before the ninth century, there were no "nations" in the modern sense, so the Norse word *ríki* is better translated as "realm." The normal pattern in early medieval northern Europe was a plenitude of small kingdoms, whose rulers from time to time attached themselves—or were forced to submit—to a powerful king, who thus became their overlord. The power of an overlord was personal—not territorial—and lasted only during his lifetime; after his death, his "underkings" were free to make new alliances. This kaleidoscopic character of fluctuating power centers with their satellites has often been overlooked in later times and, instead, been described as the "unification" of what—much later—developed into territorial and stable kingdoms.

In early medieval Scandinavia, it was not unusual for Norwegian and Swedish rulers to submit to Danish kings and act as their agents. In the late tenth and early eleventh centuries, for example, Svein Forkbeard was acknowledged as overlord by the Norwegian earls of Lade and by the Swedish king Olof ("Skötkonung," i.e., tributary king), son of Erik the Victorious.

Danish hegemony

From the eighth century (and probably earlier), much of Scandinavia was under the hegemony of the Danes, partly because of their strategic position—between the Baltic and the Atlantic, an area controlled by the rulers of Jutland. One of their main concerns was to protect Jutland from incursions by Saxons, Slavs, Frisians, and Franks, and to do that they constructed, extended, and maintained a barrier known as Danevirke (west of Schlei Fjord). One of these rulers, Godfred, was so powerful that he was considered to be a serious threat by Charlemagne. Godfred's hegemony extended well beyond Danish territories: he was acknowledged as overlord over Vestfold (west of Oslo Fjord) and presumably also by rulers along the coast east of Kattegat (which now belongs to Sweden). The Frankish annals (*Annales Regni Francorum*) report that after Godfred had been assassinated in 810, the "princes and people" of *Vestfold* refused to submit to his successors but were defeated. Vestfold probably continued for a while to be under

---

Snorra Sturlesonar: "Rétt er ok um hann konung, er undir honum eru skattkonungar, at kalla hann konung konunga. Keisari er æðstr konunga, en þar næst er konungr sá, er ræðr fyrir þjóðlandi, jafn í kenningum öllum hverr við annan í skáldskap. Þar næst eru þeir menn, er jarlar heita eða skattkonungar, ok eru þeir jafnir í kenningum við konung, nema eigi má þá kalla þjóðkonunga, er skattkonungar eru." This is not really helpful, since we do not know the older titles of these different rulers; Snorri simplifies and uses contemporary titles.

Danish overlordship, but by the end of the century the Danes were weakened by internal conflicts that enabled Harald Fairhair, a king in west Norway, who claimed to be an "Yngling," to create an independent hegemony in Norway.

Danish power was, however, restored by Harald Gormsson ("Bluetooth"), king 958–987, who claimed on his great runic monument in Jelling that he had "won all Denmark and Norway." He and his successors Svein (king 987–1014) and Knud (king 1019–1035) were acknowledged as overlords by the most powerful Norwegian ruler, Hákon Sigurdsson, earl of Lade, and his sons Svein and Eirik. Danish hegemony was interrupted by Olav Tryggvason (995–999/1000) and Olav Haraldsson (1015–1028), both supported by English rulers who sought to counteract Danish influence in Scandinavia. After Olav Tryggvason's death, Svein Forkbeard took over Norway and put it under the Norwegian earls Eirik and Svein, and after Olav Haraldsson's death at Stiklestad (in 1030), Knud the Great imposed direct rule by installing his son Svein as *king* of Norway.

"Norway"

But what was "Norway"? The name literally means "the North Way," i.e. the sea-route along the coast, the control of which was the aim of many Norwegian rulers. When Danish power diminished during the ninth century, one of them, traditionally known as Harald Fairhair, king in Sogn, succeeded in expanding his power southwards over Hordaland, Rogaland, Telemark, and Agder, the core area of his kingdom. More loosely attached were the petty kingdoms in Møre and Trøndelag. He looked for kingship models in England and sent one of his sons, Hákon, to be fostered by the English king Adalstein. After Harald's death—and the recovery of Danish influence in Norway—this first (known) attempt to unify a large part of the "North Way" failed. As mentioned above, new attempts to conquer and unify the same areas were made by Olav Tryggvason and Olav Haraldsson, who through their subjugation and Christianization of both these and vast inland areas laid the ground for the medieval kingdom of Norway, a territorial unit under an undivided royal power.

The Christian conversion of rulers was probably the most important factor in the consolidation of the Scandinavian kingdoms. The Church brought many benefits. The clergy were literate and members of an international organization based on written law that, by the twelfth century, had a relatively elaborate machinery to implement it. They emphasized the role of kings as upholders of justice and encouraged them to act as law-makers. What is more, the Church played an important part in determining the limits of the three kingdoms. At first, the whole of Scandinavia was under the archbishopric of Lund in Denmark (from 1104), but this changed in the middle of the twelfth century, when the newly established archiepiscopal provinces were, in effect, precursors of medieval Norway and Sweden (1152/3 and 1164). The province of Nidaros included Iceland, Greenland, and other Atlantic islands that had been colonized by Norwegians, although it was one hundred years before Iceland and Greenland were incorporated into the kingdom. Similarly, the Swedish archbishopric of Uppsala included the bishopric of Åbo in southwest Finland, some decades before that diocese was incorporated into the Swedish kingdom. The province of Uppsala, by joining the two Götaland sees with the three in Svealand, was an important factor in unifying these two original components of the kingdom. The provincial councils summoned by archbishops or papal legates were, indeed, the first national councils in both Sweden and Norway.[3]

The consolidation of the Norwegian kingdom took more than three hundred years to complete and was accomplished in two main phases. During the first phase, the kingdom had its roots in the coastal districts, and King Olav Haraldsson (Saint Olav) was the first to succeed in extending the royal power over most of the country (1015–1028). Between 1028 and 1035, however, Danish kings had authority over large parts of Norway, especially over Viken (the Oslofjord area). After that, Norwegian kings maintained control over the whole country, and for a few decades during the eleventh century, King Magnus Olavsson ("the Good") and Harald Sigurdarsson ("Hardrade") were on the offensive against the Danes. A period of relative stability followed, but after King Sigurd Jerusalemfarer's death in 1130, "civil wars" broke out.[4] These were not confined to Norway; they broke out at the same time in Denmark and Sweden, and among the reasons for this was rivalry between claimants to the thrones, who had allied with supporters in the neighbouring countries, not only in Scandinavia but also in Poland and Russia.[5] An important reason was the fact that legitimacy was not yet a prerequisite for being chosen as king, and as a result several sons of royal concubines succeeded in having their claims accepted. In Denmark, no fewer than five of King Svein Estridsen's illegitimate sons ruled after him, and, in 1134, after Niels, the last of them, wars between rivals and their adherents broke out in Denmark. While King Svein's sons ruled successively in Denmark, in Norway there were sometimes two or more kings who *shared* the kingship (based in different parts of the country), a symptom of the lack of real political unity.

These wars — the second phase of the unification process — ended with King Sverri's victory and full control over large parts of Norway. What remained was Østlandet, over which Sverri's grandson king Hákon Hákonsson gained control in the 1220s.

The earliest Norwegian monarchy was a result of conquest, based on the personal presence and skills of the kings themselves. A stable kingdom, however,

---

[3] Sawyer and Sawyer, "The Making of the Scandinavian Kingdoms," 268–69.

[4] The wars are conventionally called "civil wars" but were, in fact, wars of succession.

[5] See Birgit Sawyer, "The 'Civil Wars' revisited" (Norwegian) *Historisk Tidsskrift* 82 (2003): 43–73.

required much more: political organization and a common ideology, independent of the king's person. Instead of relying on voluntary cooperation with strong-willed—and often unreliable—magnates, Olav Haraldsson seems to have been the first king who tried to control the regional aristocracy. He appointed stewards (ármenn) on his estates all over the country and made leading landowners "landed-men," giving them an income from royal land in return for their service.

A common ideology was provided by the Church; kings, notably Olav Tryggvason and Olav Haraldsson, supported missionaries, had churches built, and provided for their maintenance. During the eleventh and twelfth centuries, many more churches were built, creating a valuable infrastructure. King and Church benefited mutually; in return for his support, the clergy helped the king to increase his power, and they provided him with their competence in reading and writing and—not least—their experience of advanced organization and international contacts.

Another factor promoting a stable kingdom was people's need for peace, law and order. A naval levy (*leidang*) was formed in the coastal areas (beginning already in the tenth century). As military leaders and upholders of the law, the kings contributed to the organization of law "things" (*lagting*), i.e. representative institutions for larger regions, functioning as the highest judicial assemblies. The oldest were "Gulating" (in Vestlandet), "Frostating" (in Trøndelag), and later "Borgarting" and "Eidsivating" (in Østlandet). There were also smaller—and older—general assemblies of all free men that continued to function locally in towns as well as in the country.

Last, but not least, administrative, ecclesiastical, and military bases were needed, and the kings contributed to the establishment of new—as well as the development of old—towns, thus promoting trade and crafts. From before the year of 1000 we hear about Nidaros, Borg (Sarpsborg), and Oslo; during the eleventh century Konghelle and Bergen; and somewhat later Hamar and Tønsberg. Of these towns, Oslo, Bergen, Stavanger, and Hamar were episcopal sees under the archbishop, who resided in Nidaros.

Snorri Sturluson, his life and career

We also need to know about Snorri himself and his own time. He was born in 1178/79 into the family of the *Sturlungar* but was brought up in another family, the *Oddaverjar* at Oddi, the Icelandic centre of learning, by the chieftain Jón Loptsson. Thanks to scattered information from bishops' sagas, annals, letters, skaldic verses, and—above all—data given by his nephew Sturla Thordarson in his *Íslendingasaga*, we know more about Snorri than about most contemporary authors.[6]

Snorri had a remarkable career, not only as a writer of sagas, composer of verse, and preserver of poetry and mythology but also as a chieftain, lawspeaker, and statesman. The political organization in Iceland was modelled on patterns that Norwegian emigrants had brought with them when settling there in the ninth century. Power was divided between a number of *goðar* i.e. lords of men, not of territory, whose authority was exercised in assemblies ("things"), where they were supported by their thingmen. The lordships were known as *goðorð*, and their number was gradually reduced—most often by conquest or marriage alliances—until by 1220 only five families controlled all the *goðorð* in Iceland. By marrying Herdis Bersadóttir, Snorri acquired the farm of Borg and the associated *goðorð*. He then obtained, by gift and purchase, most of the *goðorð* in that area and, as a result, had extensive power in western Iceland. In 1206 he moved to Reykholt and began to play a leading role in Icelandic politics. He was elected lawspeaker (an almost presidential position) in 1215, went to Norway in 1218, and returned in 1220. By then he and his brothers were the most powerful chieftains in northwest Iceland. In 1222 he was again elected lawspeaker and soon afterwards married the richest woman in Iceland, Hallveig Ormsdottir of Breidabolstaður (in the south). In this way he gained control of the Rangar district and many valuable farms in different parts of the country, including Bessastaðir, later the residence of the Norwegian—later Danish—king's governor and now Iceland's president. Snorri attempted to extend his power further by arranging marriages for his three daughters with some of the few remaining major Icelandic chieftains. Such an extension of power naturally excited jealousy and incited some people to look for ways to check Snorri's dominance. Two of his sons-in-law divorced their wives and became Snorri's enemies.[7]

Personally, Snorri seems to have shunned violence, cherishing an ideal of peace that was, however, difficult to maintain. Diana Edwards Whaley describes him in the following way:

> He figures variously as a reconciler, an equivocator, or a coward. His practical sense and legal expertise were often put to the service of his friends, but often used in deviously self-promoting ways; and where legal means failed, he did not flinch from inciting others to violence.[8]

---

[6] Diana Edwards Whaley, "Snorri Sturluson," *Medieval Scandinavia; an Encyclopedia*, ed. Phillip Pulsiano (New York & London: Garland, 1993), 602–3.

[7] Birgit Sawyer & Peter Sawyer, *Medieval Scandinavia: from Conversion to Reformation circa 800–1500* (Minneapolis: University of Minnesota Press, 1993), 179–80.

[8] Whaley, "Snorri Sturluson," 602–3.

By sending praise poems to Norwegian kings, Sverri, the leader of the Birchlegs, and Hákon, Snorri courted the favor of other rulers in Scandinavia, which he visited twice. During his first visit he stayed with the lawspeaker of West Götaland, learning about the political situation in Sweden. His main aim, however, was to make closer contact with the Norwegian court; he spent two winters with Earl Skule, regent to the young king Hákon Hákonsson, receiving the title of landed-man and great gifts. In return he promised to persuade the Icelanders to accept Norwegian rule.[9]

It is remarkable that—in the middle of all his activities—Snorri found time to write as much as he did. It was probably during the—relatively—peaceful period between 1220 and 1230 that he composed his *Prose Edda,* his separate *Olavs saga helga,* most of *Heimskringla,* and most probably *Egils saga.*

Norway and Iceland during Snorri's lifetime

After Iceland was included in the newly created archdiocese of Nidaros (1153), Norwegian intervention in Icelandic affairs increased rapidly. The old order, with *goðar* owning and managing the churches, was now threatened, and Bishop Thorlákr tried, in vain, to dispossess them of their church properties. In 1179 Thorlákr received a stern letter from Archbishop Eystein, addressed to the *goðar,* banning those who kept concubines, but again Thorlákr fought in vain. Even after having gone into exile, Archbishop Eystein continued to regulate Icelandic affairs: in 1189 ecclesiastics were forbidden to carry weapons, and in 1190 he forbade consecration of *goðar* to ecclesiastical offices. The result was that the Icelanders ceased to endow the Church in their wills. Further, the Archbishop continued to demand Church jurisdiction over its own men, but that was not obeyed either. In 1209 Icelandic *goðar,* among them Snorri's brother Sighvat and his nephew Sturla, banished Bishop Gudmund from Hólar and killed some of his men. After thirteen years Gudmund could return to Hólar, only soon to be driven away again. Neither the Skálholt bishop Páll nor the priests supported Gudmund, since they were loyal to the *goðar,* who refused to give up their old rights. Since they did not dare to kill Gudmund, whom they regarded as a counterpart to Thomas Becket,[10] they held him prisoner for the rest of his life. During Gudmund's time (he died in 1237), the Icelandic leaders plundered Church property, scorned Church rituals, and desecrated relics. It was in this atmosphere that many of the sagas were written, and, as Björn Thorsteinsson puts it: this "disrespect for the church has contributed to a certain freedom from prejudice in the literature."[11] All this must deeply have influenced Snorri's attitude to the

---

[9] Ibid.

[10] Thomas Becket, Archbishop of Canterbury, who was killed on royal command, was canonized in 1173.

[11] Björn Thorsteinsson, *Island,* (København: Politikken Forlag, 1985), 78.

central Church and its reforming zeal. His own foster father Jón Loptsson, as well as his nephew Sturla, had been among the principal targets of the archbishop, and as a *goði* himself, he had rights to defend.

Under King Sverre (1177–1202), the Icelandic *goðar* had followed the king's example in their independence from the Church, and after his death they had been able to mind their own business during the turbulent period that followed in Norway. As early as during the last part of the twelfth century, however, a new royal ideology began to gain ground, according to which the throne should be inherited and the king regarded as God's representative on earth, ruling on his behalf. When King Hákon Hákonsson was of age (ca. 1220), it was clear that a new era had begun, an era with close cooperation between royal power and Church, the intention being to introduce the new ideology and strengthen central power. In many different ways, Snorri demonstrates his opposition to this development.[12]

There were also other serious disturbances in Icelandic society: towards the end of the twelfth century, the Icelanders became more and more dependent on foreign trade,[13] and this gave rise to internal conflicts in which the royal power interfered on behalf of the Norwegian merchants. As a lawspeaker, Snorri supported Norwegian rights, but—contrary to his promise to support King Hákon's claims in Iceland he is said to have done little for that cause. Commercial peace was restored, but in the internal power struggle, Snorri made many enemies: in 1237 he had to flee from Iceland to Norway.

Knowing that King Hákon Hákonsson was dissatisfied with him (for not having kept his earlier promise), Snorri went to Earl Skule, who was in conflict with the king. Resenting the king´s reduction of his power Skule, took the title of king two years later.[14] What followed is well known: after defeating Skule (who was later killed by "Birchlegs" in Helgeseter monastery), King Hákon deemed Snorri a traitor and demanded that he be sent to Norway or killed. Snorri's enemies, led by his former sons-in-law, had him killed at Reykholt in 1241.

History is usually written "backwards," which makes it easy to see that Snorri had backed the wrong horse. If, instead, we try to study his policy "forward," it is easier to understand his actions. During his life, chaotic conditions prevailed in Norway; after King Sverri´s death in 1202 there were several kings in succession,

---

[12] Birgit Sawyer, "Snorri Sturluson's Two Horses," *Vi skall alla vara välkomna. Nordiska studier tillägnade Kristinn Jóhannesson* (Göteborg: Meijerbergs institut för svensk etymologisk forskning, 2008), 37–53.

[13] By then, Icelandic shipping had practically come to an end, mainly due to the lack of timber for building and repairing ships.

[14] In 1237, king Hákon had dispossessed him of his one-third of Norway and replaced it with the income from a third of the *sysler* (administrative districts) in the whole country.

a civil war between "Birchlegs" and "Bagler," a division of the kingdom between 1204 and 1217, when King Sverri´s grandson Hákon Hákonsson (then only thirteen years old) was chosen king with his rival Skule as his earl. Under Sverri the Icelandic *goðar* had followed his example in their disregard for the Church, and after his death they had been able to fend for themselves during the turbulent period that followed in Norway. When, however, king Hákon came of age, it became clear that a new era had begun, an era with strengthening of central power. A new royal ideology was gaining ground, according to which the throne should be inherited, and in 1240 (before his victory over Skule), king Hákon designated his son Hákon Unge (the young) as his successor, an important step towards hereditary kingship. This development began in Norway during the second half of the twelfth century together with the idea of the king as God´s representative on earth, ruling on his behalf. Under Sverri royal power increased immensely, and with Hákon strong kingship had the full support of the Church in creating an effective central government. Snorri demonstrates his opposition to this development in many ways.

Chapter 3
The Beginning and End of *Heimskringla*

The main purpose of this chapter is to argue that Snorri's decision to begin *Heimskringla* with *Ynglingasaga* and end it with "Magnus Erlingsson's saga" was a clear signal that his purpose was to disparage most Norwegian kings. The fact that *Ynglingasaga*, which incorporates and elaborates the poem *Ynglingatal* (= the enumeration of the Yngling kings),[1] is only known in *Heimskringla* suggests that Snorri composed it. The Yngling kings are listed by Ári at the end of Íslendingabók and, with some additional details, in *Historia Norwegiae* (1180–90). Claus Krag, however, has pointed out that the poem, only recorded in *Heimskringla*, cannot have been the source of the list of Ynglings in *Historia Norwegiae*; if earlier versions existed, they have not survived. The poem *Ynglingatal* is based on a king *list*, not a genealogy, but both Ári and the author of *Historia Norwegiae* treat it as a genealogy of the kings who ruled Norway in the twelfth century, and so does Snorri.

The beginning of *Heimskringla*

In Snorri's *Ynglingasaga*, the Ynglings first became Norwegian kings in Vestfold, but according to *Historia Norwegiae*, their original base was in Opland (*in montanis*), not on the coast, and in *Nóregs Konungatal* (from c. 1190), based on information from Sæmund,[2] they first ruled an unnamed realm in the east that Harald Fairhair inherited from his father, together with a West-Norwegian realm (Sogn) that he inherited from his maternal grandfather. With the help of *Af Upplendinga konungum* (preserved in *Hauksbók* from c. 1300, but probably much older),

---

[1] There is a *Þáttr* of the poem in "*Af Upplendingakonungum*" in *Hauksbók* about the last so-called Norwegian Ynglings with some comments about them. See Claus Krag, *Ynglingatal og Ynglingesaga; en studie i historiske kilder* (Oslo: Universitetsforlaget, 1991), 13.

[2] In a poem, dedicated to Jon Loptsson, Sæmund's grandson. The author of *Fagrskinna* used information from it; see *Fagrskinna: A Catalogue of the Kings of Norway*, translated by Alison Finlay (Leiden & Boston: Brill, 2004), 41–52.

Claus Krag has traced the gradual transfer of the Ynglings' origin from the east of Norway south to Vestfold, a transfer that is fully developed in *Heimskringla*.[3]

These changes in the Yngling tradition reflect contemporary developments in Norway.

The Danish hegemony

Danish hegemony over southern Norway from the end of the eighth century was only interrupted for short intervals (995–999/1000 under Olav Tryggvason and 1015–1028 under Olav Haraldsson). After Olav Haraldsson's death in 1030, Knud the Powerful tried to impose direct rule by installing his son Svein as king of Norway, but five years later, when Olav Haraldsson's son Magnus had been brought home from his exile in Russia, Svein was forced out of the country. Danish kings continued to claim their right to rule parts of Norway, however, especially Viken.

When the first Scandinavian archbishopric was established in Lund in 1104, Danish influence increased, since both the Norwegian and the Swedish churches were subordinated to the Danish archbishops. Fifty years later (1153/54), Norway escaped Lund's primacy with its own archbishopric established in Nidaros, but already in the 1160's, the magnate Erling Skakke had to pay homage to the Danish king Valdemar I as his earl of Viken. Erling Skakke's submission to Valdemar I must have been a serious setback, but Norwegian independence of Danish control was maintained in different ways.[4] It was in this situation that the need for a special genealogy of Norwegian kings became acute. In order to refute Danish claims to old rights in Norway, especially in Vestfold, the Norwegian genealogy began in the east: Svitjod (Sweden), proving that the Norwegian kings had their own proud lineage (during pagan times) from the important center of Uppsala. Vestfold as the starting point for the formation of Norway was thus directed against Danish claims.

It is in this world of ideas that sagas about the Ynglings, their "genealogy" and Swedish origin, become of great immediate interest, and a poem about them is presented by Snorri to prove that Norwegian kings had long established claims to Vestfold. In the sagas, Harald Fairhair is thus made a king over Vestfold, despite the fact that his "unification" had its origin in Sogn and only comprised western Norway.

---

[3] Claus Krag, *Ynglingatal og Ynglingasaga*, 143–72.

[4] In "Hendingsgang og tidrekning i kongstida til Magnus Erlingsson 1161–1177" (Norwegian) *Historisk Tidsskrift* 40 (1960–61), 232–59, Halvdan Koht shows that in the 1160s, King Valdemar's influence over Norway was much stronger than the sagas imply.

Snorri's additions to *Ynglingatal*

The tradition that *Ynglingatal* mediates, the ancient claims of the Norwegian kings to rule Vestfold, as well as their origin from a well-known royal dynasty with roots in the mythical Uppsala, made the Norwegian kings equal to the Danish and undermined Danish claims to overlordship over Norway. It was certainly in the interest of several Icelandic and Norwegian authors to mediate this message, even if today we only know about four of them: Ári, *Historia Norwegiae*, *Af Upplendingakonungum*, and Snorri. It is remarkable, however, that the tradition already in *Historia Norwegiae* focuses on the way in which the kings *die*. This is the main theme in *Ynglingatal*, in which most of the Yngling kings die ingloriously, and Snorri underlines their shameful fates in *Ynglingasaga*. His elaborations of the poem are as follows:

Ynglingatal	*Ynglingsaga*
Fjölnir dies of (in?) mead	he slips — drunk — into a barrel of mead and drowns in it
Sveigðir is devoured by a stone	into which he — drunk — has been cajoled by a dwarf
Vanlandi is killed by a nightmare	on his wife's instigation, with the help of a sorceress
Visburr is burnt to death by his sons	as a vengeance and with the help of a sorceress;[5] her condition is that after this there would always be murders within the family of the Ynglings
Álfr and Yngvi kill each other	Álfr's wife Bera prefers his brother, the viking Yngvi, to her husband; the brothers kill each other
Jörundr is hanged	by king Gýlaugr from Hålogaland, son of Guðlaugr, who had been hung by Jörundr
Óttarr is torn to pieces by birds of prey	and the Danes send a wooden crow in order to insult them further
Aðils is thrown off his horse and dies	at one of the sacrificial feasts of the "Dísir"
Eysteinn is burnt to death by the Danes	led by king Sölvi, who later became king in Svitjod until he was killed by the "Svear"
Ingjaldr burns himself to death	out of fear for the Danish king Ívarr "the Widefathomer"

---

⁵ The sorceress Hulð is said to lie behind both Vanlandi's and Visburr's deaths.

Óláfr is burnt to death	by emigrating "svear" (in Värmland)
Eysteinn drowns	in a storm, caused by magic; a ship beam throws him overboard
Guðrøðr—drunk—is assassinated	on his wife's instigation; she openly admits her intention

Snorri's ridicule of most kings in *Ynglingatal* is consistent with his tendency to criticize kings in the rest of *Heimskringla*. Only five of the twenty-two kings (from Halvdan the Black) are judged positively.[6]

By beginning his history with their inglorious reputation, Snorri strikes the tone for the rest of his narratives about the kings. Thus already in *Ynglingasaga* he shows that kings are mortals, vulnerable to natural as well as supernatural powers, and, not least, to the cunning and deceptions of women. That message was contrary to the new and elevated royal ideal that began to gain ground in Scandinavia in the twelfth century, in which kings were chosen by and responsible only to God.

With this beginning, Snorri not only casts serious doubts on Danish claims to Viken (emphasizing the bases of the Ynglings in Vestfold) but also maintains a clear resistance to royal inheritance rights and Christian rulership, which can be interpreted as his "political manifesto." There is, however, more to be found in *Ynglingasaga*; its relevance to later Norwegian history is underlined by the fact, discussed in detail later, that many episodes in it are apparently based on later developments that figure in *Heimskringla*, including fratricide and other killings within the family, Danish hegemony, the meeting of three kings at Konghelle, the leading role of East Götaland, a great but unsuccessful expedition to the east, and a revolt (against King Egil) by paupers and the landless that anticipates the revolts of the Birchlegs in the later twelfth century.

Parallels with Swedish eleventh-
and twelfth-century history[7]

Like Yngvarr in *Ynglingasaga* (*YS*), the Swedish chieftain Ingvar dies during during an expedition eastward.[8] Like Ingjaldr in *YS*, Emund (the son of Olof Eriksson) is the last of his dynasty (descending directly from father to son) to rule over

---

[6] See below, Chapters 4 and 5. Another four kings are both positively and negatively judged.

[7] See Peter Sawyer, "The Background of Ynglingasaga," *Kongsmenn og krossmenn; festskrift til Grethe Authén Blom*, ed. Steinar Supphellen (Trondheim: Tapir, 1992), 271–75.

[8] *Ynglingasaga*, herafter: *YS*, Chap. 32, Íslenzk Fornrit: *Heimskringla* (herafter ÍFH) I:61–62; *History of the Kings of Norway*, translated by Lee M.H. Hollander (Austin: University of Texas Press, 1964), hereafter: Hollander, 35.

the Svear.[9] In *YS* the line is continued through a woman: Hálfdan Goldtooth's daughter Sǫlva from Solør, who married Ingjaldr's exiled son Óláfr trételgja ("Woodcutter"); and likewise in Sweden, the line continues through Emund's daughter, who married Steinkel.[10] Like King Aun in *YS*, King Stenkil's son Inge the older was exiled from Uppsala and found asylum in West Götaland.[11] Finally, it is significant that in *YS* only the king of the *East Gauts* (King Högni) refused subordination under the Swedish king, a striking parallel to the leading position of East Götaland under King Inge the older.[12]

King Inge the older's long reign may have been an important factor in the development of the Yngling tradition; his base was in East Götaland, but in exile he found asylum in West Götaland, and he got rid of his rival Blót-Sveinn ("the pagan sacrificer") in a true Yngling fashion. The Icelanders knew Inge's history very well; Bishop Gizzur spent a year in Götaland before he attended to his episcopal duties at home, and Markus Skjeggjason was King Inge's skald before he became Icelandic lawspeaker (in 1084). These contacts probably explain the special attention devoted to King Inge's father Stenkil and the early part of King Inge's rule, presented in the list of kings attached to *Hervararsaga*. In addition to these contacts, we have Snorri's own friendship with the lawspeaker Eskil in West Götaland, a member of the important Bjälbo family in East Götaland, whose brother Earl Birger secured the royal power in Sweden on behalf of his son Valdemar (1250).

Anticipation of future events in Heimskringla

Danish hegemony

Running like a red thread throughout the whole of *Heimskringla*, the threat from Danish kings is there already in *Ynglingasaga*, supported by *Ynglingatal*: King Óttarr falls against the men of King Frode in Vendel (Jutland),[13] King Eysteinn is burnt in by a Jutlandic sea-king,[14] and King Ingjald burns himself to death for fear of the Danish king Ívarr the Widefathomer.[15] It should be noted that it is not the Norwegian but the *Swedish* Ynglings who are shown to be inferior to the Danes. As for the habit of burning enemies to death, this motif is a *topos*, which we encounter time and again in the rest of *Heimskringla*.

---

[9] *YS*, chap. 39; ÍFH I:70–71; Hollander, 42–43.

[10] *YS*, chap. 42; ÍFH I:73–74; Hollander, 44.

[11] *YS*, chap. 25; ÍFH I:47–50; Hollander, 27–29.

[12] *YS*, chap. 39: *ÍFH* I:70–71; Hollander, 42–43.

[13] *YS*, chap. 27; ÍFH I:53–55; Hollander, 31–32.

[14] *YS*, chap. 30; ÍFH I:59f-60; Hollander, 34.

[15] *YS*, chap. 40; ÍFH I:71–72; Hollander, 43.

Strategic marriages

YS gives many examples of politically planned marriages, e.g., King Ingjaldr's marriage to the princess Gauthildr from Götaland. The result was not, however, the unification of Svitjod and Götaland, since, after his father's death, their son Óláfr Trételgja had to flee to the forests in Värmland. Thanks to his marriage to Sölva, the daughter of Hálfdan Goldtooth of Solør, Óláfr becomes the link with Norway; one of their sons, Hálfdan, is chosen Norwegian king, and with him and his successors we witness the beginning of the formation of Norway. Hálfdan marries Ása, daughter of the Opland king Eysteinn "Hardrade," who ruled Hedmark; his son Eysteinn married Hildr, daughter of King Eiríkr Agnarsson in Vestfold; and his grandson Guðrøðr first married Álfhildr, daughter of King Álfr of Alvheim (the area between the Raumelv and the Göta älv) and had with her half of Vingulmark (area around Oslo). After Álfhildr's death, Guðrøðr married Ása, daughter of Haraldr the Redbeard of Agder. In the *Saga about Halvdan the Black*, Snorri later tells us how Guðrøðr's and Ása's son Hálfdan inherits the kingdom of Agder (southwestern Norway) from his mother, and with him the "unification" continues with his son Harald Fairhair, who is said to have inherited Sogn (in western Norway) after his maternal grandfather. This is not the place to list all the strategic marriages in the rest of *Heimskringla*; the method was often used both internally and externally in order to create important alliances. [16]

Women as dangerous opponents

Some of the most detailed elaborations of *Ynglingatal* concern kings whose problems were caused by women. For example:

Vanlandi leaves his wife Drifa in Finnland but promises to return after three years. When he has not come back after ten years, his wife pays a sorceress to tempt him to return or to kill him. In Uppsala he suddenly starts longing for Finnland, but his friends think it is Finnish magic that has caused his longing and dissuade him from going home. Then Vanlandi falls into a deep sleep and is suffocated by a nightmare.

Visburr rejects his first wife and their two sons. When the sons come to fetch their mother's bridal gift, a neckring of gold, Visburr refuses to give it to them. The sons then ask a sorceress to have their father killed, and Visburr is burnt to death.

---

[16] Birgit Sawyer, "Släkt, vänner och makt," *Krigføring i middelalderen; strategi, ideologi og organisasjon ca. 1100–1400*, ed. Knut Peter Lyche Arstad (Oslo: Forsvarsmuseet, 2003), 74–109.

Agni subdues Finnland and returns with Skjölf, daughter of the chieftain Frosti. They marry and she begs Agni to arrange a funeral feast for her father, and when he has got drunk, she asks him carefully to fasten the gold ring he has around his neck. When Agni has gone to sleep, Skjölf ties a thick rope in the ring, and her men throw it up in a tree, pulling it so that the king is hanged to death.

The brothers Yngvi and Álfr share the royal power. Yngvi is a great warrior, handsome, generous, and cheerful; while Álfr is always at home, taciturn, imperious, and unfriendly. Álfr's wife Bera prefers Yngvi's company and lets her husband understand that she holds his brother in much higher esteem. The jealous Álfr sticks his sword through Yngvi, who has just time to give his brother a lethal wound, before they both fall down and die.

Ingjaldr has two children with Gauthildr: Ása and Óláfr trételgja. Ása is married to a king in Scania and gets him to kill her own brother Hálfdan, father of Ívarr the Widefathomer. After this she causes also her husband's death, and it is on her instigation that her drunk father Ingjaldr burns himself to death — for fear of the expected attack of Ívarr the Widefathomer.

Guðrøðr receives half Vingulmark and the son Óláfr with his first wife Álfhildr. After her death he asks king Haraldr Redbeard of Agder to give him his daughter Ása but is refused. This leads to a fight in which both Ása's father and brother fall. Guðrøðr raids Agder, brings Ása with him home, and marries her. On his way home from a feast, Guðrøðr is assassinated by his wife's page. Ása does not conceal that she has instigated the murder.

We thus meet women who are abandoned, rejected, abducted, unfaithful, evil, or taken a war prisoner. Common for these women is their lust for revenge, a recurring theme in the rest of *Heimskringla*.

The message may seem clear enough: women are dangerous opponents. It should not, however, be taken to mean that women are generally depicted negatively in Snorri's work; he often presents women inciters with sympathy, and there are several examples of women who represent reason and sound criticism of the kings' violence.

Fratricide and other killings within the family

When Visburr's sons ask the sorceress Hulð to help them kill their father, she sets the condition that murder in the family will always be by kin. This is exactly what happens: Visburr is burnt to death by his sons, Agni is hanged on his wife's instigation, Alrekr and Eiríkr kill each other, and so do Yngvi and Álfr. Ása incites Ingjaldr to burn himself to death, and Guðrøðr (father of Hálfdan the Black) is assassinated on his wife's instigation.[17]

The murders within the family continue throughout *Heimskringla*: Eirik Bloodaxe kills his brothers, Håkon the Good is shot down on his sister-in-law Gunnhild's instigation, Sigurd Slembidiákn kills his drunk half-brother Harald Gille and is himself killed by his half-brother's sons Inge and Sigurd. After that, Inge has both brothers, Sigurd and Øystein, killed but falls in a battle with his nephew Håkon the Broadshouldered, who, in his turn, falls in a battle with his kinsman Magnus Erlingsson.

Thus, the sorceress Hulð´s prediction comes true, and even Magnus Erlingsson falls in a battle with his kinsman Sverre, but Snorri does not cover that event in his history.

Revolts of the unpropertied

In *YS* the thrall Tunni collects a fortune as King Aun's shepherd, and after Aun's death he takes a great amount of treasure and hides it. When King Egill places Tunni among the other thralls, he flees, digs up his hidden treasure, and distributes it among his followers, who choose him as their chieftain. "Therupon a great many evildoers drifted to him, and they camped out in the woods, and ever so often made incursions into the farm lands, robbing or killing people."[18]

On several occasions Tunni fights against Egill and always wins. In the end, Egill flees to King Froði in Denmark and promises him tribute if he gets Danish help. Tunni falls in a great battle, and Egill sends greats gifts to King Froði. The similarities between this story and the story about King Inge, Erling Skakke, and Håkon the Broadshouldered (towards the end of *Heimskringla*) are striking; after having had both his brothers (Sigurd and Øystein) killed, king Inge expropriated everything that they had and exiled their followers. Sigurd's disinherited son Håkon the Broadshouldered was chosen chieftain by the followers of his uncle, King Øystein. Håkon fought many battles with King Inge, who fell in the end (1161). After this the magnate Erling Skakke led the war against Håkon and went to Denmark in order to secure help from King Valdemar I. Valdemar promised his support on condition that he got the power of Viken, which was agreed. With Danish help, Erling succeeded in defeating Håkon, who fell (1162), and was forced to be Valdemar's earl and rule Viken as a fief under him.

After the fall of Håkon the Broadshouldered, the revolt continued, first led by King Øystein's nephew Olav, then by his own son, also called Øystein. He was helped by the earl Birger Brosa in Svitjod, recruited a force in Viken, and was chosen king. Snorri's description of the rebels is very similar to that he gives of Tunni´s followers in *Ynglingasaga*:

----

[17] *YS*, Chaps. 14, 19, 20, 21, 40, 48; ÍFH I:30–31, 37–42, 71–72, 79–81; Hollander, 17–18, 22–24, 43, 48–49.

[18] *YS*, Chap. 26; ÍFH I:50–53; Hollander, 29–31.

> But as they ran out of money, they robbed far and wide, so that landed-men
> and *bœndr* collected troops against them. [. . .] their clothes fell off them, so
> that they tied birchbark about their calves, whence the bœndr called them
> Birchlegs. Often they made incursions into the settlements, appearing now
> here, now there, breaking into houses wherever there were not enough peo-
> ple to oppose them.[19]

After the battle at Re, where Øystein is forced to flee, Snorri writes:

> This band which was called Birchlegs had grown to be a very numerous
> army. It was composed of tough and weapon-skilled, unruly elements who
> pursued a headlong, reckless course after they thought they had a sufficient
> force.[20]

All the main themes and ridiculing or belittling of kings in Snorri's *Ynglingas-*
aga are represented throughout the rest of *Heimskringla*, especially towards the
end.[21] The main figure in the last saga is *not* Magnus Erlingsson but his father,
the magnate Erling Skakke.

The end of *Heimskringla*

Thus, the same tone sounds in the two last chapters of *Heimskringla*; we meet
more or less useless kings, one—important—strategic marriage, Danish hegemony, a woman as a dangerous opponent, killings within the family, and the revolt of the unpropertied: Erling Skakke—of noble birth—made a real *strategic*
marriage, getting Sigurd Jerusalemfarer's legitimate daughter Kristin as his wife.
Kristin was King Inge's cousin, and Erling became Inge's loyal supporter. Kristin, in her turn, was her husband's loyal supporter and proved herself a *danger-*
ous opponent to his and king Inge's enemies. When Gregorius was expecting an
attack by King Inge's brother Øystein, it was Kristin who helped and equipped
him, and when, after Inge's fall, Håkon the Broadshouldered had subjected Norway to his rule, it was Kristin who found out what plans he and his followers had,
so that she could inform her husband about them. By mediating between Erling
and her kinsman Valdemar I, she achieved Danish support against Erling's and
Magnus' enemies in Norway. The *Danish hegemony* is clearly illustrated by the
fact that Erling was forced to subordinate himself to Valdemar, acting as his earl
in Viken.

Finally the themes *revolts of the unpropertied* and *killings within the family* are
also well represented in the end of *Heimskringla*:

---

[19] S. Magnus Erlingsson, chap. 36; *ÍFH* III:410f–11; Hollander, 815–16.
[20] S. Magnus Erlingsson, chap. 43; ÍFH III: 416–17; Hollander, 820.
[21] S. Håkon the Broadshouldered and S. Magnus Erlingsson.

Revolts of the unpropertied

King Inge had expropriated everything owned by the members of the group around his nephew *Håkon* (the Broadshouldered), who had been taken chieftain by all his uncle Øystein's followers. Håkon made several attacks against the king and his man Gregorius, but was at last defeated and killed in a fight against Erling Skakke. Then *Sigurd*, another son of King Sigurd Haraldsson and thus a brother of Håkon the Broadshouldered, was chosen king in Opland and was later chosen king also in Trøndelag. Both he and his foster-father Markus of Skog, however, were taken prisoner by Erling's men; Sigurd was beheaded, Markus hanged, and their band was dispersed. New problems faced Erling, when two second cousins and one half-brother of his son Magnus initiated rebellions. First *Olav* (a grandson of King Øystein Magnusson) gathered a troop and fought a battle with Erling, in which many of Erling's men fell and Erling himself was wounded. A second threat was *Harald* (reputed son of King Sigurd Haraldsson and Erling's own wife Kristin, thus a half-brother of Magnus), who claimed power but was beheaded on Erling's command. The next threat was more serious; a man called Øystein, considered to be the son of King Øystein Haraldsson, was proclaimed king by the people in Viken. His followers were very poor, and because of the birchbark tied around their legs they were called the "Birchlegs." Øystein was also proclaimed king in Trøndelag but was defeated in the battle at Re by King Magnus's men.

Killings within the family

As described above, there were many killings within the royal family: Kristin's uncle, Håkon the Broadshouldered was killed in battle, her cousin Sigurd was beheaded, and so was her own son (with Sigurd Haraldsson) Harald! Finally, also Øystein, likewise a cousin of Kristin, was killed in battle against Erling and Magnus.

The last kings in Heimskringla

We do not hear very much about Håkon the Broadshouldered apart from his attacks and struggle for power. Snorri obviously did not let him go down in history as a king who did anything useful for the country, and the only things we learn about King Magnus Erlingsson are that:

> 1. as a five-year old he was chosen king and promised help from the Danish king Valdemar I to maintain his power in Norway (1161);

> 2. at the age of eight or nine he was crowned by Archbishop Øystein (1163/64);

3. when he grew older he dressed splendidly (in contrast to his father) and "was of an easy-going disposition and gay, very cheerful, and a great lover of women";[22]

4. together with Orm "Kingsbrother" he defeated the Birchlegs in the battle of Re. It is made perfectly clear, however, that the decisive achievements in this battle were done not by him but by his men. Nevertheless, his saga ends:

> King Magnus then returned to Tønsberg, and he became very famous from this victory, because [before] everyone had said that between them Earl Erling was the shield and leader for both of them. But after King Magnus had obtained the victory over so strong and numerous a host with a smaller force of his own, everyone thought that he would surpass all [other generals] and that he would as a warrior become as much greater than the earl as he was younger.[23]

There is no mistaking Snorri's irony; he knows very well what happened to King Magnus later. Far from being a "much greater" warrior than his father, he fell against Sverre in the battle at Fimreite (1184). Snorri could not possibly foresee what would happen to King Håkon Håkonsson, but if *Heimskringla* was finished towards the end of the 1230s, it was still an open question; would Håkon—like Magnus Erlingsson—be defeated by a rival in the end?

There is much to indicate that Snorri has compared the balance of strength between King Håkon and Earl Skúli with that between King Magnus and Erling Skakke: Erling had *personally* defeated several revolts (led by Håkon the Broadshouldered, Sigurd Sigurdsson, Olav, and Øystein), while it was King Magnus's *men* who ended the revolt of Øystein and the Birchlegs. The only thing we hear about King Magnus's contribution is that he dwelt in the room of a yeoman, warming himself by the fire, when Øystein's corpse was brought to him.[24] This can be compared with the contributions of Earl Skúli, who *personally* struck down the revolts of both the "Slittungs" and the "Ribbungs," while, during a new revolt of the "Ribbungs" in Värmland, the contribution of king Håkon Håkonsson was not a military triumph; the only thing he did was to burn the areas, from which the inhabitants had already fled. Snorri could hardly more clearly have elevated the experienced earls at the cost of the young kings.

A parallel to this contrast between a young, inexperienced king and his older supporter can be found in *Gesta Danorum*, where Saxo elevates Archbishop Absalon at the cost of King Valdemar I. In all the many battles in which they both took part, it was always Absalon who did the most: he was on the lookout, he

---

[22] S. Magnus Erlingsson, chap. 37; ÍFH III: 411–12; Hollander, 816.
[23] S. Magnus Erlingsson, chap. 44; ÍFH III: 417; Hollander, 821.
[24] S. Magnus Erlingsson, chap. 42; ÍFH III:415–16; Hollander, 820.

fought, made cunning plans, negotiated, and undertook dangerous commissions, while King Valdemar is described as hesitant, undecided, easily exhausted, more often asleep than awake.[25]

---

[25] Birgit Sawyer, "Valdemar, Absalon and Saxo," *Revue Belge de Philologie et d'Histoire*, 63 (1985): 685–705, especially 691–93.

Chapter 4
Kings and Magnates (I)

In this and the following two chapters, the contents of *Heimskringla*—apart from *Ynglingasaga*—are summarized and analyzed. Most kings, with the main contemporary magnates, are discussed in separate sections, but the roles of the women who figure are discussed in Chapter 6. Most sections refer to two or more of the sagas into which *Heimskringla* is conventionally divided. Each section begins with Snorri's explicit characterization, followed by a summary of the narrative and my comments on both.

1. Halvdan the Black, his mother and his wives

Explicit characterization

"King Halvdan was a very wise man, both truthful and fair-dealing. He both made laws and kept them himself. He compelled all to keep them; and in order that violence should not overthrow the laws, he set up penalties, fixing everyone's compensation according to his birth and position."[1]

Summary

Guðrøðr, king in Vestfold and Vingulmark, had taken Ása, daughter of the king in Agder, by force (having killed her father), and in revenge she instigated her husband's death. Then she took their one-year-old son Halvdan to Agder to inherit her father's kingdom. Halvdan and his elder halfbrother had inherited Vestfold from their father, and Halvdan acquired Romerike, Toten, and Hadeland.

He was first married to a daughter of the king in Sogn, and their son inherited his (maternal) grandfather's kingdom. After the son's death, Halvdan claimed Sogn as his heir, and after his wife's death, he married Ragnhildr, daughter of the king in Ringerike. She was a wise woman who had significant dreams: in one of them she seemed to be in her garden, removing a thorn from her shirt.

---

[1] S. Halvdan the Black, chaps. 7, 9; ÍFH I:91; Hollander, 57–58.

The thorn grew into a long twig, one end touched the ground, the other reached high in the sky. "The lowest part of it was red as blood, but farther up the trunk was fair and green, and its branches white as snow. [. . .] The limbs of the tree extended so far that they seemed to her to spread over all Norway and even much farther."[2] King Halvdan found it strange that he never dreamed and asked advice from a wise man, who told him to sleep in a pigsty. He did so and dreamed that he had the longest hair of any man, some touching the ground, some reaching to the middle of his leg, some sprouting out of his skull like little horns. This was interpreted to mean that a great line of descendants would come from him, "and that they would govern the land with great distinction, though not all equally so; but that one would arise out of his line who would be greater and nobler than all the rest."[3]

Halvdan the Black drowned at the age of 40:

> There had been excellent seasons during his rule; and people were so affected by his death that when they learned of his demise and that his body was being taken to Ringerike in order to be interred there, men of influence came from Romerike, Vestfold, and Hedmark and prayed, all of them, to take the body with them to be buried in their lands; for it was thought that he who got possession of it could expect good seasons. They reached an agreement in this wise; that the body was assigned to four places: the head was laid in a mound at Stein in Ringerike, but each of the others carried away their share and interred them in burial mounds in their homelands, and all are called the Mounds of Halvdan.[4]

Comments

The treatment of Halvdan's corpse reveals uncertainty about his real power basis. The oldest source, written by the Icelander Sæmund the Learned (1056–1133), now lost but used by the author of *Nóregs konungatal*, described Halvdan as king in the Oppland region[5] with his base in Ringerike, as does also an older manuscript of *Fagrskinna*, although a younger manuscript expands Halvdan's power and reports that his corpse was divided into three parts, the intestines in Hadeland, his body in Ringerike, and his head in Vestfold. Snorri thus makes yet another division.

The claim that Vestfold was the startingpoint for the unification of Norway appears rather late; according to *Historia Norwegiae* (from the end of the twelfth

---

[2] S. Halvdan the Black, chap. 6; ÍFH I:90; Hollander, 56.
[3] S. Halvdan the Black, chap. 7; ÍFH I:91; Hollander, 56–57.
[4] S. Halvdan the Black, chap. 9; ÍFH I:93; Hollander, 58.
[5] Oppland comprised Gudbrandsdalen, Valdres, Hadeland, Ranrike, and Hedmark.

century), Halvdan the Black was king *in montanis*, i.e., the Oppland region, so the addition of Vestfold as the basis of Norway's unification is clearly an invention of thirteenth-century authors.[6] The younger manuscript of *Fagrskinna* only includes Vestfold, but Snorri treats Halvdan as *mainly* a Vestfold king, making him the prototype for his son Harald Fairhair.[7]

Snorri also makes Halvdan the Black the true ancestor of later Norwegian kings, by having both his second wife and himself prophesizing many descendants, good as well as bad.

Like the author of *Fagrskinna*, Snorri tells us about Halvdan's dream, but unlike him he also has Ragnhildr, "a wise woman," dream and thus be the first to prophesy the rich offspring of Halvdan. Dreams are an important motif, and in other Old Norse sources there are many variations on the theme of sleeping in a particular location in order to have a prophetic dream. To sleep in a pigsty is known from other peoples and has been explained in terms of associating the pig with fruitfulness and veracity.[8]

Like so many of his forefathers, Halvdan expands his realm by marrying strategically, but in *Heimskringla*, women are not only pawns in the political game; as we will see, Snorri puts a great weight on the roles of influential women all through his work. Unlike *Fagrskinna*, Snorri has a woman play a key role: Halvdan's mother Ása, who not only has her husband killed but also enables her son to inherit Sogn, her father's kingdom.

In all, Snorri gives a favorable portrait of Halvdan; his narrative does not contradict his explicit characterization. During Halvdan's rule there had been excellent seasons, and he was deeply mourned. In fact, king Halvdan represents all the four cardinal virtues: prudence, justice, temperance, and fortitude. Snorri emphasizes that he measured fines according to people's birth and status, something the magnates wanted but was ignored by Olav Haraldsson.[9]

2. Harald Fairhair (*c.* 900–932); his women and his sons

Explicit characterization

"Men versed in history say that Harald Fairhair was of exceedingly handsome appearance, very strong and tall, most generous of his substance and extremely well liked by his men. He was a great warrior during the earlier part of his

---

[6] See Chapter 3 above.

[7] Claus Krag, "Rikssamlingenshistorien og Ynglingerekken." (Norwegian) *Historisk Tidsskrift*, 2012, 159–89.

[8] *Fagrskinna: A Catalogue of the Kings of Norway*, translated by Alison Finlay (Leiden & Boston: Brill, 2004), 42–43, note 3.

[9] See section on Saint Olav below.

life."[10] King Harald "had made slaves of all the people in the land and oppressed them."[11]

Summary

At the age of ten, Harald took over his father's power in eastern Norway. Many chieftains invaded his areas, but Harald defeated them all and then subjugated many districts in the central and southern parts of the country. His continued expansion was incited by Gyða, a beautiful maiden, daughter of the king in Hordaland. She agreed to be his concubine, only on condition that he first conquered all Norway.[12] Taking her challenge seriously, he subdued also the western part of Norway, fighting and killing many kings.[13] In Trøndelag he gave Earl Håkon Grjotgardsson rule over the Strinda district.

Harald's expansion was threatened by an attack from people in Hordaland, Rogaland, Agder, and Telemark. The battle in Hafrsfjord was the turning point; Harald won and was then the sole ruler of all Norway. As such, he claimed that all ancestral lands belonged to him and demanded tax from all landowners, both the great and the humble. In each district (*fylke*) he placed an earl with four or more subordinate rulers (*hersar*) and with the duty of serving the king with sixty soldiers. This caused conflicts with his many sons, who opposed this organization; they drove some earls away and even killed some of them. Harald yielded and gave all his sons the title of king; and he decided that all his descendants on the male side were to inherit the kingdom after his father, while his descendants on the female side were to inherit earldoms. This, however, did not put a stop to his conflicts with his many sons, and because each of them considered his share too small, they went on plundering expeditions. Harald's favourite son Eirik wanted all power for himself, and—with his father's consent—he began by burning his brother Ragnvald in his hall. Later he killed another brother: Bjørn. At the age of eighty Harald let only three of his sons take over his power: Eirik "Bloodaxe"[14] as "over-king," Olav as king in Viken, and Sigrød as king in

---

[10] S. Harald Fairhair, chap. 42; ÍFH I:148; Hollander, 94.

[11] S. Håkon the Good, chap. 1; ÍFH I:151; Hollander, 96.

[12] S. Harald Fairhair, chap. 3; ÍFH I:96; Hollander, 61. Harald vowed not to cut or comb his hair before he had conquered all of Norway. After his success—with his hair now properly dressed—he got the surname "Fairhair." Chap. 23; ÍFH I:122; Hollander, 78.

[13] The kings Snorri mentions were rulers in Orkdalen, Gauldalen, Strinda District, Verdalen, Skaun, Sparbyggja District, Inderøya, Naumdalen, Nordmøre, South Møre, Fjordane, Hordaland, Rogaland, Agder, Hadeland, Toten, Gudbrandsdalen, Hedmark, Ringerike, Vingulmark, and Ranrike.

[14] So called because he had killed his own brother Bjørn, king in Vestfold.

Trøndelag. He had also organized royal strongholds in Álrekstad, Seim, Fitjar, Utstein, and Avaldsnes (Karmøy).[15]

Many of Harald's opponents fled, either east to Jämtland and Hälsingland (now in Sweden) or west to the Atlantic islands: Iceland, the Faroes, and Shetland. Others became outlaws, going on viking expeditions, staying in the Orkneys and the Hebrides in the winter, harrying in Norway in the summer.[16]

Comments

Snorri has Harald Fairhair's expansion start in eastern and southern Norway and continue with the western part, including Trøndelag, but it is generally recognized that this is a later construction. Harald's startingpoint was most probably Sogn in Vestlandet, and his sphere of power included mainly the western (coastal) districts of Norway. Rulers in the east never yielded to him, and the southern districts (including Vestfold) were under Danish royal rule; the attackers that he defeated in Hafrsfjord seem to have had Danish connections.[17]

At the same time as Harald established his realm, another ruler, Håkon Grjotgardsson, established his own, based on Lade near Nidaros, wielding power over an even larger area than Harald. He began cooperating with Harald and became his earl. Recent studies have shown that medieval authors underestimated the role of Earl Håkon, who was probably as important in unifying Norway as Harald. The earls of Lade retained power until 1029.[18] Thanks to Snorri's great influence, however, the conviction that his depiction of Harald Fairhair as solely responsible of the "unification" is still widely accepted. The fact is that—before Snorri—we hear very little about Harald Fairhair's life and career[19] and must treat his account with skepticism.

That Harald Fairhair seized the property (*odal* = hereditary right to the land) of the landowners was still believed well into the twentieth century, but modern studies have shown that this view is due to misunderstandings; the saga authors generalized from what they knew about Harald's confiscations and his demand that all were obliged to provide hospitality to him and his agents (*veitsler*).[20] Snorri's claim that the exodus to the Atlantic isles started because of Harald's expansion cannot be right, since we know it started already in the last quarter of the ninth century, while Harald's victory in Hafrsfjord is now dated to *c.* 900.

---

[15] S. Harald Fairhair, chap. 37; ÍFH I:142–43; Hollander, 91.

[16] S. Harald Fairhair, chap. 19; ÍFH I:117–18; Hollander, 76.

[17] Claus Krag, *Norges historie fram til 1319* (Oslo, Universitetsforlaget, 2000), 46.

[18] Krag, *Norges historie fram til 1319*, 48–49.

[19] Cf. Sverrir Jakobsson, "Erindringen om en mægtig Personlighed," (Norwegian) *Historisk Tidsskrift* 81 (2002): 213–30.

[20] Krag, *Norges historie*, 213.

Another idea that has been hard to correct is that all Norwegian kings were descendants of Harald Fairhair, a "fact" that legitimized the power of all his successors. Already Sæmund the Learned was convinced that Harald's line included Olav Tryggvason, Olav Haraldsson, and Harald "Hardrade,"[21] and this idea was accepted by later authors. Snorri tries his best to persuade his readers/listeners that this was really so; in addition to making Harald's father Halvdan the Black a ruler of Vestfold as well as Romerike and Hedmark, he also described his parents' dreams about their rich offspring. *Fagrskinna* claims that Harald had more than twenty sons with many women, but Snorri is more detailed, giving us the names of several of them: Ása, daughter of Earl Håkon Grjotgardsson (Trøndelag);[22] Gyða, daughter of king Eiríkr (Hordaland);[23] Ragnhildr, daughter of Eiríkr in Jutland;[24] Svanhildr, daughter of Earl Eysteinn (Ringerike);[25] Áshildr, daughter of king Hringr Dagsson (Ringerike);[26] Snœfriðr (daughter of Svási (a Finn);[27] and Þóra "Mosterstong."[28] Apart from letting women play important roles in his history, Snorri (unlike the author of *Fagrskinna*) makes it plausible that Harald Fairhair could be the ancestor of so many pretenders to the throne. In fact, the real founder of the Norwegian royal dynasty was Harald Hardrade, son of a petty king in Ringerike.[29]

Fagrskinna says nothing about Gyða's key role in Harald's decision to conquer the whole of Norway.[30] Snorri's incredible claim illustrates his ambiguity, of which we will see many more examples. At the same time as he wants to prove that the Norwegians had power over Vestfold at least since the middle of the ninth century, thereby dismissing Danish claims, he follows his own agenda in criticizing Harald, the "founder of Norway," for not planning the expansion himself but acting on the challenge of a woman he coveted.

The only virtue Snorri allows Harald is fortitude, but even that is qualified by stating that this was only in the earlier part of his life. The implicit characterization of Harald is of a man lacking most virtues but guilty of the sins of pride, greed (expropriating land and introducing taxes), lust, and wrath. While the author of *Fagrskinna* has only positive things to say about Harald, his conquests

---

[21] Krag, *Norges historie*, 215.

[22] S. Harald Fairhair, chaps. 9, 17; ÍFH I:100–102, 114; Hollander, 64, 73.

[23] S. Harald Fairhair, chaps. 3, 4, 20; ÍFH I:96–97, 118; Hollander, 61–62, 76.

[24] S. Harald Fairhair, chap. 21; ÍFH I:118–20; Hollander, 76.

[25] S. Harald Fairhair, chap. 21; ÍFH I:118–20; Hollander, 76.

[26] S. Harald Fairhair, chap. 21; ÍFH I:118–20; Hollander, 76.

[27] S. Harald Fairhair, chap. 25; ÍFH I:125–27; Hollander, 80–81.

[28] S. Harald Fairhair, chap. 37, related to the magnate Hortha-Kári; ÍFH I:142–43; Hollander, 91–92.

[29] Krag, *Norges historie*, 215.

[30] Nor is the Gyda-episode found in earlier sources like *Historia Norwegiæ*, Theodoricus Monachus, and Ágríp.

and achievements, Snorri underlines the resistance he met, the problems he had with his own family, and how he enslaved the Norwegian people, taking their "odal" away from the *bændr*.[31] Thus, in contrast to *Fagrskinna*, Snorri gives a very negative portrait of Harald Fairhair, emphasizing his troubles with both opponents and his own sons.

3. Eirik Bloodaxe (*c.* 930–934)[32]

Explicit characterization

"Eirik was a large and handsome man, strong and of great prowess, a great and victorious warrior, violent of disposition, cruel, gruff and taciturn. Gunnhild, his wife, was a very beautiful woman, shrewd and skilled in magic, friendly of speech, but full of deceit and cruelty."[33]

Summary

What Snorri explicitly says about Eirik and his wife is well illustrated in his narrative, split between the saga of Harald Fairhair and the saga of Håkon the Good. Only two of Harald Fairhair's many sons became kings in Norway: first Eirik and then Håkon, who had been fostered by King Adalstein in England. When King Harald died, Eirik succeeded as ruler in Norway after having defeated his brothers, two of whom were killed in battle, while Tryggve and Gudrød fled to the Oppland region. It is remarkable that Snorri has nothing to say about Eirik's rule in Norway, only that he left for the British Isles as soon as Håkon had returned and won support from many chieftains.

In England, King Adalstein offered him Northumberland to defend against Danes and other Vikings. Eirik agreed to be baptized together with his wife, children, and men. Finding his land too small (1/5 of England), Eirik continually went on plundering expeditions, harrying in Scotland, the Hebrides, Ireland, and Wales, and gaining wealth for himself. After Adalstein's death in 939, Eirik and many Norwegians fell in battle against Adalstein's brother Edmund. His widow Gunnhild and their sons left via the Orkneys to Denmark and were well received by Harald Bluetooth, who adopted Gunnhild's foremost son, Harald "Greycloak."

---

[31] I.e., their rights to their ancestral estates.
[32] In two sagas: S. Harald Fairhair and S. Hákon the Good.
[33] S. Harald Fairhair, chap. 43; ÍFH I:149; Hollander, 95.

Comments

Snorri's depictions of Eirik, Gunnhild, and their sons (hereafter referred to as Gunnhild's sons) are entirely negative, especially that of Gunnhild, with her intrigues, lust for power, and use of magic. Snorri has little to say about Eirik; we hear much more about his wife, who figures in no fewer than four sagas (in five, if the saga of Earl Håkon is counted as a separate one)[34] and has great influence over her sons, who are real troublemakers, repeatedly challenging Håkon the Good, Earl Håkon, and Olav Tryggvason (see below).

4. Håkon the Good (c. 934–961) vs Gunnhild's sons

Explicit characterization

"While Håkon was king in Norway good peace obtained for both farmers and merchants, so that no one harmed the other or his property. Abundance reigned both on sea and land. King Håkon was a most cheerful person, very eloquent, and most kindly disposed. He was a man of keen understanding and laid great stress on legislation. He devised the Gulathings Law with the help of Thorleif the Wise; and the Frostathings Law, with the advice of Earl Sigurth and other men from the Trondheim District who were accounted wisest."[35]

Summary

King Adalstein had given Håkon ships to return to Norway, where he allied with Sigurd, the earl of Lade. With Sigurd's support, Håkon was chosen king in Trøndelag and gave the landholders all their possessions back. He also gave his nephews Tryggve and Gudrød the title of "king": Tryggve over Ranrike and Vingulmark, and Gudrød over Vestfold. After Eirik Bloodaxe's flight, Håkon became king in the whole of Norway with Sigurd as his earl in Trøndelag. On one of Håkon's stays in Lade, Sigurd's wife gave birth to a boy child, and the same day, Håkon sprinkled the boy with water and gave him his own name. King Håkon drove the plundering Danes out of Viken, destroyed all viking ships in the Sound, and harried in Denmark.

This angered the Danish king Harald Bluetooth, who had welcomed Eirik's widow Gunnhild and their sons, accepting Harald Greycloak as his foster son. Gunnhild's sons plundered in Norway, and this drove many Norwegians away to Jämtland and Hälsingland. Håkon the Good, however, made peace with people in these districts and gave them law. He also managed to stop an attack

---

[34] S. Harald Fairhair; S. Håkon the Good; S. Harald Greycloak, and S. Olav Tryggvason.

[35] S. Håkon the Good, chap. 11; ÍFH I:163–64; Hollander, 104.

by Gunnhild`s sons (who fled back to Jutland) and divided Norway into "ship-levies," organizing how many ships there should be in every district.

Håkon was a confirmed Christian and sent for a bishop and priests from England, but his attempts to christianize Norway were strongly opposed. When he requested everyone to let themselves be baptized at the Frostathing Assembly, people refused, and Åsbjørn from Melhus eloquently defended their old laws, after which Håkon yielded.[36]

Gunnhild's sons attacked Håkon several times but were always defeated until, after twenty-six years as king, Håkon was attacked by the eldest of them: Harald Greycloak. Before the battle (of Stord at Fitjar), "it is said" that the king cast off his coat of mail. "King Håkon was easily recognized—more easily than other men. His helmet glittered as the sun shone upon it."[37] In front of his men, King Håkon was fatally struck by an arrow: according to some, shot by Gunnhild's page. On his deathbed, Håkon bequeathed Norway to Gunnhild's sons, requesting that they should exercise forbearance to his friends and kinsmen. Although himself a Christian, he allowed for a heathen burial, and thus, after his death, a great mound was raised over him.

Comments

Like the author of *Fagrskinna*, Snorri gives a very positive picture of King Håkon, emphasizing his restoration of the landholders' rights to their inherited properties[38] and—with advice of wise men—giving good laws,[39] not only in Norway but also in Jämtland and Hälsingland. His nephews Tryggve (future father of Olav Tryggvason) and Gudrød are restored to power, and he was on most friendly terms with the powerful earl in Trøndelag. He defended Norway against Danish attacks but died almost a martyr, being killed allegedly on the evil Gunnhild's instigation. Snorri praises Håkon not only for being a good Christian[40] but also for compromising with his pagan subjects, listening to their advice, and tolerating heathen practices. King Håkon represents all four cardinal virtues and no vices. We are told that he was deeply mourned and that Øyvind Skaldaspiller composed a poem, "Hákonarmál," in his memory. All in all, Håkon the Good seems to be Snorri's ideal king.

---

[36] S. Hákon the Good, chap. 15; ÍFH I: 169–70; Hollander, 109. For Åsbjørn's speech, see Appendix 4 in this volume.

[37] S. Hákon the Good, chap. 30; ÍFH I:189; Hollander, 120.

[38] S. Hákon the Good, chap. 1; ÍFH I:150–51; Hollander, 96.

[39] S. Hákon the Good, chap. 11; ÍFH I:163; Hollander, 104.

[40] S. Hákon the Good, Chaps. 12, 13; ÍFH I:164–67; Hollander, 104–6.

5. Gunnhild's sons; Harald Greycloak (961–965/970)[41] vs. Earl Håkon

In some editions, a separate "Saga of Earl Håkon" has been created, consisting of Chapters 6–16 in the saga of Harald Greycloak.[42] This creates problems, since we read even more about Earl Håkon in the "Saga of Olav Tryggvason," where Gunnhild's sons, led by their brother Harald Greycloak, also figure prominently. Above all, we meet Gunnhild in no fewer than four (five) sagas: of Harald Finehair, Håkon the Good, Eirik's (Gunnhild's) sons, (Earl Håkon), and of Olav Tryggvason.

Explicit characterization of Gunnhild's sons

"All the sons of Gunnhild were held to be avaricious, and it was rumored that they hid valuables in the ground. [. . .] They required much for their upkeep, and they were most rapacious and did not abide by the laws King Håkon had established except when it suited them. [. . .] They were all very handsome men, strong and of great stature, and accomplished in bodily skills."[43]

"During the time when the sons of Gunnhild ruled in Norway there were bad seasons, and they became worse the longer they ruled, and the *bœndr* attributed that to the kings, and also complained that they were grasping and treated the *bœndr* harshly. It went so far that the people in all parts hardly had any grain or fish. In Hålogaland there was such famine and starvation and scarcely any grain grew there. The snow lay in all parts in midsummer, and the cattle had to stay in their stalls."[44]

Explicit characterization of Earl Håkon

«During the time Earl Håkon ruled over Norway there were good harvests and a good peace reigned within the land among the farmers. For the greater part of his life the earl was popular with them."[45] [. . .] Håkon" had many qualifications for leadership: first, an exalted lineage, and therewith shrewdness and sagacity to use his power, briskness in battle as well as a lucky hand in winning the victory and slaying his enemies. [. . .] Earl Håkon exceeded everyone in generosity. . ."[46]

---

41 Three sagas: S. Harald Fairhair; S. Hákon the Good; S. Olav Tryggvason.
42 Laing (1844, 1914, 1930), Gyldendal (1942), Holtsmark & Seip (2003).
43 S. Harald Greycloak, chaps. 1+2; ÍFH I:200, 204; Hollander, 130–31.
44 S. Harald Greycloak, chap. 16; ÍFH I:221; Hollander, 142.
45 S. Olav Tryggvason, chap. 45; ÍFH I:290; Hollander, 187.
46 S. Olav Tryggvason, chap. 50; ÍFH I:298; Hollander, 193.

Summary

On his deathbed, King Håkon had exhorted Harald Greycloak and his brothers to be forbearing to his friends and kinsmen, a request they totally ignored. They based themselves in the middle of Norway, since they did not feel safe in areas where King Håkon's best friend (Earl Sigurd) and other nephews (Tryggve and Gudrød) lived, i.e., Trøndelag, Østfold, and Vestfold. The brothers had accepted Christianity in England but did not attempt to convert the Norwegians, though they did their best to destroy pagan cult centres. They all kept their own followers, who had to be maintained at great cost, and since there was also a severe crop failure under their rule, their subjects suffered.

Gunnhild urged her sons to take over the whole of what their forefathers had owned. She wanted them to get rid of Earl Sigurd, but since he was a very powerful ruler, they hesitated. With the help of Gunnhild, however, Harald Greycloak and his brothers made a plan, tempting Earl Sigurd's brother Grjotgard with their friendship and the title of earl, if he helped them to betray Sigurd. They burnt Sigurd and his people to death, but the people of Trøndelag gathered around Sigurd's son Håkon and drove Gunnhild's sons out of the district. Friends of both parties managed to reconcile them on the terms that Earl Håkon would have the same power as his father, and Gunnhild's sons the same power as King Håkon the Good. The terms were not held; there were many and serious conflicts between them, but Earl Håkon nevertheless found time to raid in the east every summer.[47] When he allied with the kings Tryggve and Gudrød (nephews of King Håkon the Good), Gunnhild suspected that some treason against them was planned and had her sons kill them both. Since Tryggve's widow had been expecting a child, Gunnhild urged her sons to find out about it, and on hearing that the child was a boy (Olav), she made several attempts to get hold of him. In vain, however, her men looked for Olav both in Norway and Sweden.

In the meantime, Earl Håkon had allied with the Danish King Harald ("Bluetooth"), and during a long stay in Denmark he tried to persuade the king to get rid of Harald Greycloak and his brothers. The Danish king was unwilling to betray his foster-son, but in the end he yielded and, advised by Håkon, deceitfully invited Harald Greycloak to come to Jutland to accept fiefs from him. Inspite of his doubts—and hoping to rescue Norway from a famine—Harald Greycloak accepted the invitation, but according to Earl Håkon's plan, he was attacked by the Danish king's nephew and fell in the battle that followed. After this, Gunnhild and her sons fled to the Orkneys, and Håkon became Harald Bluetooth's vassal/tributary earl in Norway.

---

[47] To avoid being hindered by Gunnhild's sons, he had brought his ships to Hälsingland (in Sweden), from where he set out on raiding expeditions every summer.

Comments

Being sonless, King Håkon decided that Gunhild's sons should be kings after him; they had defeated him and were, after all, his nephews, grandsons of Harald Fairhair. Unlike earlier sources, however, Snorri actually renders some legitimacy also to Earl Håkon's rule, since in *Heimskringla* the king has sprinkled him with water and given the boy his own name.

Even though Gunhild's sons have been baptized and Earl Håkon is a heathen, Snorri does not contrast Christianity with paganism; instead, he contrasts the brothers' ruthless destruction of old cult centers with Earl Håkon's restoration of them. As a whole, Snorri treats his paganism lightly and presents his maintenance of the temples and sacrifices as a sign of respect for old order and customs. The brothers' lavishness and greed lead to the impoverishment of the country, while Earl Håkon builds his own wealth on plunderings in the east, and during his rule the country is flourishing. As the fosterson of Harald Bluetooth, Harald Greycloak (together with his brothers) is fully dependent on Denmark, while, thanks to his cunning, Earl Håkon manages to free Norway from Danish hegemony.

The only positive things Snorri has to say about Gunnhild's sons is that they were handsome, strong, of great stature, and accomplished in bodily skills.[48] Their fortitude, however, was not of the virtuous kind, and (though Christian) their vices were many, above all their pride, envy, greed, and wrath. Their rule was disastrous. In contrast, Earl Håkon's rule over Norway is said to have been fortunate for the country:

> The first winter Håkon ruled over Norway, shoals of herring came near land all over the country, and during the fall before, the grain had matured wherever it had been sowed. And in the spring *bœndr* provided themselves with seed corn, so that most of them could sow their fields, and a good season was promising.[49]

Earl Håkon's qualities are illustrated in the poem *Vellekla*, of which Snorri quotes four stanzas.[50]

Snorri's explicit characterizations of both Gunhild's sons and Earl Håkon correspond totally with what is implied in his narrative. His favorable picture and opinion of the earl contrast with earlier sources, and we will return to this after dealing with Håkon's relationship with Olav Tryggvason (p. 51–56.).

---

48 S. Harald Greycloak 2; ÍFH I:204; Hollander, 131.
49 S. Olav Tryggvason, chap. 16; ÍFH I:243; Hollander, 156.
50 S. Olav Tryggvason, chap. 16; ÍFH I:241–42; Hollander, 155.

6. Olav Tryggvason (995–999/1000) vs. Earl Håkon

Introduction

"The Saga of Olav Tryggvason" contains 113 chapters (= 100 pages in Holland-er), and in almost a third of them Earl Håkon plays a leading role.[51] This raises the question why the editors who created a special saga of Earl Håkon did not include these chapters in it. It is one of the many indications that the division into separate "Kings' Sagas" is not original but a result of the editorial work on Snorri's original *Heimskringla*.

Explicit characterization of Olav Tryggvason

Olav was the strongest and most handsome man you could see, better in sports than any other Norwegian there are stories about.[52] He "was of a most cheerful disposition and full of fun; he was friendly and affable, impetuous in all matters, exceedingly generous, and a fine dresser. He exceeded everyone in bravery when in battle. When angered he was very cruel, inflicting tortures on his enemies. Some of them he burned with fire, some he let wild dogs tear to pieces, others he had maimed or cast down from high cliffs. For these reasons he was beloved by his friends and feared by his enemies. And he had such success, because some out of friendship and good will did what he wanted done, and some, because of their fear of him."[53]

Comment

Olav is praised for his looks and bravery, but what is said about his friendliness is immediately contradicted by the description of his violence and cruelty. The narrative will reveal what prevails.

Summary

Olav's youth

After King Tryggve Olavsson had been killed by Gunnhild's sons, his widow Astrid, who was expecting their child, fled to her father. Having given birth to Olav, she and her son were chased by Gunnhild's spies, so together with Olav's fosterfather they fled again (via Svitjod), planning to join Astrid's brother Sig-urd in Gardarike. On their way across the Baltic, however, they were attacked by

---

[51] S. Olav Tryggvason: 34 chaps.: 9–20; 23, 24; 26, 27; 33–42; 45–50; (59, 83).
[52] S. Olav Tryggvason, chap. 8; ÍFH I:232; Hollander, 149.
[53] S. Olav Tryggvason, chap. 85; ÍFH I:333; Hollander, 218.

vikings, who killed Olav's fosterfather, separated mother and son, and sold both as slaves in Estonia.

When Olav was six years old, he was found by his uncle Sigurd, who took him to Holmgard, where—three years later—he killed his fosterfather's murderer (Klerkon) with an axe. After this he was taken care of by Queen Allogia until he was eighteen years old, when he decided to leave Holmgard and sailed into the Baltic, where he harried and got much booty.

In Vendland he married Geira, daughter of its ruler Burislav. Here he collected tax from areas belonging to her and raided, killing many people and confiscating much land. He also raided in Skåne and on Gotland. After three years of marriage, Geira died, and Olav left Vendland to raid in Frísia, Saxland, the land of the Flemings (Flanders), England, Scotland, the Hebrides, the Isle of Man, Ireland, Wales, and Valland (France), finally arriving at the Scilly Islands (west of England). There he met a hermit, who prophesized that Olav would become a famous king who would convert many people to Christianity. The hermit also predicted what would happen to Olav in the next few days, and since his prediction turned out to be true, Olav believed him to be a real prophet. Together with all his men, Olav was persuaded to be baptized, and he remained for a long time with the hermit, learning about the Christian faith. Taking with him priests from the Scilly Islands, he sailed to England but proceeded peaceably, "for England was Christian."[54] In an assembly there, he met Queen Gyda, married her, and then went harrying in Ireland.[55]

Earl Håkon's rule

Having defeated all Gunhild's sons, Earl Håkon ruled over all coastal Norway, and he did not pay any tribute to the Danish king.[56] When King Harald Bluetooth was threatened by the German emperor Otto, however, he summoned Håkon, who came to his help with a big army. Håkon's defence of Danevirke was successful, but Emperor Otto attacked Jutland again, and this time King Harald was defeated. In order to avoid further attacks from the emperor, King Harald accepted the Christian faith and forced Earl Håkon and his followers to do the same. The earl, however, put the priests he had been given in order to christianize Norway ashore, and then he left, raiding both sides of the Øresund and the Götaland region on his way home. Not long after this, Harald Bluetooth fell in battle with his own son Svein ("Forkbeard"), who cooperated with

---

[54] S. Olav Tryggvason, chap. 32; ÍFH I:267; Hollander, 171.

[55] Gyda was the sister of the Irish king Olav Kváran in Dublin. Olav's harrying in Ireland is remarkable, since Ireland had been Christian long before England!

[56] S. Olav Tryggvason, chap. 23; ÍFH I:254; Hollander, 163.

the Jómsvikings, whose plan it was to drive Earl Håkon out of Norway.[57] Their attempt failed, however, and after his victory Earl Håkon ruled over sixteen districts along the coasts and had sixteen earls under him.

When Earl Håkon heard a rumour that a man in the British Isles, calling himself "Åle," was regarded as a man of royal descent, he suspected this man to be Olav, the son of Tryggve Olavsson. He then sent his friend Tore Klakka to Dublin in order to find out if his suspicion was right and, if so, make Olav come to Norway by telling him lies about Earl Håkon's unpopularity there. On hearing this, Olav Tryggvason immediately set out for Norway (via the Hebrides and Orkney, forcing Christianity on the rulers and people there). He landed at Moster and had a church built there. It was soon known that Tore's lie about Earl Håkon's unpopularity had actually become true; by now, Håkon had upset many powerful landowners because of his "licentious" behaviour, abducting their daughters, bringing them to his residence, and lying with them for a week or more before sending them back home.[58]

The anger of the landowners forced Earl Håkon to flee, and now also challenged by Olav Tryggvason, he and his thrall Kark took shelter in a pigsty belonging to his friend Tora of Rimul. When Olav Tryggvason arrived there in search for Håkon, he could not find him, but he loudly announced that the person who could damage the earl would be richly rewarded. Hearing this from their hiding-place, Kark waited until Earl Håkon was asleep and cut off his head. Presented with Håkon's head, King Olav "rewarded" Kark by having him beheaded and put both heads on gallows in the island of Nidarholm (outside Nidaros), where many people came to stone them.

Comments

Even though Earl Håkon—like Olav Tryggvason—was Harald Fairhair's great grandson, all sources used here emphasize that he did not strive for kingship himself. Having driven away Gunhild's sons, he ruled Norway as earl with sixteen earls under him, but he feared that Olav Tryggvason would claim royal power over the whole country. By that he appears as a representative of the old political system, opposed to the new centralizing ideas of Christian kingship, and as such he obviously has Snorri's sympathy.

Neither in *Fagrskinna* nor in *Heimskringla* does Håkon take any part in the hunt for the newborn Olav. This is consistent with the positive portraits both works paint of the earl—in contrast with the earlier sources. *Historia Norwegiae* makes Håkon the sole hunter for the baby, in *Ágrip* both Gunhild and Håkon are

---

[57] The Jómsvikings were a band of vikings who were based in Jómsborg, a stronghold on the island of Wollin, situated at the mouth of the river Oder. S. Olav Tryggvason, Chaps. 34, 35; ÍFH I:272–75; Hollander, 174–76.

[58] S. Olav Tryggvason, chap. 45; ÍFH I:290–91; Hollander, 187.

hunting, while Theodoricus and Oddr Snorrason have Gunhild *force* Håkon to go searching. This illustrates the development in the opinions of Håkon; according to *Historia Norwegiae* and Theodoricus, he is totally evil; in Ágrip and Oddr, he is still bad but has at least some good qualities. *Fagrskinna* presents a nuanced picture of Håkon, calling attention to his positive features, and in *Heimskringla* the metamorphosis is accomplished. In his whitewash of "Håkon the bad," Snorri even goes so far as to introduce another Håkon, said to be a chieftain and close friend of Gunnhild, to find Olav. Snorri's description of Astrid's flight, Olav's childhood and youth in the east does not differ significantly from earlier sources, but reading about Olav's stay in the British Isles we are led to question Olav's evangelical disposition: as newly baptized (in the Scilly Islands), he abstains from plundering in England, since the country was Christian, but he goes on harrying in Ireland, which had been Christian much longer!

After Emperor Otto's victory, King Harald Gormsson is seriously weakened, and for Håkon, time is ripe to break with the Danes. Like Theodoricus and *Fagrskinna*, Snorri describes Håkon's demonstrative refusal to obey King Harald's order to christianize Norway and, instead, goes plundering areas under Danish influence. When the Danes retaliate, Snorri is careful to point out that Håkon restores all that had been destroyed during their attacks, yet another example of the earl as the defender of old order, customs, and traditions. As such, he has to stop Olav Tryggvason from claiming his royal rights in Norway, and Theodoricus describes in detail how cruelly Håkon behaves to this purpose: knowing that Olav would not believe any messengers but his own uncles, he threatened them with death unless they obeyed his command, which was to tell Olav that Earl Håkon was dead and that the whole country anxiously awaited him.[59]

In *Heimskringla*, however, Olav Tryggvason's uncles play no part in the deceit, neither does Håkon instruct the messenger Tore Klakka what to say to Olav, only that "he was to get the better of him by some treachery, if he could."[60] Far from spreading a false rumour about Håkon's death (as in Theodoricus' version), Tore stresses the earl's strength and power, which incites Olav, especially as Tore adds that many *bændr* would welcome him in Norway. Thus, Snorri does not depict Olav as an innocent victim, lured to Norway, but as a powerful warrior, intent on grasping royal power.[61]

It should be noted that in *Historia Norwegiae*, *Ágrip*, and *Fagrskinna*, Olav Tryggvason has nothing to do with Earl Håkon, while Snorri seems to build his story

---

[59] Theodoricus, chap. 7; Theodoricus Monachus, *The Ancient History of the Norwegian Kings* (Viking Society for Northern Research; London: University College of London, 1998), 10–11.

[60] S. Olav Tryggvason, chap. 46; ÍFH I:291; Hollander, 188.

[61] S. Olav Tryggvason, chap. 47; ÍFH I:292; Hollander, 188.

on Theodoricus and expand it to suit his purpose, i.e. to vindicate Håkon and defame Olav. The expansion includes a scene where Olav hurls the tiller of his rudder at a swimming man whom he believes to be Håkon, thereby killing Håkon's son Erlend instead.

In all sources used here, Håkon is killed by his thrall Kark, but it is only in Oddr and *Heimskringla* that he has been egged on by Olav. All but one of the sources agree that, in the end, it was Håkon's immoral behaviour that provoked anger and caused the revolt.[62] "He went so far as to abduct the daughters of powerful chieftains and to have them brought to his residence, where he lay with them for a week or two before sending them home."[63] Snorri, however, makes little of this and instead states that it was typical of the people of Trøndelag to "murmur menacingly if anything displeased them."[64]

In *Heimskringla*, Håkon "the Bad" has turned into a great defender of Norway, outshining the powerful Danish king. Even Oddr Snorrason admits that there were some good things in him:

> Although we have harsh and negative things to say about Jarl Håkon, it is nonetheless said of him that his rule lasted for a long time and was popular at first, but as his life advanced, his rule became harsher and more aggressive to live under. It is also told of him that he was a very handsome man and very wise, and in many ways the most preeminent among all those of his rank. He was in addition a great warrior.[65]

Snorri, however, does not criticize Håkon at all and tones down the negative points made in earlier sources. His judgment of the earl is entirely positive:

> There was such fierce hatred against Earl Håkon among the Trønders that no one might call him by any other name than the evil earl. And that name stuck to him for a long time. But the truth of the matter is that he had many qualifications for leadership: first, an exalted lineage, and therewith shrewdness and sagacity to use his power, briskness in battle as well as a lucky hand in winning the victory and slaying his enemies [. . .] Earl Håkon exceeded everyone in generosity, and it was great ill fortune that a chieftain such as he should have died as he did. But the reason for this was chiefly that the time had come when heathen worship and idolators were done away with and Christianity took their place.[66]

---

62 *Historia Norwegiae* mentions nothing about his immorality.
63 S. Olav Tryggvason, chap. 45; ÍFH I:290–91; Hollander, 187.
64 S. Olav Tryggvason, chap. 45; ÍFH I:290; Hollander, 187.
65 Oddr Snorrason, chap. 20; Andersson, 68.
66 S. Olav Tryggvason, chap. 50; ÍFH I:298–99; Hollander, 192–93.

It is hardly surprising that ecclesiastical works, like *Historia Norwegiae* and *The-odoricus*, condemn a pronounced pagan, but it is noteworthy that the portrait of him is more nuanced in both Oddr and *Fagrskinna*. In *Heimskringla*, however, Earl Håkon is a hero. Snorri tones down Earl Håkon's paganism, praises his wit and long-lasting good rule, emphasizing how Norway flourished during his time. While *Historia Norwegiae* describes Earl Håkon's path to power as usur-pation, Snorri admiringly describes his manipulation of King Harald Gormsson into giving him the whole of Norway. In all, Harald Gormsson is portrayed as incredibly gullible and simply has to accept first that Håkon stops paying tribute, and then that he breaks their alliance and frees Norway from Danish overlord-ship.

But how could such a skillful politician and leader as Earl Håkon fall in the way he did? Like the authors of *Ágrip* and *Fagrskinna*, Snorri answers that his *flight* was due to his appetite for women, but for his *death* Snorri blames Olav Tryggvason. As far as the earl's appetite for women is concerned, Jan Rüdiger has offered an interesting explanation,[67] which Snorri might have embraced: there was a tradition about the divine origin of the earls of Lade, according to which the dynasty was founded by a pagan god and a giant woman, representing the earth ("hierogamy").[68] Their sexual relationship could explain why the successors continued the hierogamic habit, leading to Earl Håkon's wish to own as many women as possible within his realm. What Earl Håkon had obviously not real-ized, however, was that attitudes were changing, and that Christian rules were now more widely accepted. This is exactly what Snorri remarks, commenting on Earl Håkon's ignominious end: "the time had come when pagan sacrifices and sacrificers (idolators) should be condemned to be replaced by the holy faith and right (good) habits."[69]

Thus, Snorri shows a better understanding of Earl Håkon's behaviour than the earlier authors, who all criticize him for his immorality. Considering the cru-elty with which Olav Tryggvason forced Christianity on people, Snorri's remark could be interpreted as irony; true Christians could hardly approve of King Olav's ruthlessness and brutality. Thus, Snorri's explicit praise of Olav has no basis in his narrative, which, instead, illustrates Olav's cruelty and dark sides.

---

[67] Jan Rüdiger, "Polygynie im Hochmittelalter im europäischen Vergleich," unpub-lished manuscript.

[68] I.e. a marriage between a god and a goddess, and also when human participants represent the deities. It is the harmonization of opposites; the ruler representing the god, and the woman the land.

[69] S. Olav Tryggvason, chap. 50. My translation of the Icelandic text (in ÍFH I, p. 299). Cf. Hollander, p. 93: "." . .the time had come when heathen worship and idolators were done away with and Christianity took their place."

7. Olav Tryggvason as king of Norway

After Earl Håkon's death, his sons Eirik and Olav fled to Sweden, and Olav Tryggvason was chosen king over all Norway at a general assembly in Nidaros. He immediately began his christianizing enterprises—characterized by threats, treachery, force, and violence—in Viken, Agder, Hordaland, Rogaland, Sogn & Fjordane, Møre & Romsdal, Ringerike, Hålogaland, and Iceland.

Examples of Olav Tryggvason's methods

Ch. 53: Viken
In Viken King Olav demanded that all people convert to Christianity, and those who refused, he punished severely; some were killed, others were mutilated, and others exiled.

Ch. 54–55: Rogaland
At an assembly in Rogaland, Olav asked people first in mild words to convert to Christianity, but then he threatened with punishments if they did not obey. All people at the thing were in the end baptized.

Ch. 59: Sogn and Fjordane; South Møre and Romsdal
At the thing with people from these areas, King Olav appeared with a great following, demanding that they convert—else they would have to fight him. The people yielded and everyone was baptized.

Ch. 62–64: The sorcerers
(Ch. 62:) Once in Tønsberg, Olav proclaimed that all those who practiced magic and sorcery must leave Norway. He had a search made for such persons and summoned them to him, had them all put in one room, and entertained them with strong drink. When they were drunk, he had the house set afire, and all except a skilled sorcerer, called Øyvind, were burnt inside.

(Ch. 63:) When Olav prepared to celebrate Easter at Avaldsnes, Øyvind came there with a ship fully manned with warlocks and other kinds of sorcerers. Øyvind's sorcery did not function, so he and his whole crew were caught by the king's men. Olav had them all taken out to the skerries, where they lost their lives when, at high tide, the skerries were covered with water.

(Ch. 64:) At a feast held in Avaldsnes, King Olav was visited by an old one-eyed man. Olav sat up a long time in the night listening to this man, who turned out to be Odin himself, and the bishop had to interrupt their conversation twice, before he could make Olav go to bed.

Ch. 76: Øyvind in Hålogaland

Here Olav´s men had another Øyvind, also a pagan, caught and brought to Nidaros, where he was led to King Olav. The king first asked him gently to convert to Christianity, then offered him presents, but Øyvind flatly refused. He still did not yield when Olav threatened him with mutilation or death. Then Olav had a basin full of live coals brought in and put on Øyvind's belly, which soon burst.

Ch. 80: Raud in Hålogaland

Raud, a farmer in Hålogaland, was powerful and a great sorcerer. King Olav sailed to find him and seized him in his home. His housecarls were captured, some were beaten, others killed. When Raud refused to believe in Christ, the king was enraged and promised him a most terrible death. Raud was tied with his back to a beam with a stick between his teeth to keep his mouth open. Then he had a snake put before his mouth, but it wriggled away when Raud blew against it. Then the king had the hollow stem of an angelica-stalk put into his mouth (some say he had his trumpet put into it), inserted the snake into it, poking it down with a glowing iron bar. Then the snake wriggled down Raud´s throat and gnawed its way out through his side. From that Raud died. On that journey, trolls and evil spirits taunted both Olav and his men.

In Gulathing, Olav met with such resistance that he had to negotiate with the magnates. The chieftains' condition to accept Christianity was that Olav's sister Astrid should marry their leader Erling Skjalgsson, which Olav accepted. When Astrid refused, Olav simply forced her to obey. After their wedding, King Olav planned a marriage for himself. He sent messengers to ask for the hand of Queen Sigrid of Sweden, and a betrothal was agreed on. On their first meeting Olav demanded that Sigrid should be baptized; when she refused, he broke their engagement, insulted her, and slapped her in the face with his glove. Sigrid stood up exclaiming: "This may well be your death!"—a threat that would prove to come true. Instead, Sigrid married the Danish king Svein (Forkbeard), who became the stepfather of her son Olof (with the Swedish king Erik.) The two kings were great friends with Olav Tryggvason's enemy, the Norwegian Earl Eirik Hákonsson (see ch. 7).

Also in Trøndelag, the resistance to Olav was very strong. At an assembly in Nidaros, all *bændr* were armed, and realizing that he could not defeat such a large force, Olav pretended that he yielded to their demand and promised to attend their greatest sacrifice at Mære. He invited chieftains and other important *bændr* to a big feast at Lade and treated them generously in the evening but told them his true intentions in the morning, announcing that he would arrange the greatest sacrifice ever made, even to sacrifice humans. The guests got the message and yielded, let themselves be baptized, promised to abolish all sacrifices, and had to leave their sons and closest kinsmen as hostages to the king. This maneuver made it possible for Olav to destroy the cult site at Mære and have the pagan leader Jernskjegge killed. Having offered Jernskjegge's kinsmen atonement, they were reconciled, and Olav married Jernskjegge's daughter Gudrun. On their first night together, however, Gudrun drew a knife to kill him, but he managed to wrest it from her. After this, Gudrun and her men left the place. All people present at the site of Mære were baptized, and Olav demanded hostages from them to make sure they would hold fast to Christianity. After this, the resistance in Trøndelag was broken, and the whole district was converted. Olav had a market town founded in Nidaros with a royal residence erected above a small inlet there.[70]

Olav's missionary zeal also extended to Iceland and Greenland. He sent the priest Thangbrand to convert the Icelanders, but when he came back, reporting that his mission had been a failure, King Olav became so angry that he wanted all Icelanders who were then staying in Nidaros to be killed. Thanks to the interventions of wise Icelanders, Olav changed his mind and, instead, had all Icelanders in the town baptized.[71] On his second attempt to convert the Icelanders, Olav sent Gizzur and Hjalte together with the priest Tormod and other ordained men—but kept four noble Icelanders with him as hostages. This attempt was successful: Christianity was adopted in Iceland by law, and all the people were baptized.[72]

Olav Tryggvason's fall

The Danish king Svein Forkbeard was first married to Gunnhild, the daughter of Burislav, king of the Vends, to whom he had promised his sister Tyre. She refused to marry "a heathen king who also was old" but was nevertheless sent to Vendland bitterly weeping.[73] Soon after the wedding, however, she fled to Norway where she met Olav Tryggvason, who found her both well spoken and handsome, and they married. After their wedding she urged him to recover the property she had lost in Vendland. Despite the advice of his friends, he agreed to help her, assembled a large fleet, and sailed to Vendland, where Burislav agreed to release her property.

---

[70] S. Olav Tryggvason, chap. 70, ÍFH I:318; Hollander, 208.

[71] S. Olav Tryggvason, chap. 84; ÍFH I:332–33; Hollander, 217–18.

[72] S. Olav Tryggvason, chap. 95; ÍFH I:347; Hollander 227–28. Later he commissioned Leif Eriksson, who had earlier been baptized at his court, to lead a company with clerics to preach in Greenland. On their journey Leif discovered Vínland ("the Good") and rescued a crew, marooned on a wreck. Leif's father Eirik commented thus: "the two things balanced each other—that Leif had rescued that crew and that he had brought the hypocrite to Greenland." Snorri adds: "by that he meant the priest," chap. 96; ÍFH I:347; Hollander, 228.

[73] S. Olav Tryggvason, chap. 92; ÍFH I:342; Hollander, 224–25.

Not having forgotten Olav Tryggvason's insult, Sigrid incited her new husband, Svein Forkbeard, to wage war against him, saying that his having married Tyre without Svein's consent consent was sufficient reason.[74] Svein was persuaded to follow her advice and, with the support of the Swedish king Olof and the Norwegian earl Eirik, he attacked Olav on his way back to Norway. In the battle at Svolder, Olav was wounded, fell overboard, and drowned.[75] Now Svein had power over the whole of Norway, and he granted Earl Eirik Romerike and Hedmark, while Eirik's brother Svein was given the earldom of Lade by the Swedish king. Both earls were baptized, and Snorri writes:

> . . . during the time they ruled over Norway they let everyone do as he pleased about the keeping of Christianity, whereas they kept well the old laws and all customs of the land, and they were greatly beloved and governed well. Earl Eirik had most to say of all his brothers in matters dealing with the administration of the country.[76]

Comments

In contrast to the two earls, who are said to be tolerant, just, competent and diligent, Olav Tryggvason is both explicitly and implicitly described as having no virtues. He is

- shrewd rather than prudent,
- intent on breaking old laws instead of keeping them,
- selfish and avaricious—generous only to his friends,
- cruel instead of merciful to his enemies,
- feared by his enemies instead of being popular, and
- hard, ruthless and imperious, not temperate.

As Snorri describes them, his Christianization methods are *political conquests* rather than attempts to spread the new faith. Snorri actually casts suspicion on Olav's own faith; apart from lacking all Christian virtues, he is so fascinated by Odin's tales that the bishop has to intervene. He spares not even his family to reach his goals, simply forcing his sister to obey him. When he does not use direct violence or torture, he finds other ways of forcing people, for example, taking hostages; this was how he converts both Trøndelag and Iceland. For a couple of years he is successful, but he prepares his own fall by behaving like a political idiot, challenging both the Swedish queen and the Danish king. His brutal treat-

---

[74] S. Olav Tryggvason, chap. 98; ÍFH I:349; Hollander, 229.

[75] S. Olav Tryggvason, chaps. 101–11; ÍFH I:353–72; Hollander, 231–41. See more in Chapter 7 below.

[76] S. Olav Tryggvason, chap. 113; ÍFH I:372; Hollander, 244.

ment of Queen Sigrid, breaking their engagement and hitting her in her face, rouses her wrath and drives her to marry his worst enemy, King Svein, whom she incites to take revenge. In addition, Olav is foolish enough to yield to his wife's demand for her property in Vendland and sets out on a voyage that leads him right into the arms of his enemies. His rule lasted for less than five years and ended with Norway's loss of independence: the country was split by the victors. Svein Forkbeard took Viken, and the rest of Norway was split between Earl Håkon's sons, Erik and Sven (earl under the Swedish king).

As far as Olav's interest in women is concerned, it is uncertain whether Snorri wanted to characterize him as driven by lust or strategic planning, but the fact remains that Olav is polygamous. After the death of his first wife, the Wendish princess Geira, he married the Irish Queen Gyda, and soon after that the Norwegian Gudrun; his proposal to the Swedish queen Sigrid misfired, and finally he married the Danish princess Tyre. The last two women were largely responsible for his fall.

8. Olav Haraldsson ("Saint Olav," 1015–1028); Erling Skjalgsson; Tore the Hound; Einar Tambarskjelve; Kalv Arnesson

The saga of Saint Olav is an adaptation of Snorri's earlier "Separate Saga of St. Olav." It takes up almost one-third of the work, and much has been written about it. My purpose is not to compare Snorri's version with those of his predecessors; suffice it to say that in *Fagrskinna*, the story about Saint Olav only takes up less than one-tenth of the contents.[77] A widely held view is that Snorri arranged his saga like a classical tragedy: initial success, turning point, ultimate failure and death,[78] but this is disputable. In *Heimskringla's* version, neither Olav's way to power or his rule could be called a story of success. Instead, both were riddled with opposition and serious conflicts, both internal and external. The only success he had was after his death, as a saint. The structure of Snorri's St. Olavsaga is as follows:

Section	Chapter(s)	Contents
1.	1–31	Childhood and youth; fights in England
2.	32–66	Fights for power in Norway; forced Christianization
3.	67–94	Conflicts with the Swedish king Olav
4.	95–129	Conflicts with Norwegian magnates

---

[77] *Fagrskinna, A Catalogue of the Kings of Norway.* Translated with Introduction and Notes by Alison Finlay (Leiden & Boston: Brill, 2004).

[78] E.g., Sverre Bagge, *Society and Politics in Snorri Sturluson's Heimskringla* (Berkeley & Los Angeles: University of California Press, 1991), 37.

5.	130–161	Conflicts with the Danish king Knud the Powerful
6.	162–191	Decline and flight
7.	192–229	The battle at Stiklestad: Olav's death
8.	230–251	After the Battle

Explicit characterization

Olav was "an accomplished man, handsome and of middle height [. . .], clever and eloquent.[79] He was "of stout frame and great strength," had light brown hair, a broad face of light complexion and ruddy, unusually fine eyes, bright and piercing, so that "it inspired terror to look into them when he was furious."[80] He was good at sports (shooting, swimming, hurling spears). He was nicknamed Olav the Stout, spoke boldly and quickly, early mature in both strength and shrewdness, liked by all relatives and friends. He was ambitious in games, always wanting to be foremost.[81] He changed laws according to the advice of the wisest men and gave Christian laws with the help of bishop Grimkjell and other clergy. He used all his power to abolish paganism and ancient practices that were contrary to the spirit of Christianity. He was well-mannered, a man of rather few words, openhanded, but eager to have possessions. He carefully inquired well-informed men how the Christian faith was held in the tributary countries and on Iceland.[82] "We are told that King Olav led a pure life and was diligent in his prayers to God all the time he lived; but when he found his power diminishing and his opponents waxing strong, he concentrated all his mind on serving God. [. . .] He let punishment go over both the great and the small. But that seemed presumptuous to the people of the land, and a hate against him arose among them who had lost kinsmen through a just verdict of the king, even though there was good cause for it. That was the reason for the revolt against King Olav that they would not stand for his exercising justice.[83] [. . .] He was most generous toward his friends."[84]

Comments

At first sight, this description of Olav Haraldsson gives a rather positive impression of him and his achievements, but that is deceptive. It is obviously because of Olav's sanctity that, *explicitly*, Snorri must do a balancing act. The narrative has many negative implications, which we find already in his explicit characterization of Olav, which is full of contradictions. At the same time as Olav's eyes

---

79 S. Saint Olav, chap. 1; ÍFH II:3; Hollander, 245.
80 S. Saint Olav, chap. 3; ÍFH II:4; Hollander, 245.
81 S. Saint Olav, chap. 1; ÍFH II:3; Hollander, 245.
82 S. Saint Olav, chap. 58; ÍFH II:74; Hollander, 289–90.
83 S. Saint Olav, chap. 181; ÍFH II:330; Hollander, 474–76.
84 S. Saint Olav, chap. 181; ÍFH II:330; Hollander, 476.

are fine and bright, they are also piercing and inspire terror; likewise, he is both handsome and stout, eloquent and "a man of rather few words," generous toward his friends—and greedy. He is described as shrewd and ambitious and is liked—obviously—only by relatives and friends. Snorri does not maintain that Olav led a pure life, praying to God, but carefully refers to what "we are told." Thus, we read almost nothing about his Christian belief but all the more about his zeal to abolish paganism. His letting punishment go over both the great and the small is, in effect, a criticism of his breaking old laws.

Summary

According to Snorri, Olav Haraldsson was the son of Harald Grenske, who is said to be Harald Fairhair's great grandson.[85] This makes the two Olavs close relatives (see genealogy, Appendix 2), but the descent is a construction, made all the better by Snorri, who has Olav Tryggvason convert Olav Haraldsson's mother and stepfather—and become his godfather.[86]

In the beginning of Olav Haraldsson's career he collected great wealth, due to his raiding and fighting for the English king Adalråd against the Danes. That is why he could return to Norway as a rich man with good ships and well-armed crews. Through generous gifts he acquired many followers but met hard resistance, above all from Earl Svein Hákonsson, Einar Tambarskjelve, and Erling Skjalgsson. After defeating them in the Battle of Nesjar,[87] there was a temporary reconciliation, but after new conflicts, they broke with the king. Other magnates who had originally been Olav's men (Hårek of Tjøtta, Tore the Hound, and Kalv Arnesson) also broke with him, and after Olav's man killed Erling Skjalgsson, many other magnates abandoned Olav and joined the Danish king Knud.

Olav Haraldsson's christianization of Norway

Snorri's presentation of Olav's evangelical methods is full of violence and detailed descriptions of the king's cruel methods. After his victory at Nesjar, Olav went to the Oppland region to investigate how Christianity was being kept there. Snorri writes:[88]

> . . . if he found anyone who did not want to abandon heathendom, he drove him out of the land. Some he had maimed, having their hands or feet lopped off or their eyes gouged out, others he had hanged or beheaded, but

---

[85] Harald Grenske was the son of Gudrød, son of Bjørn, son of Harald Fairhair.
[86] S. Olav Tryggvason, chap. 60; ÍFH:I:310; Hollander, 200.
[87] S. Saint Olav, chap. 49; ÍFH II:60–62; Hollander, 281–82.
[88] S. Saint Olav, chap. 73; ÍFH II:101; Hollander, 309–10.

left no one unchastised who refused to serve God. And thus he proceeded in all the district. Always he punished both the mighty and the humble.

Hearing about this, the kings in the districts of Romerike, Hedmark, Gudbrandsdalen, and Hadeland decided to oppose Olav and sent spies to find out every move that he made on his way through Romerike. When the kings had made their plans, they called landed men and landowners from all districts to attend a meeting. One of them, Kjetil from Ringnes, betrayed the kings, however, and told Olav about their plans, showing him where the kings were sleeping. Olav had them all taken prisoner, had King Rørek blinded and King Gudrød's tongue cut out. The other kings had to swear to leave Norway never to return; some of their accomplices were exiled, some were mutilated, but with some he was reconciled. "After that Olav was sole king in Norway."[89]

More examples of Olav Haraldsson's methods

Ch. 105: Namdalen District
In Namdalen District, Olav was accepted as king in all assemblies, and—as everywhere else—he ordered the people to accept Christianity. He punished those who refused with the loss of their limbs, lives, and property. He severely punished many people there, the powerful in the same way as the humble.

Ch. 111: Lesja and Dovre
When Olav had been king of Norway for seven years, he went to the Oppland District, took all the best men in both Lesja and Dovre prisoners, and forced them either to accept Christianity or die. Those who accepted the new faith had to give their sons to Olav as hostages. In the area called Lom, he sent word to say that people there, as well as in Vågen and the Dale, had to fight him and have the whole area burnt if they did not convert and give him their sons as hostages. Most became his men, but a few escaped south to Gudbrandsdalen.

Ch. 121: Valdres
When Olav had been king for ten years, he forced the people in Vors (Hordaland) to become Christian, and after that he joined his fleet in Osterfjorden and went to Valdres, which was still pagan. He took the *bœndr* by surprise, took all their ships, and held an assembly, ordering Christianity to be accepted. The yeomen who attended the assembly were fully armed and cried to the king to keep quiet and made so much noise that he could not pursue the matter by talking. Instead, he had his men spread out in the area, plundering and burning, whereupon the army of *bœndr* dissolved in order to go home and look after their properties.

---

[89] S. Saint Olav, chap. 75; ÍFH II:104–7; Hollander, 314.

It ended with the *bœndr* asking Olav's mercy, offering to become his men. He stayed in the area during the autumn but did not move far from his ships, since he did not trust the yeomen.

Comments

It is remarkable that, according to Snorri, Olav Haraldsson converted the same areas as Olav Tryggvason: Viken, Sogn, Hordaland, Møre and Romsdal, the inner of Trøndelag, and Hålogaland. Snorri does not comment on this. The districts that Olav Tryggvason is not said to have converted—and were left for Olav Haraldsson—were in the interior of Norway, namely Oppland, Romerike, Hedmark, Gudbrandsdalen, and Hadeland.

Summary

Apart from his Norwegian enemies, Olav had problems with the neighboring kingdoms. The Swedish king Olof Eriksson was furious because Olav had occupied land that was tributary to him and expelled Earl Svein. Olav sent Earl Ragnvald to Sweden to negotiate a peace treaty and a marriage between him and Olof's daughter Ingegjerd. Olof Eriksson refused but was then harshly rebuked by the lawspeaker Torgny at the Uppsala Assembly.[90] The two kings were reconciled, and the Swedish princess Ingegjerd was to be married to Olav Haraldsson. This did not happen, however, since Olof changed his mind and married her to the Russian ruler Jarisleiv instead. The Norwegian Olav had to make do with Olof Eriksson's illegitimate daughter Astrid (the daughter of a servant girl). Relationships with Denmark were no less strained; Knud, king of both England and Denmark, had claims on Norway, considering it his inherited possession. Earl Håkon also had claims on part of Norway, thinking he had lost it dishonourably. As long as Olav Haraldsson had seemed popular in Norway, they had not raised their claims, but when many Norwegian magnates and sons of powerful yeomen fled from Norway to join King Knud, they did so. When Knud invaded Norway, King Olav could not get enough people to support him and had to flee with his young son Magnus via Sweden to Holmgard/Russia.

After two years there, Olav heard that Norway was without a ruler (Earl Håkon had perished on his way to England), so he decided to return and regain power in Norway, leaving Magnus with King Jarisleiv and Queen Ingerid. Receiving help from the Swedish king Anund, he travelled north, and when the Norwegian landowners heard that he was approaching Verdalen (in Trøndelag),

---

[90] S. Saint Olav, chap. 80; ÍFH II:115–16; Hollander, 320–21. For Torgny's speech, see Appendix 4 below.

they mobilized a great army. King Knud's bishop Sigurd was in the army and often spoke to the landowners, encouraging them to resist Olav.[91]

Comments

Torgny the Lawspeaker's speech at the Uppsala Assembly is directed to a Swedish king and concerns Swedish politics, but no doubt it also contains Snorri's and many of his contemporaries' views on the duties of a king. It is also remarkable that Snorri has Sigurd, a Danish bishop, say the same things about Olav that Snorri himself has already told us: according to the bishop, Olav had in his youth robbed and killed men far and wide. He had taken possession of land tributary to Knud of Denmark and Olof of Sweden and expelled the earls Svein and Håkon. Further, Olav had driven all the kings from the Oppland districts, having mutilated them and appropriated their dominions. Snorri has Sigurd emphasize how Olav had killed the best landmen and gone through the country raiding and burning. Reminding the landowners about Olav's cruelty and lack of mercy, Sigurd is quoted admonishing them to fight Olav and receive the freedom that King Knud had promised them.

Summary

After Olav's fall, the Norwegians were not given the promised freedom; Knud sent his son Svein to rule as king in Norway together with his mother Alfiva, and they became extremely unpopular. There were soon rumours about miracles happening to people who had come close to "Saint" Olav. When talk of his sanctity increased, many of his former enemies also began to confirm it, heaping reproaches on those who had urged them to be hostile to him. The people of Trøndelag invited Olav's bishop Grimkjell in the Oppland region to return; he was well received by Einar Tambarskjelve, and "they came to agree on all matters."[92] Together they went to the place where Olav's body had been interred and had the coffin dug up. Even though Olav had been dead for more than a year, it was reported that the king's countenance had not changed and that his hair and nails had grown since his death. Alfiva, however, was not impressed but said: "Mighty little do bodies decompose when buried in sand. It would not be the case if he had lain in earth."[93] In answer to that, Bishop Grimkjell cut the king's hair and whiskers, trying to convince Alfiva that they had grown since his death, but she answered: "That hair would seem to me a holy relic only if fire does not burn it. We have often seen wholly preserved and undamaged the hair of persons who

---

[91] S. Saint Olav, chap. 217; ÍFH II:370–71; Hollander, 505ff. For Bishop Sigurd's speech, see Appendix 4 below.

[92] S. Saint Olav, chap. 244; ÍFH II:403; Hollander, 527.

[93] S. Saint Olav, chap. 244; ÍFH II:404; Hollander, 528.

have lain in the ground longer than this man has."[94] Bishop Grimkjell laid Olav's hair in a fire he had blessed and could show that it did not burn. Alfíva did not yield but demanded that the hair be tested in an unconsecrated fire, but then "Einar Tambarskjelve bade her be silent and used hard language against her."[95] After this, Olav was declared a true saint by Bishop Grimkjell, with the consent of King Svein and the people.

Comments

While the author of *Fagrskinna* does not waste many lines on the individual magnates who opposed Olav, Snorri gives detailed portraits of many and has four of them play leading roles: Erling Skjalgsson, Tore the Hound, Einar Thambarskjelfir, and Kalv Arnesson. In contrast, *Fagrskinna* mostly treats Olav's enemies collectively, as trouble-making *landed men*: "When men of power saw that the king gave equal judgement to great and small, they began to be ill-pleased, because [they] were so quarrelsome and unyielding that some would not give way in their suits to kings or jarls."[96] Thus, while in *Fagrskinna* these magnates are described as "false to the king in their schemes," Snorri explains why each of the main leaders opposed and abandoned Olav.

Summary: Erling Skjalgsson

We meet Erling in the sagas of Olav Tryggvason and Saint Olav. According to Snorri, Erling was "the noblest and most powerful of men in Norway, excepting only those of princely rank."[97] He belonged to an important family whose representatives were powerful enough to present an ultimatum to Olav Tryggvason: either give his sister Astrid in marriage to Erling or fight them. As we have seen, Olav chose the first alternative, and now as his brother-in-law, Erling became— and remained—loyal to him. After Olav's fall, Erling refused to be reconciled with Earl Eirik, who begrudged him his power and control of all the royal land that King Olav had granted him. After Eirik had left Norway, however, Erling was reconciled with his brother Earl Svein, who confirmed all Olav Tryggvason's grants. When Olav Haraldsson arrived in Norway, Erling joined in the resistance to him, and even after Olav had been accepted as king, Erling continued to rule his part of the country, which led to many serious conflicts between them. One of them was due to Olav's prohibition of sending grain to the north. Despite this, Erling allowed his thralls to sell grain to his nephew Asbjørn. On his way home, Asbjørn was stopped by the king's steward Tore

---

[94] S. Saint Olav, chap. 244; ÍFH II:404; Hollander, 528.

[95] S. Saint Olav, chap. 244; ÍFH II:404–5; Hollander, 530

[96] *Fagrskinna*, chap. 31; trans. Finlay, 146.

[97] S. Saint Olav, chap. 176; ÍFH II:318; Hollander, 468.

Seal, who confiscated the whole shipload. Asbjørn took revenge and killed Tore, and since King Olav refused to accept compensation for the slaying of his steward, Asbjørn was put in irons, expecting execution. Thanks to Erling's—and the bishop's—intervention, King Olav accepted reconciliation on condition that Asbjørn became his steward instead of the man he had killed. What happened after that we will see in connection with Asbjørn's paternal uncle, Tore the Hound. In the end, the conflicts become more serious and the situation untenable, whereupon Erling, together with his sons, joined Knud and began recruiting supporters against Olav Haraldsson.

In the final confrontation between Erling and King Olav, Erling's fleet was defeated, and "so complete was the slaughter of Erling's crew, that not a single man was left standing at the end except he alone." Snorri adds: "He defended himself so nobly that no one could remember any one man having stood off the attack of so many so long; and never did he attempt to escape nor did he ask for quarter."[98] Obviously impressed, King Olav asked Erling to swear allegiance to him. Erling did so, took off his helmet, and laid down his sword and shield, but his trust was misplaced; he was humiliated by Olav who pricked him on his chin with the point of his axe, saying: "A mark he shall bear, the betrayer of his king."[99] Immediately one of Olav's men rushed forward and killed Erling, a deed that so upset the king that he burst out: "Wretch that you are, to strike him down. With that blow you struck Norway out of my hand."[100]

Comments on Erling

This famous quotation is found also in *Ágrip* and *Fagrskinna*, and having the king himself realize that the killing of Erling would be the beginning of his downfall underlines Erling's power, popularity, and importance. Snorri deplores the fact that there was no one who could avenge the killing of "the noblest and most powerful of men in Norway." As Snorri characterizes Erling Skjalgsson, he illustrates most virtues; he is the ideal landowner and—not least—a great defender of the traditional social and political order. The portrait of Erling is one of the most flattering in *Heimskringla*: he was one of the handsomest, largest, and strongest men, a better warrior than any other. He was wise, generous, and good to his servants and thralls, giving them opportunities to improve their status, helping all to prosperity.

It should be added that Erling was commemorated not only by Sigvat skald but also by a priest who had a runic cross erected after him.[101] In fact, Erling and

---

[98] S. Saint Olav, chap. 176; ÍFH II:315; Hollander, 466.

[99] S. Saint Olav, chap. 176; ÍFH II:317; Hollander, 466.

[100] S. Saint Olav, chap. 176; ÍFH II:317; Hollander, 467.

[101] The cross is now in Stavanger. See *Norges innskrifter med de yngre runer*, ed. M. Olsen (Oslo: 1941–50), no. 252.

other men like him played as important a role in the conversion of Norway as Olav Tryggvason, and it is in Erling's territory (the West of Norway from Sogn Fjord to Lindisness, the southern tip of the country) that most of the early Christian crosses were erected.

Summary: Tore the Hound

The main story about Tore the Hound is in Saint Olav's saga; in the saga of Magnus the Good we only read that, shortly after King Olav's fall, he left Norway and went to Jerusalem and is said to have never returned.[102] Snorri describes Tore as the most powerful man in the North, living on the island of Bjarkøy. He was very well connected; his sister Sigrid was married to Olve, the magnate at Egge, with whom she had two sons (Tore and Grjotgard), and his brother Sigurd was married to Erling Skjalgsson's sister Sigrid, with whom he had the son Asbjørn. Tore was originally a landed man of Olav Haraldsson, but when four of his kinsmen had been killed by Olav, he joined the king's enemies. Tore was himself partly responsible for the fate of his nephew Asbjørn, since it was on his advice that Asbjørn refused to become Olav's steward, and this refusal led to his death. Egged on by two women, his sister and his sister-in-law, he had four men to avenge, and his revenge was threefold: first he killed Asbjørn's murderer and—on an expedition to Bjarmaland—seized all the king's booty, paying only one-third of the penalty for this offence, and then disappeared with all his riches to England. By joining King Knud, he enriched himself still more and took his third revenge at Stiklestad, piercing Olav's stomach with his spear.[103]

After Olav's fall, however, Tore immediately changed sides: he took care of the king's body and spread a cloak over it, and when urged by the *bœndr* to pursue the fugitives from Olav's army, he did so less than half-heartedly. Later, when the king's holiness came to be generally known among the people, Tore testified that the wound on his hand had healed speedily when touched by Olav's blood, and he was among the first of the king's enemies to give witness to his sanctity.[104] When hearing a rumor that King Olav was not dead but had managed to escape, Tore thought it better to be safe than sorry and left Norway for good.

---

[102] S. Magnus the Good, chap. 11; ÍFH II:22; Hollander, 549.
[103] S. Saint Olav, chap. 228; ÍFH II:385; Hollander, 515.
[104] S. Saint Olav, chap. 230; ÍFH II:387; Hollander, 516.

Comments on Tore

Both *Ágrip* and *Fagrskinna* mention Tore the Hound as one of the leaders for
the *bœndr* at Stiklestad, but it is only in *Ágrip* we read that he was also one of
the two who dealt Olav his death blow.[105] In *Heimskringla* we hear much more
about Tore, and Snorri describes him as one of the king's most dangerous enemies, much feared by Olav himself. When Tore disappeared to England, Snorri
has Olav react with relief: ". . . the further [Tore is] from us, the better."[106] Tore
is shrewd and escapes unhurt from difficult situations; he is also proud and constant in his opposition to the king but plays his cards well in the unstable political situation after Olav's fall at Stiklestad. Like Einar Tambarskjelve, he shows
many examples of a ready wit and the art of survival, for which he was no doubt
admired by Snorri. Tore's character is almost impossible to pinpoint; Snorri does
not seem to measure him according to virtues and vices but stresses his commitment to the old political order.

Summary: Einar Tambarskjelve and Kalv Arnesson

Einar, son of Eindride, earned his surname by his skill as an archer, Tambarskjelve meaning "he who twangs the gut-string of the bow." We read about him
in no fewer than five sagas,[107] first about his descent and then about his in-
laws: he was married to one of Earl Håkon's daughters, Bergljot, whose maternal grandfather was the magnate Skage Skoftesson and was thus very well connected.

Already as a young man, fighting for Olav Tryggvason, Einar showed his
prowess, being both quick-witted and a good warrior. Later he excelled in practical politics, changing loyalty whenever necessary. After Olav's fall he quickly
allied with his enemies, the earls Svein and Eirik, and married their sister. After
Earl Svein's death, however, Einar soon allied with Olav Haraldsson but abandoned him when he realized the growing discontent. After staying with Earl
Eirik's son Håkon in England, he turned to the Danish King Knud and became
his man. Disappointed with Knud, however, he began to plan a reconciliation
with King Olav Haraldsson and thus avoided taking part in the battle at Stiklestad. Instead, after the king's fall, he was quick to proclaim king Olav's sanctity,
cooperating with the king's bishop Grimkjell and silencing the skeptical Alfiva
(see above, p. 67). Realizing how much the Norwegians hated Svein's and Al-

---

[105] The other one was Torstein Knarresmed. Ágrip, chap. 31; Ágrip, af Nóregskonungasogum, ed. M. J. Driscoll. (Viking Society for Northern Research, London:
University College London), 1995, 44.

[106] S. Saint Olav, chap. 139; ÍFH II:253; Hollander, 422.

[107] S. Harald Greycloak; S. Olav Tryggvason; S. Saint Olav; S. Magnus the Good;
S. Harald Sigurdarsson.

fiva's rule, Einar and Kalv Arnesson made plans to replace them with Olav's son Magnus, whom they were convinced would be easily led.[108]

We meet Kalv in three sagas, first supporting then opposing Olav Haraldsson, later supporting—and falling out with—Magnus the Good, and, in the end, first opposing then supporting and at last being betrayed by Harald Sigurdarsson/Hardrade. He was one of Arne Armodsson's seven sons, and his sister Ragnhild was married to the powerful magnate Hårek of Tjøtta. All brothers (Kalv, Finn, Torberg, Åmunde, Kolbjørn, Arnbjørn, and Arne) became Olav Haraldsson's men, and Kalv requested the king to let him marry Sigrid, the widow of Olve at Egge, a chieftain of noble descent, who had had great influence before he was killed by King Olav's men. Kalv was granted permission and all Olve's possessions, thus becoming Sigrid's husband, the stepfather of her and Olve's sons, a landed man, and the ruler of Trøndelag. After King Olav had both stepsons killed;[109] however, a break between Kalv and the king was inevitable. When Earl Håkon had gathered a great warforce in Trøndelag against Olav, Kalv and many others suddenly left the king to join the earl.[110]

Karl hesitated when Earl Håkon asked him to enter his service, but at home he was urged by his wife Sigrid to accept this offer in order to take revenge on Olav for his killing of her family. In the end, Kalv was persuaded to enter the earl's service and next spring went to England, where Knud promised him the earldom of Norway if he bound himself to raise a force against Olav. Kalv agreed and, having received splendid gifts from Knud, returned to Norway. Before the battle of Stiklestad, Kalv was chosen chief of the *yeoman* army, inciting it against King Olav, who, among his men, had four of Kalv's brothers. It should be noted that Snorri takes care to point out that it was uncertain which Kalv wounded King Olav, Kalv Arnesson or his relative Kalv Arnfinsson. After the battle, Kalv searched for his brothers and, finding two of them wounded, brought them home to Egge.

Growing more and more displeased with the rule of Knud's young son Svein and his mother Alfiva, many Norwegians began to blame the people in Trøndelag for having been the cause of Saint Olav's death and, thereby, such tyranny. People in Trøndelag acknowledged the truth of this reproach, and the chieftains, led by Einar Tambarskjelve and Kalv Arnesson, discussed what was to be done. Kalv felt badly deceived by Knud, who had broken his promise to give him rule over all Norway. The result was that Kalv and Einar went to Novgorod to entreat Saint

---

[108] We will meet Einar Tambarskjelve later; see pp. 75f., 77, 80, 82, 108f.

[109] King Olav had discovered that one of them (Tore) was King Knud's man and that the other one (Grjotgarth) had tried to avenge his brother.

[110] S. Saint Olav, Chaps. 165, 166, 178; ÍFH II:300–03, 322–23; Hollander, 454–57, 470–71.

Olav's son Magnus to be the king of Norway. Magnus accepted and became Kalv's foster-son, promising full reconciliation, and Kalv—on his part—promised to do all he thought necessary to extend Magnus' dominion and make it independent (of Denmark).[111] All people were glad that Magnus came, King Svein and his mother fled to Denmark, and Kalv was praised by Bjarni Gullbrárskald:

> Kalv, through you the king did
> Come into his own; and
> You it was who, warrior,
> Won Magnus his title.[112]

Comments on Einar and Kalv

Thus the founding fathers of a Norway free from Danish overlordship are in fact the two magnates Einar Tambarskjelve and Kalv Arnesson. Both of them are good navigators in dangerous water, especially Einar, who avoids the fight at Stiklestad and can therefore not be blamed for Olav's death. Thanks to his power and shrewdness he manages to outlive several rulers, including king Magnus, and to cause much trouble for Harald Hardrade, as we will see later. As Magnus' foster-father also, Kalv has great influence. His path to power was complicated, however, since his loyalty to his family caused him much trouble; he felt obligation both to his brothers and his stepsons and was thereby torn between opposite lords, Olav and Knud. When he joins Earl Håkon he has taken the first step to oppose Olav, but it takes his wife's incitement to make him become the earl's man, thereby openly siding with Knud. This decision forces him to fight against his own brothers at Stiklestad, but after the battle he nevertheless takes care of the wounded Torberg and Finn, sending them back to their homes, generously equipped. His loyalty is repaid, when—during his long exile—Finn manages to have him restored to his old position in Norway, which, ironically, causes his fall.

We are left in the dark about Kalv's role in Olav's death; probably Snorri here gives Kalv the benefit of the doubt, at the same time explaining the suspicions later cast on him. Whatever role Kalv played, he—like other magnates—is very quick to accept Olav's sanctity. According to Snorri, Kalv's willingness to replace Svein and his mother with Olav's son is due to the fact that Kalv felt deceived when Knud had given not *him*, but his own son Svein, rule over Norway.[113]

---

[111] S. Saint Olav, chap. 251; ÍFH II:414–15; Hollander, 536–37.

[112] S. Magnus the Good, chap. 5; ÍFH III:11–12; Hollander, 543.

[113] We will meet Kalv again, in connection with King Magnus the Good (see Chapter 5 below).

Comments on Olav Haraldsson and the magnates

Three of Olav's most dangerous enemies survive him and have successful careers, while one of them, Erling Skjalgsson, is killed by Olav's man and dies almost a martyr. Erling gets his revenge after his death, however, since this deed—as Olav himself realizes—causes the general revolt against him. Snorri contrasts Erling and Olav, Erling having all virtues, Olav none, being envious of and angry about Erling's power and popularity. Tore the Hound and Einar Tambarskjelve are not measured according to virtues and vices; what Snorri emphasizes is that they are clever tacticians, constant in their opposition to King Olav and after his fall, trimming their sails according to the wind. Nor is Kalv Arnesson characterized according to virtues and vices; he is also described as a clever tactician, but Snorri paints a very humane portrait of him and his split loyalties: setting out as King Olav's man—like his brothers—he gradually distances himself from the king, one contributing factor being his marriage with Sigrid, the widow of Olav's enemy Olve, and his loyalty to her and her sons. At the same time he is torn, feeling loyalty also to his brothers who side with king Olav.

As will be more fully dealt with in Chapter 6, Snorri often lets women voice his own opinions. Alfiva's skepticism concerning Olav's sanctity is a very good example, reflecting Snorri's own attitude. Admittedly, he reports that rumours about Olav's sanctity began to spread very soon after his death, but it is clear that he tries to distance himself from these rumours; he uses such expressions as "this was taken to be a true miracle";[114] "That winter there arose much talk among the people of Trøndelag that King Olav was in truth a saint. . .";[115] ". . . he [= Bishop Grímkel] believed there might be truth in what was said about the miracles and the sainthood of King Olav."[116] We are told that Tore the Hound is the first of Olav's opponents to accept his sanctity, but Snorri stresses that it is Tore's own story he relates,[117] and that Tore does not tell others about it until the sanctity of Olav has already become known.[118]

Snorri also makes it clear that many of Olav's enemies soon take advantage of the rumours, especially after Knud has sent his son Svein with his mother Alfiva to rule Norway. They institute new—harsh—laws and become very unpopular. Einar Tambarskjelve, who "was mindful of the fact that Knud had promised him the earldom over Norway, and also that the king had not kept his promise," is the first among "men of influence" to maintain Olav's sanctity. Snorri points

---

114 S. Saint Olav, chap. 189; ÍFH II:342; Hollander, 485.

115 S. Saint Olav, chap. 240; ÍFH II:401; Hollander, 526.

116 S. Saint Olav, chap. 243; ÍFH II:403; Hollander, 527.

117 S. Saint Olav, chap. 230; ÍFH II:387; Hollander, 516: according to Tore his wounded hand was cured, when Olav's blood touched it.

118 S. Saint Olav, chap. 230; ÍFH II:387; Hollander, 516.

out that Einar boasts that he did not join in the rebellion against Olav.[119] Together with Kalv Arnesson, Einar makes plans, resulting in their refusal to pay tribute to Knud and, instead, set out to fetch Olav's son Magnus from Gardarike. There is no doubt that Snorri thinks that the magnates Einar Tambarskjelve and Kalv Arnesson have played their cards well, especially as Kalv manages to become the foster-father of his enemy's own son Magnus!

Snorri does not depict Olav Haraldsson as a saint but balances this by reporting many miracles that happened *after Olav's death*. The living Olav has no virtues. His fortitude is inspired by wrath, he is shrewd instead of prudent, he is not temperate, and his—new—justice (treating great and small equally) is not accepted by the magnates. Further, he is proud, greedy, and envious. Snorri also casts suspicion on Olav's Christianity: apart from attending masses, the only Christian feature Snorri gives him is that he punishes himself for having "worked" on a Sunday.[120] It has been suggested that Olav shows another Christian virtue before the battle of Stiklestad; when several *bœndr* in the area had refused to join his force, he asked his men for advice how to deal with them. Finn Árnason recommended harsh treatment, harrying all districts "with fire and sword," robbing the *bœndr* of all their possessions, and burning down all settlements completely. Finn's advice was welcomed by many, but King Olav did not take it, declaring his wish to show forgiveness, since—this time—the *bœndr* had misbehaved against himself, not "transgressed against God." This seems to be a truly Christian attitude, but Snorri reveals the true reason for Olav's "clemency": if he were victorious, the houses and properties of his enemies would be destroyed, if they followed Finn's advice.[121]

As has been shown above, Olav Haraldsson's evangelical methods were very much like the ones used by his predecessor Olav Tryggvason. Both were ruthless and cruel, using threats and torture to attain their aims. The portrait that Snorri paints of Saint Olav is certainly not flattering.

After Olav Haraldsson, Christian faith was not an issue, nor was royal power questioned but generally accepted, *as long as the magnates controlled it*.

---

[119] S. Saint Olav, chap. 241; ÍFH II:401–2; Hollander, 241ff.

[120] S. Saint Olav, chap. 190; ÍFH II:342; Hollander, 485: During his exile in Gardarike Olav cut ships from a piece of wood, but being reminded that it was a Sunday he swept all the shavings he had cut into his hand, set fire to them, letting them burn his palm. See Chapter 7 below.

[121] S. Saint Olav, chap. 205; ÍFH II:354–57; Hollander, 495–96.

CHAPTER 5
KINGS AND MAGNATES (II)

From 1035 to 1169 there were four periods with under-age kings, led by the magnates: first under Magnus Olavsson; second under Magnus Bareleg's sons Øystein, Sigurd, and Olav; third under Harald Gille's sons Øystein, Sigurd, and Inge; and finally under Magnus Erlingsson.[1] The impression Snorri gives is that everything went smoothly as long as the young kings listened to their advisors but badly when they stopped doing so. Rulers who took over royal power as adults: Harald Hardrade, Magnus Barelegs, and Magnus "the Blind" never became popular; their self-interest and warlike natures met with strong opposition.

9. Magnus Olavsson ("the Good," 1035–1047)[2], Kalv Arnesson, and Sigvat the Skald

Explicit characterization of Magnus

"King Magnus was of middle height, with regular features and light complexion. He had light blond hair, was well-spoken and quick to make up his mind, was of noble character, most generous, a great warrior, and most valorous. He was most popular as a king, both friends and enemies praising him."[3] The death of him was mourned by all people.[4]

Summary

Persuaded by Einar Tambarskjelve and Kalv Arnesson, (the ten-year-old) Magnus left Russia and sailed to Sweden, where he was welcomed by his stepmother Astrid, who lived there now.[5] She immediately summoned a numerous assembly,

---

[1] I.e., a couple of years after, respectively 1035, 1103, 1136, and 1161.

[2] In three sagas: S. Saint Olav; S. Magnus the Good; and S. Harald Hardrade.

[3] S. Hardrade, chap. 30; ÍFH III:107; Hollander, 600.

[4] S. Hardrade, chap. 28; ÍFH III:105; Hollander, 599.

[5] Snorri makes no secret of the fact that Magnus was the illegitimate son of Saint Olav and Alfhild, a servant girl, admittedly pointing out that the mother descended from a good family.

at which she most eloquently forwarded his case. "And so successful was Astrid, what with her speech and her active support of Magnus, that a great host was willing to join [her] in accompanying him to Norway."[6] With a large force, Magnus set out to Trøndelag and was accepted as king at the Øre Assembly.[7] Svein fled from Norway and died the same year as his father Knud (1035). In the beginning of King Magnus' reign, Kalv Arnesson had great influence, but as an adolescent Magnus listened less and less to his advisors, became vengeful, and punished many of his father's enemies hard. Even his foster-father Kalv had to flee his wrath, being suspected of having taken part in the killing of Olav; he sailed westward, raiding in the British Isles.[8] Dissatisfaction with Magnus' rule spread widely throughout the country, and the people of Sogn planned a revolt. Then friends of the king cast lots to select a man to inform the king of this dissatisfaction, and it fell on Sigvat the Skald. In his "Outspoken Verses," Sigvat criticized Magnus for not reconciling himself with the *bœndr*, warned him of a revolt, and urged him to change his mind. This warning helped: the king took counsel with the wisest men and had a law-book written (*Grágás*). After this, Magnus became popular and beloved by the people, and because of this he was called "the Good."[9]

After Knud's death, his son Hardeknud ruled in Denmark. He and Magnus had planned to fight each other, but because both were young and "of childish mind," the influential men in charge of the government made the kings conclude peace for so long as either lived, "and if one of them died without a male heir, the one who survived was to take over his land and subjects."[10] Thus, when Hardeknud died (in 1042), Magnus succeeded him as king of Denmark, which caused many problems. Against Einar Tambarskjelve's advice, Magnus made Knud's nephew Svein Estridsen his earl in Denmark,[11] but when Svein began to call himself *king* of the Danes, Magnus quickly remonstrated. After having successfully defended the Danish coasts against the attacking Vends (and having hewn down many of them himself), he turned against Svein, whom he defeated in several battles.

Next we meet King Magnus, Einar, and Kalv in the Saga of Harald Sigurdsson (Hardrade).

---

⁶ S. Magnus the Good, chap. 1; ÍFH III:5; Hollander, 539. In *Morkinskinna* we hear nothing about his stepmother's help. Here, instead, it is Einar Tambarskjelve who forwards Magnus's cause by bribing influential men in Norway to accept him as king.

⁷ S. Magnus the Good, chap. 3; ÍFH III:9; Hollander, 540–41.

⁸ S. Magnus the Good, chap. 4; ÍFH III:25; Hollander, 330–31.

⁹ S. Magnus the Good, chaps. 15–16; ÍFH III:31; Hollander, 551–55.

¹⁰ S. Magnus the Good, chap. 6; ÍFH III:12–13; Hollander, 543.

¹¹ Svein is called Ulfsson in Hollander.

Comments

Earlier sources give a very favorable picture of Magnus Olavsson, but in *Heimskringla* it is more nuanced. Even if, explicitly, Snorri has only praise for Magnus, implicitly the portrait is tainted because of the stress put on his suspicions and desire for vengeance. Not only does Magnus appropriate all the goods Kálf left behind but also he:

> took possession of many other large estates which had belonged to those who had fallen in the yeomen's army at Stiklestad. Also, he dealt out heavy punishment to those who had fought against King Olav in that battle. Some he drove out of the country, and from some he took great sums of money, and in the case of still others he had their cattle slaughtered. Then the farmers began to murmur and said to one another, 'What can this king be thinking of, breaking thus the laws with King Håkon the Good has given us? Doesn't he remember that we have never tolerated acts of injustice? He is likely to have the same fate as his father and other chieftains whom we have slain when we grew weary of their overbearing and lawlessness.'[12]

In using direct speech, Snorri has the *bœndr* express his own criticism towards Magnus's behavior, and he emphasizes the need Magnus had for wise guidance in his rule. The episode when Sigvat openly criticizes Magnus' harsh rule is very important, since it illustrates the important role of skalds; they played a key role in warning and advising rulers and could say what others did not dare.[13] No doubt Snorri sympathizes with Sigvat and admires his endeavor to guide King Magnus. After this turning-point in Magnus's rule, his portrait is more favorably painted.

Einar Tambarskjelve fares better than Kalv, even if he has to realize that the young king is not as easily led as first assumed. Foreseeing trouble when Magnus makes Svein Estridsen his earl, Einar wisely advises against this but only receives a scornful reply.[14] Snorri lets us soon see that Magnus should have listened to Einar. In *Heimskringla*, Einar Tambarskjelve and Kalv Arnesson figure as liberators from the Danish yoke; their initiative to bring Saint Olav's son back to Norway and make him a king turned out to be a masterly move. With very young kings, the magnates had the real power, something that would happen again in 1103 and in 1161. Einar, who had changed his loyalties three times earlier, nevertheless remained loyal to Magnus and is favorably portrayed because of his commitment to the old political order. The same commitment was entertained

---

[12] S. Magnus the Good, chap. 15; ÍFH III:25–26; Hollander, 552.

[13] Roberta Frank, "Skaldic Poetry," in *Old Norse-Icelandic Literature: A Critical Guide,* ed. Carol J. Clover and John Lindow (Ithaca and London: Cornell University Press, 1988), 181f.

[14] S. Magnus the Good, chap. 23; ÍFH III:37; Hollander, 558.

by Kalv, and it is with great sympathy that Snorri describes his dilemma, being torn between loyalty to his brothers (Olav Haraldsson's men) and to his stepsons (who had been killed on Olav's order).

Despite his criticism of Magnus's vengefulness, Snorri shows a certain sympathy for him. As only a child Magnus is more or less forced to become king of Norway and is from the beginning totally dependent first on his stepmother Astrid, later on his foster-fathers and other counsellors—and on his dead father, who advises him in his dreams.

10. Magnus the Good (Olavsson) and Harald Hardrade (Sigurdsson)

Summary

King Magnus was challenged by his uncle, Saint Olav's halfbrother Harald, who as a young man had taken part in the battle of Stiklestad, where he was hurt but rescued by a yeoman. After many adventures in the East (see below), Harald came back in order to claim his right to the throne. In Sweden he met Svein Estridsen, his wife's kinsman, with whom he allied. Faced by this threat, Magnus followed his councillors' advice and offered to share the kingship with Harald, who immediately broke with Svein. In revenge, Svein took in all royal tithes in Denmark, whereupon Magnus and Harald led a fleet that brought the country under their sway. There was, however, soon discord between the two kings, and Snorri calls the claims of those who sided with Harald in the conflicts "unreasonable."[15]

While in Denmark Magnus dreamed that Saint Olav asked him to choose between going to him or becoming the most powerful of all kings and do unforgivable misdeeds. In his dream Magnus answered that he wanted his father to choose for him. Soon after that, Magnus fell ill and on his deathbed gave Norway to Harald and Denmark to Svein Estridsen.

Comments

One wonders why Snorri avoids elaborating on the conflicts but only says, "Then many things occurred about which the kings each had his own opinion; though little is written about that here."[16] The cause of Magnus's illness and death is not made clear, which leaves the reader suspicious. What is made clear, however, is that Magnus does not trust Harald, for on his deathbed he sends a message to Svein Estridsen, not only giving him the Danish realm but also asking him to

---

15 S. Harald Hardrade, chap. 27; ÍFH III:104; Hollander, 598.
16 S. Harald Hardrade, chap. 27; ÍFH III:104; Hollander, 599.

help his brother Tore, whenever he needed it.[17] As we shall see below, King Magnus and King Harald are depicted as each other's contrasts; Snorri does not make a secret of his dislike of Harald and sympathy for Magnus, who may well come close to his ideal of a king. After Magnus changed for the better, he exemplifies not only fortitude but also prudence and temperance. The fact that Magnus died young (only *c.* 20 years old) and — at least towards the end — was careful to take advice from his councillors probably contributed to Snorri's positive image of him.

11. Harald Hardrade (Sigurdsson)1046/47–1066)
Einar Tambarskjelve, Kalv Arnesson, Finn Arnesson, and Håkon Ivarsson

Explicit characterization

King Harald was a powerful and strong ruler, sage, deepminded, quick to make up his mind, a brave warrior, stronger and more dexterous in arms than any other man. He was a great friend of the Icelanders.[18] He "was of an imperious nature, and grew the more so as he consolidated his rule in Norway. And eventually it became worse than useless to oppose him or to promote matters other than those he wished."[19]. . . He "was a handsome man of stately appearance [. . .] ruthless with his enemies, and given to harsh punishment of all who opposed him."[20] He "was inordinately covetous of power and of valuable possessions of all kinds. He bestowed great gifts on his friends and those of whom he thought much."[21]

Summary

After the battle at Stiklestad, Harald Sigurdsson set out for Gardarike, where he and his followers were welcomed by king Jarisleiv, who made him chieftain of the men charged with the defence of the country. Later he went to Byzantium, where he became the leader of all Varangians. Harrying in Africa for many years, Harald acquired great quantities of valuable things, some of which he sent to be taken care of by Jarisleiv in Holmgard. After many adventures in both the Saracen lands and Sicily, he wanted to return to the North. When he gave up service in Byzantium, Queen Zoë was enraged and accused him of having stolen the property of her co-ruler, the Greek king Konstantinus Monomakus, during his

---

17 S. Harald Hardrade, chap. 28; ÍFH III:105; Hollander, 599.
18 S. Harald Hardrade, chap. 36; ÍFH III:119; Hollander, 607.
19 S. Harald Hardrade, chap. 42; ÍFH III:123; Hollander, 610.
20 S. Harald Hardrade, chap. 99; ÍFH III:199; Hollander, 661.
21 S. Harald Hardrade, chap. 99; ÍFH III:199; Hollander, 661.

expeditions. Her fury was due to Harald's wish to marry not her but her beautiful niece Maria. To prevent him from leaving, Zoë had him imprisoned, but he was helped to escape by an unknown lady. Together with the Varangians he took a cruel revenge on Konstantinus, abducted Maria, and forced their way through the chains of the Golden Horn. Before sailing into the Black Sea, Harald put Maria ashore, bidding her tell Queen Zoë how powerless she had been in preventing him from doing what he wanted.[22]

In Holmgard he took hold of his treasure, married Jarisleiv's daughter Elisabet (Ellisiv), sailed north, and—as related above—was offered to share the kingship with Magnus. After Magnus' death, Harald had difficulties in maintaining his power in Denmark, which he claimed to have inherited from Magnus. When he bade his army to support him, Einar Tambarskjelve refused to obey, saying that he preferred "to follow King Magnus in death rather than any other king in life.,"[23] and then brought King Magnus's body to Nidaros to be buried. Being left with only a part of his army, Harald soon had to abandon his claims, and Svein Estridsen was acknowledged king in Denmark retaining power despite Harald's repeated attacks.

Also within Norway the resistance to Harald was growing. There were several conflicts between him and Einar, who was the most powerful of all landedmen in Trøndelag. Einar knew the law well and did not lack courage to forward his cause, even if the king was present, always supported by the yeomen. This infuriated Harald so much that Einar took to having a large company of men about him, both at home and when out. Friends of both parties sought to reconcile them, and a meeting was agreed on, but as soon as Einar and his son Eindride arrived, they were treacherously killed by the king's men. Snorri writes: "After the fall of Einar, King Harald was so strongly detested on account of his deed that the only reason the king's stewards and the yeomen did not attack and do battle with him was the lack of a leader to raise the standard for the yeomen's army."[24]

Thus, there was no open revolt, but fearing that Einar's kinsman Håkon Ivarsson intended to avenge the deed, Harald asked his steward Finn Arnasson to reconcile him with the *bøndr*. Finn's condition was that Harald pardon his brother Kalv, who was still in exile, and allow him to return to Norway. This was granted, but it soon turned out that Harald wanted to get rid of Kalv, whom he sent at the head of a force to attack Denmark. Although he had promised his assistance, he did not give any, so Kalv and many other Northmen fell in the battle against the Danes. Realizing that he had been deceived, Finn left Harald and went to serve King Svein, who gave him an earldom in Halland with the commission to defend it against the Northmen. When Håkon Ivarsson also became Svein's man, since his conditions for reconciliation had not been

---

[22] S. Harald Hardrade, chap. 15; ÍFH III:88–89; Hollander, 589.

[23] S. Harald Hardrade, chap. 29; ÍFH III:107; Hollander, 600.

[24] S. Harald Hardrade, chap. 44; ÍFH III:126; Hollander, 612.

accepted, Harald changed his mind and gave him the earldom of Oppland (and Magnus the Good's daughter Ragnhild in marriage). Their reconciliation did not last long.

In his next attack on Denmark, Harald defeated the Danish fleet, but Håkon helped King Svein escape from the battle and was highly and widely praised — also in Norway — for this and his fighting skills. Furious over this and jealous of Håkon's popularity, Harald decided to kill Håkon, who was staying in Oppland during the winter. Warned in time, however, Håkon had time to hide all his movable property and flee to Sweden, from where he continued to levy rents and revenues not only from Oppland but also from Värmland, which the Swedish king had given him to rule. Thus, when Harald tried to collect his rents and fines in Oppland, the people refused to pay, declaring their loyalty to Håkon. It was obviously the threat of Håkon's power and popularity that forced King Harald to conclude peace with Svein, and when that was obtained, he attacked and defeated Håkon. He then took a harsh revenge on the Oppland *bøndr*; in Romerike he had them seized, some maimed, others killed, confiscating the property of many. Then he laid not only Romerike waste but did the same to Hedmark, Hadeland, and Ringerike. "After that the *bøndr* submitted unconditionally to the king."[25]

In England, Edward the Confessor had adopted his nephew Harold Godwinson, who was chosen to succeed him. Harold's brother Tostig, however, thought he was no less entitled to the English crown and sought the help of his uncle, King Svein. When Svein refused, Tostig turned to Harald and persuaded him to gain possession of England. Many people, including two of the king's men, had dreams foretelling King Harald's fall, and Harald himself was warned by Saint Olav in a dream. He nevertheless left one of his wives (Tora) in Norway, taking the other (Ellisiv) and his children with him to England. After raiding in various regions, Harald defeated two earls in York but was himself defeated and killed by King Harold Godwinson's men in the battle at Stamford Bridge (1066).[26]

Comments

The saga of Harald Hardrade is one of the longest in *Heimskringla* (101 chapters, covering 86 pages in Hollander's edition), and Snorri's narrative corresponds closely with his explicit characterization of the king, illustrating several of the deadly sins (*superbia*, *avaritia*, *luxuria*, *invidia*, and *ira*). In the East he is always victorious, and what he cannot win with weapons he wins with different clever

---

[25] S. Harald Hardrade, chap. 73; ÍFH III:166; Hollander, 63–40.

[26] S. Harald Hardrade Chaps. 78–92; ÍFH III:72–91; Hollander, 645–56. William's army defeated and killed Harold Godwinson (Hastings 1066), and William had himself proclaimed king of England; Chaps. 95–97; ÍFH III:172–91; Hollander, 658ff.).

stratagems. He outwits the general of the Greek army, cheats and outmaneuvres him. In advancing his case, he uses people ruthlessly, charming Queen Zoë and her co-ruler Konstantinus Monomakus, obviously also the "lady of high degree" who came to his rescue, and playing with Zoë's young niece Maria—and leaves them all disgraced. He punishes King Konstantinus most cruelly, putting out both his eyes, and the abducted Maria is sent home with a sarcastic greeting to Queen Zoë.[27]

The only positive things Snorri says about Harald are that he was strong, dexterous in arms, brave, and a great friend of the Icelanders. His negative portrait of Harald is a clear contrast to *Morkinskinna* and *Fagrskinna*, where Harald is favorably treated. While in *Heimskringla* the magnates' reasons for abandoning King Harald are perfectly intelligible, the author of *Fagrskinna* criticizes their behaviour: "At this time the landed men were so over-confident that as soon as anything was not wholly to their liking with the king they ran off out of the country to King Svein in Denmark, and he made great men of them."[28]

From the start, Harald has great ambitions and obviously long-term plans to win what he regarded as "his own ancestral possessions."[29] By raiding far and wide, he accumulates wealth in order to reward retainers and gain power, and by marrying strategically, he can all the easier ally with King Magnus's enemy, Svein Estridsen. Even though Snorri does not openly question Harald's rights to kingship in Norway and Denmark, it is made clear that they were disputable since he is only the halfbrother of Magnus's father.[30]

As king of Norway, Harald is most unpopular, especially after the killing of Einar and his son, and Snorri deplores the fact that there was no one to lead a revolt against him. When Finn trusts Harald's promise to pardon Kalv, Snorri relates that many people thought it was very childish of Finn to believe that Kalv would obtain the king's sincere friendship, "considering that the king had shown his vindictiveness in the case of smaller offences than those which Kalv had committed against him."[31] By treating magnates like Finn Arnesson and Håkon Ivarson badly, Harald drives them into Svein Estridsen's arms, and the fact that it was one of his own men who warned Håkon in time shows that there was discontent also among his retainers.

---

[27] S. Harald Hardrade, chap. 15; ÍFH III:88–89; Hollander, 589.

[28] *Fagrskinna*, chap. 57; trans. Finlay, 210. Cf. the author's criticism of Saint Olav's enemies above, p. 67.

[29] S. Harald Hardrade, chap. 13; ÍFH III:85; Hollander, 587.

[30] Like earlier sources, Snorri presents Harald's father, Sigurd Syr, as Harald Fairhair's great grandson (S. Olav Tryggvason, chap. 60; ÍFH I:310; Hollander, 200), but this alleged royal descent is not mentioned in connection with Harald's claims to the Norwegian throne.

[31] S. Harald Hardrade, chap. 53; ÍFH III:134; Hollander 617–18.

Towards the end of Harald Hardrade's Saga, Snorri presents a comparison of the ways of Saint Olav and Harald, quoting the chieftain Halldor:

> 'I was in great favour with both brothers, and I knew the disposition of both. I never saw two persons whose disposition was more alike. Both men were exceedingly sagacious and skilled in arms, avid for wealth and power, imperious in manner, not very affable, jealous of their authority, and given to meting out stern chastisement. King Olav forcibly converted the people to Christianity and the true faith, and cruelly punished those who turned a deaf ear to it. The leaders of the country would not accept his jurisdiction and equitable judgments, and gathered an army against him, laying him low in his own land. It was therefore he became a saint. But Harald made war to gain fame and power, subduing all those he could, and fell in the realm of other kings. Both brothers were as a rule well mannered and highminded. They were also widely travelled and men of great energy, and as such became famous and gained a great name.'[32]

Since Snorri describes Halldor as a "man of discernment," we ought to take this characterization seriously: what is emphasized are both men's greed, lust for power and cruelty. Again we are reminded how King Olav's jurisdiction met disapproval, and, as far as King Harald is concerned, it is clear that he only made war for his own "fame and power." The last sentences are neutral and could be interpreted as either positive or negative.

Driven by pride and greed, Harald set out as a viking, raiding and gaining much wealth in the East, some of it belonging to his lord, the Greek emperor. Snorri describes him not only as a shrewd and ruthless warrior—and womanizer (Queen Zoë, Princess Maria, and—presumably "the lady of high degree"), but also as a tactical bigamist (Ellisiv and Tora). In Norway his greed and envy makes him plunder and confiscate many properties, and his pride drives him to expand his power to encompass not only Norway but also Denmark and England. His cruel punishment of the Oppland yeomen illustrates both his greed and wrath (*ira*), and, always intent on warfare, he is not known to have done much constructive in Norway. Apart from some building enterprises in Nidaros,[33] he had a market town built in Oslo, where he often resided, because its location was good, "both to protect the land against an attack of the Danes and to make incursions in Denmark"—which he often did![34]

---

[32] S. Harald Hardrade, chap.100; ÍFH III:200–201; Hollander, 662.

[33] In Nidaros, King Harald had the building of Saint Olav's Church (begun by King Magnus Olavsson) completed, laid the foundation of Saint Mary's Church, and had a royal residence built below it by the river. S. Harald Hardrade, chap. 38; ÍFH III:121; Hollander, 608–9.

[34] S. Harald Hardrade, chap. 58; ÍFH III:139; Hollander, 621.

King Harald had many enemies both outside and inside Norway and obviously also found it difficult to keep the loyalty of his own men. He ruled for nearly twenty years, and Snorri's concluding words about him are: ". . . in all that time he lived in constant turbulence and war."[35]

12. Harald Hardrade's sons: Magnus Haraldsson[36] (1066–1068) and Olav Haraldsson ("the Gentle"), 1066/68–1093[37]

Introduction

With his second wife Tora, King Harald had two sons: Magnus and Olav. The eldest, Magnus, ruled Norway during the first year after his father's death and thereafter together with his brother Olav until, after two years, he died. He left a son called Håkon, fostered by Steigar-Tore. According to Snorri, King Magnus had been beloved of all the people.[38]

Olav Haraldsson ("the Gentle") *Explicit characterization*

Olav was large and well proportioned. "All are agreed that no one ever saw a handsomer man nor one of more stately appearence. He had flaxen, silky hair of great beauty, and a fair skin. His eyes were unusually fine, and his limbs well-shaped. As a rule he was a man of few words and spoke little at assemblies. But he was merry at ale and a great drinker, talkative and soft-spoken, peacably inclined during his rule."[39] "He was much beloved as king, and during his rule Norway had grown greatly in wealth and honor."[40]

Summary

We are introduced to Olav the Gentle already in the saga of Harald Hardrade, where we learn that he had fought with his father in England. After Harald's death, Olav returned to Norway together with his stepmother Ellisiv and friend Skúli, who became the leader of his retinue. Since Skúli was a wise man, advising

---

[35] S. Harald Hardrade, chap. 99; ÍFH III:200; Hollander, 661.

[36] S. Harald Hardrade, chap. 101; ÍFH III:201–2; Hollander, 663.

[37] In two sagas: S. Harald Hardrade and S. Olav the Gentle.

[38] S. Harald Hardrade, chap. 101; ÍFH III:202; Hollander, 662.

[39] S. Olav the Gentle, chap. 1; ÍFH III:203; Hollander, 664.

[40] S. Olav the Gentle, chap. 8; ÍFH III:209; Hollander 667. The question is whether Olav the Gentle was" a man of few words" or "talkative."

the king in all matters of government, Olav gave him valuable estates near the market towns, the most valuable estates in every place.[41] He also gave his cousin Gudrun, the niece of Saint Olav and Harald Hardrade, to Skule in marriage. King Olav himself was married to the Danish king Svein's daughter Ingerid, while Svein's son was married to King Olav's sister, so the ties between Norway and Denmark were made firmer. Together with his concubine Tora, Olav also had a son called Magnus, who grew up at the king's court.

The story about him is the shortest in *Heimskringla*. The Saga of Olav the Gentle contains only eight chapters (= four pages in Hollander's edition), two of which deal not with him but with Saint Olav. What we hear is that he kept the peace and did not have any enemies outside or inside Norway, and we are told about internal developments, such as the establishment of new towns and the growth of the already existing ones. Further, he had the foundations laid for the large Christ Church in Bergen and established guild places in many market towns. Other initiatives King Olav took were not so momentous; we are told that many foreign customs and fashions in the cut of clothes were introduced, as well as new habits imported from the courts of foreign kings, for example, letting his grand-butler stand at the end of the table and fill the table-cups for himself and his guests, and using torchbearers who held as many candles at the table as there were guests present. King Olav also had a much greater retinue than the law allowed, which was questioned by the *bœndr*. After twenty-six years as king, he died of a sickness.

Comments

Since we know from other sources that many much more important initiatives were taken during King Olav's reign, not least the establishment of several bishoprics, one wonders why Snorri ignores them and, instead, dwells on changes in fashion and court habits. A plausible explanation is that since his intention was *not to praise but to criticize* kings, one of the few Norwegian kings whose rule was successful gets known more for minutiae rather than his much more important initiatives. We should pay attention to the information about the royal grants to Skule, which laid the foundation of the family's wealth and powerful position, inherited by one of his direct descendants Skule Bårdsson, Snorri's friend and King Håkon Hákonsson's rival.

Does Snorri paint a positive or a negative portrait of Olav the Gentle? It is difficult to give a straight answer, since so many advances were made during his reign that Snorri does not mention. The reason we hear so little about this peaceful king must be that most sagas were woven by dramatic events, which were obviously not to be told about Olav. Still, Snorri states that Norway prospered

---

[41] I.e. the towns of Konghelle, Oslo, Tønsberg, Borg, Bjorgvin, and Nidaros; S. Harald Hardrade, chap. 98; ÍFH III:197–98; Hollander, 660.

under his rule.[42] The brevity of Olav's story supports the hypothesis that *Heimskringla* is basically a criticism of "bad" kings, who therefore get most space.

13. The cousins Håkon Magnusson (1093–1094) and Magnus Olavsson ("Barelegs," 1093–1103)

Introduction: Håkon Magnusson and Magnus Olavsson

After Olav the Gentle's death, his son Magnus was chosen king at an assembly in Viken, but the people in Oppland chose his cousin Håkon (the foster-son of Steigar-Tore) instead. Håkon was also accepted in Trøndelag, and King Magnus so much disliked the great concessions that Håkon had made to the *bændr* there that he prepared to fight his cousin. It never came to a battle, however, since King Håkon was taken ill and died (in 1094).[43] Snorri characterizes him as "one of the chieftains who was most beloved by all the people in Norway."[44]

Magnus Olavsson, son of Olav Magnusson ("the Gentle") *Explicit characterization*

Magnus Olavsson ("Barelegs") was "a vigorous man, warlike and active, and in every respect more like his grandfather Harald in disposition than his father."[45] "In his days there was good peace within the land, but people had much labour and expense from his expeditions abroad. By his followers King Magnus was greatly beloved, but the yeomen considered him stern."[46]

Summary

After Håkon Magnusson's death, his foster-father Tore allied with a Danish viking and turned against Magnus, plundered Bjarkøy, and harried in Hålogaland. King Magnus captured Tore, had him hanged, and punished all the traitors severely.[47] After this he sailed to Orkney and captured the earls Pål and Erlend and sent them back to Norway, replacing them with his son Sigurd, whom he later married to the Irish princess Bradmynja. Before returning home he went harrying, burning, and killing in the Hebrides.

---

[42] Both *Morkinskinna* and *Fagrskinna* treat Olav favorably.

[43] S. Magnus Barelegs, chap. 1; ÍFH III:211–12; Hollander, 668.

[44] S. Magnus Barelegs, chap. 3; ÍFH III:212; Hollander, 670.

[45] S. Magnus Barelegs, chap. 7; ÍFH III:218; Hollander, 674.

[46] S, Magnus Barelegs, chap. 26; ÍFH III:237; Hollander, 686.

[47] S. Magnus Barelegs, chaps. 4–7; ÍFH III:214–18; Hollander, 670–74.

Ireland and Man.[48]

In Norway King Magnus demanded all land west of (the Swedish lake) Vänern and raided in Götaland. The Swedish king Inge offered the Norwegians free retreat, but in vain. In a battle with the Götar, the Norwegians were defeated, and King Magnus was forced to flee.[49] A peace meeting was arranged to take place at Konghelle on the Göta älv, where King Magnus met the Swedish King Inge and the Danish king Erik. It was agreed that King Magnus was to obtain King Inge's daughter Margret (thereafter called Fredkulla = Peace Woman).[50] Before marrying her, Magnus had children with other women: Øystein, whose mother was of low birth; Sigurd, whose mother was Tora; and Olav, whose mother was his mistress Sigrid, daughter of Saxi of Viken, a chieftain in Trøndelag.

In the battle with the Götar, the magnate Ogmund had rescued Magnus, changing clothes with him. Ogmund's son Skofte, however, fell out with Magnus, quarrelling about an inheritance. Due to this quarrel, King Magnus made new enemies; together with his sons. Skofte left Norway with five well equipped warships (and is said to be the first Norwegian to sail through Norva [Gibraltar] Sound.[51] King Magnus continued his attempts to expand his power and prepared another expedition with a large army. He sailed first to the Orkneys, then to the Hebrides and to Ireland, where he subdued Ulster. In a battle against the Irish he was wounded and died (1103). He was revenged by Vidkunn, who slew the man who had killed the king, for which he was in great favor with King Magnus's sons.

Comments

Snorri's explicit characterization of Magnus Barelegs corresponds closely with his narrative; here we meet a warrior king, who cost his country a great deal but did not do much for its inhabitants. Like his grandfather Håkon (Sigurdsson) Hardrade, Magnus Barelegs had—and made—many enemies. He lacks all virtues; his fortitude is not of the virtuous kind. Instead, Snorri illustrates his envy (of his cousin's popularity), greed, and lust for power (external expansion), and lust—for both women and luxurious (British) fashion. His preference for this fashion, with short kirtles, rendered him the nickname Barefoot or Barelegs, and another nickname was "Styrjaldar Magnus," meaning "Magnus of the turbulence/warfare." Thus, Snorri is very critical of Magnus Barelegs, who is said to have been loved only by his followers.

---

[48] S. Magnus Barelegs, chaps. 8–9; ÍFH III:219–22; Hollander, 675–76.

[49] S. Magnus Barelegs, chaps. 12–14; ÍFH III:225–28; Hollander, 678–80.

[50] S. Magnus Barelegs, chap. 15; ÍFH III:228; Hollander, 680.

[51] S. Magnus Barelegs, chap. 20; ÍFH III:232; Hollander, 682.

14. Shared Kingship I:
The sons of Magnus Barelegs:
Øystein 1103–23,
Sigurd ("Jerusalemfarer") 1103–30,
Olav 1103–15
and
Harald Gille 1130–36

Introduction

After King Magnus's death, his three young—illegitimate—sons succeeded to
the kingdom in Norway. Øystein (14–15 years old) ruled in the northern part
and Sigurd (13–14 years old) in the southern part. Olav was only 4–5 years old,
so his third part of Norway was administered by his elder brothers.[52] According
to Snorri, the brothers were greatly beloved by both the common people and the
chieftains; they abolished many taxes that had been imposed by the Danes under
Svein Alfivason's rule,[53] and they gave Earl Pål's son Håkon the earlship over the
Orkneys, of which his father and uncle had been deprived.[54] After twelve years
of shared kingship, Olav died from a disease, and Snorri has only positive things
to say about him. The elder brothers were very different, both in appearance and
character:

Explicit characterization

Øystein was handsome, had wide and blue eyes, blond and curly hair, and was of
middle height. He was wise, knowledgeable about everything, laws and stories,
quick in counsel, eloquent, merry, friendly, and beloved by everyone.[55]

Sigurd "Jerusalemfarer" was stout, brown-haired, masculine but not handsome,
well proportioned, quick of temper, of few words and seldom friendly, good to
his friends, and faithful, formal and dignified, imperious and severe with punishments. He observed the law well, was generous, powerful and able. The problem with Sigurd, however, was that he showed signs of madness more and more
often.[56]

---

[52] S. Magnus's sons, chap. 1; ÍFH III:238; Hollander, 688.
[53] S. Magnus's sons, chap. 17; ÍFH III:256; Hollander, 700
[54] S. Magnus's sons, chap. 2; ÍFH III:239; Hollander, 688.
[55] S. Magnus's sons, chap. 16; ÍFH III:256; Hollander, 700.
[56] S. Magnus's sons, chap. 22; ÍFH III:262; Hollander, 704–5.

Olav was of tall and slender build, handsome, of cheerful disposition, affable, and popular.[57]

Summary

Øystein and Sigurd

Øystein's and Sigurd's different characters are well illustrated in Snorri's narrative; while King Øystein remained in Norway, doing much good for the country, Sigurd almost immediately left the country with sixty ships, spending three years abroad.

Øystein did much to serve the land well, while his brother Sigurd was away: he established the monastery in Bergen on the North ness and endowed it with much wealth, and he built the Church of Saint Michael, a splendid stone minster. On the site of the royal palace in Bergen he built the Apostle Church, a wooden edifice, and erected the great hall, the most magnificent wooden structure in Norway. Further, he built a church at Agdenes and made a fortification and a harbor where before had been a harborless coast. He also built the Saint Nicholas Church in the royal palace in Nidaros (richly adorned with woodwork and all kinds of artistry). He built another church in Vågen in Hålogaland and endowed it with a prebend (for its maintenance). Øystein had won over the wisest and most powerful men of Jämtland, and "the outcome of their friendly intercourse was that the people of Jämtland brought all their land under the sway of King Øystein." As Snorri puts it: "Thus King Øystein won the land of the Jämtar by wisdom not by force as had some of his forebears."[58]

In Nidaros, king Øystein had a large ship constructed (on the same scale as Olav Tryggvason's "Long Serpent") and also had two boathouses built, "both so large that it was considered a great achievement."[59] After a feast at Stim, however, Øystein fell suddenly ill and died (in 1122, after twenty years as king). He was buried in Christ Church. Snorri writes: "It is said that over no man's body in Norway had ever stood so many men in sorrow, since the death of King Magnus, the son of King Olav, as over him."[60]

Sigurd first sailed to England, then proceeded to France and Galicia, taking much booty. He fought against some vikings in Spain and won eight galleys from them. In Cintra and Alcasse (Spain) he won an immense amount of booty, and after successful raids in Iviza and Minorca he sailed to Jersusalem, where he was well received by King Balduin, who gave him many sacred relics, above all a splinter taken from the Holy Cross. This relic was given on condition that King

---

[57] S. Magnus's sons, chaps. 17, 18; ÍFH III:256; Hollander, 700–701.
[58] S. Magnus's sons, chap. 15; ÍFH III:256; Hollander, 700.
[59] S. Magnus's sons, chap. 23; ÍFH III:262; Hollander 705.
[60] S. Magnus's sons, chap. 23; ÍFH III:263; Hollander 705.

Sigurd (and twelve of his men) swear an oath that Sigurd was to promote Christianity and establish an archbishopric in Norway and that the piece of the cross should be deposited where Saint Olav was interred. King Sigurd also promised to promote the payment of tithes. Then Sigurd joined King Balduin on an expedition to Syria, where they took possession of Sidon. Finally, Sigurd sailed to Miklagard, where the Byzantine emperor had the castle gate opened, through which Sigurd and his men passed with great pomp. After having been treated to great games, he made ready for the journey home, giving the emperor all his ships. In return, the emperor gave him many horses and guides, and, thus well equipped, Sigurd travelled through Bulgaria, Hungary, Pannonia, Swabia, and Bavaria, where he met Lothar, the emperor of Rome. In Denmark he was welcomed by King Niels, who gave him a ship that brought him back to Norway. "It was thought that no more honorable expedition had ever sailed from Norway than this one."[61]

In contrast to his brother Øystein, King Sigurd does not appear to have done very much within Norway; admittedly, he did much to improve the market town Konghelle, where he built a church and a large stronghold, surrounded with a great moat. By placing the piece of the Holy Cross there (instead of Nidaros), however, he failed to keep his promise to king Balduin,[62] and according to Snorri this turned out to be most ill-advised, since the holy relic was then within the reach of the heathens, "as was evident later on."[63] Snorri here refers to the Vendish attack on Konghelle (in 1135), when the church was burnt down. The holy cross, however, was saved.

King Sigurd was obviously more interested in exploits abroad than internal affairs. When his stepfather, the Danish king Niels (now married to Sigurd's mother), asked him to join his crusade to Småland (in Sweden), King Sigurd summoned a full levy in Norway of both troops and ships. When he arrived in Öresund (the agreed meeting place), he found that Niels had tired of waiting for him and had departed with the whole fleet. King Sigurd was displeased and planned to avenge this by plundering in Denmark. After having seized a village in Skåne, the Norwegian army harried in Kalmar and in Småland, "levying contributions of food, to the extent of 1.800 head of cattle."[64] King Sigurd returned to Norway with valuable goods and property, won on what came to be called "the Kalmar expedition."[65]

---

[61] S. Magnus's sons, chaps. 3, 4, 5, 11, 12, 13; ÍFH III: 239–43, 250–54; Hollander, 689–90, 691, 696, 697–98, 698–99, 699.

[62] S. Magnus's sons, chap. 19; ÍFH III:257–58; Hollander, 701. However, he did establish tithes in Norway, as promised.

[63] S. Magnus's sons, chap. 19; ÍFH III:258; Hollander, 701.

[64] S. Magnus's sons, chap. 24; ÍFH III:264; Hollander, 705–6.

[65] S. Magnus's sons, chap. 24; ÍFH III:264; Hollander, 706.

A great problem with King Sigurd was that he often showed signs of insanity; for different reasons, he had such fits of laughter "that his mind was unhinged."[66] One morning he was so glum and silent, "that his friends feared that he had one of his seizures." It turned out that he had had a bad dream, which he interpreted as foreboding the arrival of a man, who, together with his offspring, would be of great importance in Norway.[67] King Sigurd's interpretation proved to be correct: soon Harald Gille came from Ireland, claiming to be a son of Magnus Barelegs and, thus, King Sigurd's half-brother. After Harald had undergone the ordeal of walking over nine red-hot ploughshares without being burnt, Sigurd accepted their kinship but made Harald promise not to claim the kingdom as long as Sigurd himself or his son Magnus was alive.

King Sigurd was married to Malmfrid,[68] but she was not the mother of Magnus. His mother was a Norwegian woman called Borghild, whom King Sigurd had taken as his concubine.[69] Magnus disliked Harald Gille, whose Irish ways and inadequate knowledge of Norwegian was ridiculed by many. Once when they were both drunk, Magnus overheard Harald telling another man about matters in Ireland, among other things about Irish men who could run faster than horses. Immediately Magnus challenged Harald, demanding him to show his own prowess as a runner. He organized a race between his own horse and Harald, and even though the rules of the game were most unfair, Harald won the race three times, thereby earning the ring Magnus had put up as pledge but refused to give him. Having heard about this, King Sigurd was angry with his son:

'You call Harald foolish, but it seems to me you are a fool. You are not acquainted with the ways of other peoples. Did you not know before that people in other parts train themselves in other sports than filling their bellies with drink and rendering themselves senseless and unfit, so they don't know what they do? Give Harald his ring and make no more sport of him while I am alive.'[70]

After twenty-seven years of rule, at the age of forty, King Sigurd died (in 1130) and was buried in Saint Hallvard's Church (in Oslo).

---

[66] S. Magnus's sons, chap. 22; ÍFH III:262; Hollander, 704–5.

[67] S. Magnus's sons, chap. 25; ÍFH III:265; Hollander, 707.

[68] Malmfrid was the daughter of "Harald Valdemarsson" = Mstislav, Grand Duke of Kiev, and Kristin, daughter of Inge Stenkilsson, king of Sweden. S. Magnus' sons, chap. 20; ÍFH III:258; Hollander, 702.

[69] S. Magnus's sons, chap. 19; ÍFH III:257; Hollander, 701. King Sigurd did this after Borghild had cleared herself from rumors about a relationship with king Øystein.

[70] S. Magnus's sons, chap. 27; ÍFH III:268; Hollander, 708–9.

Comparison between Øystein and Sigurd

The differences between Øystein and Sigurd are very well illustrated by Snorri
in his comparison of their accomplishments. After having compared their different talents in wrestling, swimming, shooting, and knowledge of law, Sigurd accused Øystein of not being true to his word, truckling to those who happened to
be present. Øystein explained that his method was to please both parties and, if
possible, reach a compromise. He preferred this to the method he accused Sigurd
of, i.e., "to promise everyone ill; and I have not heard anyone taunting you for
not sticking to that." When Sigurd boasted about his great expedition abroad,
ridiculing Øystein for having stayed at home as a daughter of his father, Øystein replied that he had dowered Sigurd, as though he were his sister, before he
went away. Sigurd answered that he had been victorious in all of his many battles
and had acquired many valuable things, to which Øystein replied that his own
building enterprises at home were more useful for the country. Even though the
brothers were both furious after this conversation, Snorri maintains that peace
was maintained between them.[71]

Comments

Since Magnus Barelegs's sons were so young when their father died, the magnates obviously had great influence over their rule at first, though this is not
what Snorri reports. In his story about the sons of Magnus, Snorri highlights
the question of what a king's duty to his country should be. It is clear that he admires—and prefers—Øystein's responsibility to improve conditions in Norway
as well as his diplomacy, but the picture of Sigurd is not all negative. Sigurd's
successful expedition to the East and his acquisition of a piece of the Holy Cross
are presented as worthy of praise, even if Snorri criticizes his choice of Konghelle to house this precious relic. One gets the impression that Snorri feels some
sympathy with Sigurd, his illness, and his troubles with his son Magnus, who is
presented as not very promising, and his understanding of Harald Gille's diffi-
culty in being accepted because of his Irish habits and language problems. Even if
Snorri judges Sigurd favorably,[72] it seems, however, that he values Øystein more
highly than Sigurd and that his main sympathies lie with those rulers who con-
centrate on ruling and improving matters in Norway. Øystein is presented with
all the cardinal virtues and no vices, while Sigurd has some virtues (fortitude and
justice) at the same time as he illustrates the vices of pride and greed. Admittedly, Snorri lets him show some prudence and temperance in his dealing with
Harald Gille, but then his mental illness took over. The praise Snorri bestows on
the youngest brother Olav seems to be in line with the praise bestowed on oth-

---

[71] S. Magnus's sons, chap. 21; ÍFH III:262; Hollander, 702ff.

[72] "His reign was blessed for the people of the land with both peace and good harvests." S. Magnus's sons, chap. 33; ÍFH III:277; Hollander, 714.

ers who died young.[73] It should be added that Snorri also values the peace that prevailed in Norway under Øystein's and Sigurd's rule—in contrast to the conditions under the sons of Harald Gille.

15. Shared kingship II:
Magnus Sigurdsson ("the Blind," 1130–35)[74]
and Harald Gille (1130–36)[75]

Explicit characterization of Magnus and Harald

Magnus Sigurdsson "was handsomer than any man then living in Norway. He was a man of a haughty disposition, cruel, and a great athlete; but it was his father's popularity that brought him the friendship of the people. He was much given to drinking, greedy for money, unfriendly, and hard to get along with."[76]

Harald Gille "was a man of tall and slender stature. He had a long neck and rather long face, black eyes, and dark hair."[77] He "was an affable man, merry and gay, not haughty; and he was generous, so that he begrudged his friends nothing. He was open to advice, letting others give him counsel on whatever they would. All this made him popular and earned him praise. As a consequence, men of power attached themselves to him no less than to Magnus."[78]

Summary

Harald Gille heard of King Sigurd's death when he was in Tønsberg, where he summoned the Haugathing Assembly, in which he was chosen king of half the country. Since Magnus had a smaller force, he had no choice but to share the kingdom with Harald. After three and a half years, however, Magnus mobilized against Harald and defeated him in battle. Harald fled to Denmark, where he hoped to secure the support of King Erik Emune, now married to his sister-in-law Malmfrid, widow of King Sigurd. Harald's hope was not ill-founded; the Danish royal family was furious with Magnus, for he had sent back his wife, King Erik Emune's niece Kristin, since he did not like her. King Erik assigned Harald the province of Halland and gave him eight warships. With these he

---

[73] Cf. the praise of Magnus Olavsson above.

[74] In three sagas: S. Magnus's sons; S. Magnus the Blind & Harald Gille; and S. Harlald's sons.

[75] In two sagas: S. Magnus' sons; and S. Magnus the Blind & Harald Gille.

[76] The saga of Magnus the Blind and Harald Gille, chap. 1; ÍFH III:278; Hollander, 715.

[77] S. Magnus's sons, chap. 27; ÍFH III:267; Hollander, 708.

[78] S. Magnus the Blind and Harald Gille, chap. 1; ÍFH III:278; Hollander, 715.

returned to Norway and was well received in Tønsberg, where a great force joined him.

King Magnus resided in Bergen when he heard of this, and he asked his men for advice. His landed man Sigurd Sigurdsson advised him to offer Harald reconciliation, which Magnus refused. Sigurd then reminded the king how his earlier advice to keep the troops in the Viken had been ignored by Magnus, who had sent them home. Therefore, Sigurd's second suggestion was that Magnus kill all those who stayed at home and refused to help him now. Magnus refused to follow this advice on the grounds that it would create much ill will against him. Sigurd's third suggestion was to proceed north to Trøndelag and gather all the men they could on their way there. When Magnus refused also this, Sigurd at last advised him to remain in Bergen until Harald came with his big army, saying, "then either death or disgrace will be in store for you."[79]

Harald Gille arrived at Bergen on the day before Christmas but did not want to do battle during the "Holy Season." On Twelfth-night, however, he ordered his fleet to leave the harbor and attack.[80] King Magnus's men abandoned him, and he was taken prisoner on board his ship.[81] Harald asked his counsellors what to do with the king, and it was decided to dethrone and depose him. Harald's thralls then mutilated Magnus, putting out his eyes, cutting off one of his feet, and finally gelding him.[82] Inquiries were made about Magnus's treasures, and Bishop Reinald of Stavanger, a close friend of Magnus, was charged, but when he denied having them, he was hanged, an action that earned King Harald much reproach.[83]

After this, Magnus was put in the monastery Munkholm outside Nidaros, and Harald Gille was sole king in Norway. His rule was not unchallenged however; just as he had himself claimed the right to the kingdom by referring to Magnus Barelegs as his father, he was now challenged by Sigurd Slembedjakn, who also claimed to be Magnus Barelegs's son (and thus Harald Hardrade's half-brother). Harald asked his friends for advice how to act and was advised that the claim was just a fraud. With the help of conspirators at the court, however, Sigurd succeeded in having Harald killed.

Comments

Magnus and Harald are each other's contrasts: while Magnus is presented as having no virtues, only vices (pride, greed, envy, wrath, and gluttony), Harald is presented as easy-going, perhaps not very virtuous but free of serious vic-

---

[79] S. Magnus the Blind and Harald Gille, chap. 5; ÍFH III:285; Hollander, 719ff.
[80] S. Magnus the Blind and Harald Gille, chap. 6; ÍFH III:286; Hollander, 721.
[81] S. Magnus the Blind and Harald Gille, chap. 7; ÍFH III:287; Hollander, 723.
[82] S. Magnus the Blind and Harald Gille, chap. 8; ÍFH III:287; Hollander, 723.
[83] S. Magnus the Blind and Harald Gille, chap. 8; ÍFH III:288; Hollander, 724.

es—apart from lust. We have already seen that, from the start, Magnus disliked Harald and tried to trick him (ref. page 91). Magnus is described as a drunkard and hard to get along with, and again Snorri lets us meet an experienced counsellor (Sigurd) who tries to persuade an unwise king, though this time in vain. In contrast to Magnus, Harald is always ready to take counsel, which is praiseworthy in Snorri's eyes. Still, many historians have interpreted this as a sign of Harald's incompetence as a ruler, and in an interesting article Knut Arstad has shown that this interpretation is based on the bad reputation Harald has been given by Saxo and the author of *Morkinskinna*.[84] In both *Fagrskinna* and *Heimskringla*, however, Harald is favorably treated, and Arstad explains the negative opinion of him as follows:

> Why he was described in this way is [. . .] a result of the general views on society predominant in the 19th century and which Munch and his fellow historians were part of. The general views of 19th century historians in the fields where they aimed to find evidence of Harald's character, a womaniser and drunkard who neither commanded the language nor had knowledge of the Norwegian spirit, did not make him a suitable role model on which to build a nation. Neither his background nor the thoughts of society on moral issues or what the 19th century historians believed were the results of his reign, were destined to gain honour and recognition in a century of Norwegian nationalism.[85]

Both explicity and implicitly, Snorri emphasizes Harald's positive sides, and he puts the blame for the cruel treatment of Magnus not on Harald but on his thralls. It seems that some of Magnus's men, however, harbored hatred towards Harald and therefore brought about his death. We will hear more about Magnus, when Sigurd Slembediakn returns during the rule of Harald Gille's three sons, Inge, Sigurd, and Øystein.

---

[84] Knut Arstad, "En undersøkelse av Harald Gilles ettermæle," (Norwegian) *Historisk Tidsskrift* 4 (1999): 435–60.

[85] Arstad, "En undersøkelse av Harald Gilles ettermæle," 459–60.

16. Shared kingship III:
Harald Gille's sons: Inge, Sigurd, and Øystein;
Sigurd Slembedjakn and Håkon the Broadshouldered;
Erling Skakke, and Gregorius Dagsson

Harald Gille's sons:
Inge ("Hunchback") 1135–57/61 (two sagas)[86]
Sigurd ("Munn") 1135–55
Øystein 1142–57

Introduction

The saga of Harald Gille's sons is the most complicated saga in *Heimskringla* (32 chapters; 32 pages in Hollander), no doubt reflecting the troubled time it describes. In addition to the three kings, it deals as much with the two pretenders, Sigurd Slembedjakn and Håkon the Broadshouldered, and with the magnates Erling Skakke and Gregorius Dagsson. The saga ought to be treated together with the saga of Håkon Sigurdsson ("the Broadshouldered") and the saga of Magnus Erlingsson. Following are first the explicit characterizations of the three kings, sons of Harald Gille.

Explicit characterization

Inge "had an exceedingly handsome countenance. His hair was yellow, rather thin, and very curly. He was of low stature and could hardly walk alone because one of his legs was withered, and he had a hump both on his shoulders and his chest. He was kindly of speech and good to his friends, generous with his possessions. He let the chieftains share in the government of the country and was popular among the people. All this contributed to draw most of the people to his side."[87]

Sigurd "as he matured grew to be a most overbearing man, unruly in all respects, as was Øystein who yet was somewhat more moderate, though he was a most avaricious and covetous man. King Sigurd grew to be a tall and strong man of stately appearance. He had brown hair and an ugly mouth, but good features otherwise. He was exceedingly ready and skilful of speech."[88]

---

[86] S. Harald's sons; S. Håkon the Broadshouldered.
[87] S. Harald's sons, chap. 22; ÍFH III:331; Hollander, 756–57.
[88] S. Harald's sons, chap. 21; ÍFH III:330; Hollander, 756.

Øystein "was a man with black hair and a dark complexion. In stature he was somewhat over medium height. He had a good mind and keen understanding. What most contributed to his unpopularity was his avarice and stinginess.[89]

Summary

Harald Gille's widow, Queen Ingerid (a niece of the Swedish king Inge the older), commanded the people in Trøndelag to accept the illegitimate four-year-old Sigurd as king, while she herself took her legitimate son, the two-year-old Inge, to Viken, where he was accepted as king at the Borgar-thing. Their rule was soon disturbed by the pretender Sigurd Slembedjakn, who fetched Magnus the Blind from the monastery (1137) in the hope of getting support from Magnus's men. In Oppland Magnus obtained a great following, and a great battle with King Inge's men followed, during which Inge (then only five years old) injured his back and one of his feet. Magnus lost and fled to Denmark, asking King Erik Emune for help. King Eirík burnt Oslo but was himself plundered by King Inge's men. In the meantime, Sigurd Slembedjakn raided in Denmark, Hålogaland, Vågen, Hordaland, and Viken.

Since both Inge and Sigurd were children, Inge's men sent a letter to Sigurd's men asking for help against Sigurd Slembedjakn, and during the battle at Holmengrå (Grey Holm), both Sigurd Slembedjakn and Magnus the Blind were defeated. Magnus died, while Slembedjakn threw himself overboard, was betrayed, caught and—under great self-control—tortured to death. A couple of years after this, King Inge's and King Sigurd's elder half-brother Øystein (now 17 years old) came from Scotland and was accepted as king over one-third of Norway (at Øre-thing). Due to discord between him and the *bœndr* on (the island of) Hisingen, he burnt there, after which he harried in Caithness, Scotland, and England. During a stay in Viken he begot a son with a maiden of a yeoman: Håkon "the Broadshouldered."

Gregorius Dagsson and Erling Skakke

According to Snorri, the brothers got on well, as long as their foster-fathers ruled the kingdom, but after a couple of years the elder brothers, Sigurd and Øystein, planned to get rid of Inge. In the following conflicts Inge was supported by two important magnates: Gregorius Dagsson and Erling Skakke. Gregorius, whose estate was in Bratsberg (not far from Skien), was of noble birth and well connected. His father had been in King Magnus Barelegs's army in Ireland, and his (maternal) grandfather had been a powerful chieftain in Giske (South Møre) and a steward of King Magnus. Gregorius is described as King Inge's "best support,"

---

89 S. Harald's sons, chap. 22; ÍFH III:331; Hollander, 756.

and according to Snorri, he kept his housecarls better than other landed men: all his following was helmeted.[90]

Erling was also of noble birth (a descendant of the great Earl Håkon, who was his paternal grandmother's father), "a man of excellent understanding and a great friend of King Inge,"[91] through whose influence he was able to marry Kristin, the daughter of Sigurd Jerusalemfarer and Malmfrid. Erling owned an estate at Støle in south Hordaland and had been in Jerusalem on a much praised expedition.

When King Inge heard about his brothers' plan to get rid of him and that they were to meet in Bergen, he went there with a great force together with Gregorius Dagsson, who provided two warships at his own expense. King Sigurd was already in the town, and when one of his men killed one of Gregorius's housecarls, Gregorius wanted to attack Sigurd, but King Inge was against that. Even when one of his own men had been killed on King Sigurd's order, Inge did not act but was willing to accept compensation. His mother Ingerid reproached him for this passivity and egged him to take revenge. King Inge was furious at her reproaches, but Gregorius agreed with the queen and finally persuaded Inge to let him attack Sigurd himself, saying, "Sigurd and I shall this night have it out. Not only are you poorly off on account of your disabilities, but I think you have little desire to protect your friends." King Inge yielded and called for his armour.[92] In the following fight (1155), many of Sigurd's men deserted and asked for quarter, and Sigurd himself was killed.

After this, King Øystein came from the East with thirty ships, and Gregorius immediately wanted to attack them. Since many were against this and wanted reconciliation, Gregorius had to yield; King Inge sailed to Nidaros, and there was "peace of a sort" between him and Øystein, "though they did not meet personally."[93] The peace did not last long; Øystein planned to attack Gregorius on his estate, but Gregorius was warned in time and escaped to Hardanger, where he was helped and equipped by Erling Skakke's wife Kristin. Meanwhile, King Øystein burnt Gregorius's farm and killed all his cattle. A new reconciliation between Inge and Øystein was attempted but failed, and both of them collected forces. Many of King Øystein's retainers were tempted by Inge and Gregorius to join them, and when Øystein's force fled instead of confronting Inge's army, he was left alone in the woods, where he was killed by one of his own men.[94]

Among Øystein's men was his nephew Håkon the Broadshouldered (son of King Sigurd), who—at the age of ten—had been chosen chieftain of the large group that had followed King Øystein. King Inge expropriated everything that

---

[90] S. Harald's sons, chap. 26; ÍFH III:338; Hollander, 761.

[91] S. Harald's sons, chap. 17; ÍFH III:323; Hollander, 751.

[92] S. Harald's sons, chap. 27; ÍFH III:340; Hollander, 762.

[93] S. Harald's sons, chap. 28; ÍFH III:341; Hollander, 763.

[94] S. Harald's sons, chaps. 29–32; ÍFH III:341–46; Hollander, 763–67.

they owned in Norway and exiled them. Gregorius stayed in Konghelle in order to defend the country. When Håkon attacked Konghelle with a large force, Gregorius defeated him with a much smaller army, but Håkon escaped and went to Trøndelag, where he was chosen king over one-third of Norway. Gregorius wanted to go north and pursue him but was again advised against this attack.[95]

The third time we hear about Gregorius being advised against an attack is when Håkon had returned south, gathering his force at the (Göta älv) River. This time the advice came from Erling Skakke, whom King Inge regarded as the wisest and bravest man in his army. Gregorius felt thwarted, but since Erling soon changed his mind, the king also changed his own and decided to attack Håkon, who lost the battle but managed to escape.[96] The enmitities continued: Håkon and Gregorius had several of each other's men killed, and Gregorius was now determined to confront Håkon. He set out from Konghelle late in Christmas, planning to cross the (Göta älv) River on the ice. Håkon, however, had set a trap for him, having cut ice and covering it with snow. When Gregorius came to the river, the ice appeared to him to be unsound, but challenged by his own men he went on it—and fell through. A shot by one of Håkon's men killed him. King Inge vowed to avenge him and insisted on leading a new battle against Håkon himself, during which, however, he fell.[97]

Comments

Snorri states that people accepted the brothers as kings "because their father was called holy,"[98] but he also makes it clear that both decisions were made by the magnates. We are not told whether they also lay behind the rumor about Harald's holiness, but it is obvious that they preferred kings of minor age, so that they themselves could have the power.

Snorri's narrative corresponds closely with his explicit characterization of the three kings; his half-brothers Sigurd and Øystein are presented as strong-minded and illustrating several vices, not least pride, envy, wrath, and greed. In contrast, (the legitimate) Inge seems to lack vices, but at the same time, he does not excel in any of the virtues either: he is physically weak, irresolute, and helpless without his advisors, including his mother. He is guided above all by Gregorius, after whose death he "cried like a child" and said:

> There now has passed away the man who has done most for me and has kept
> the land together for me. Until now I had thought that death would not

---

[95] S. Håkon the Broadshouldered, chaps. 1–3; ÍFH III:347–49; Hollander, 768–70.

[96] S. Håkon the Broadshouldered, chaps. 5–6, 9–11; ÍFH III:350–52, 355–60; Hollander, 769–72, 774, 778.

[97] S. Håkon the Broadshouldered, chap. 18; ÍFH III:368–69; Hollander, 785.

[98] S. Håkon the Broadshouldered, chap. 1; ÍFH III:303; Hollander, 736.

separate us for long. Now I shall do my utmost to proceed against Håkon and his band, and then one of two things will happen: either I shall fall or else triumph over Håkon and his men. Nor is a man like Gregorius avenged sufficiently, even though all of them perish.[99]

Like King Inge, Snorri is full of admiration for Gregorius:

It was everybody's opinion that he had been the greatest chieftain among the landed-men of Norway in the memory of men then living, and that he was the man best disposed to us Icelanders ever since the passing of King Øystein the Elder.[100]

17. Håkon the Broadshouldered, Erling Skakke, and Magnus Erlingsson

Explicit characterization

Håkon Sigurdsson "was rather handsome, well-grown, tall and slender. He was very broadshouldered, for which reason his followers called him Håkon the Broadshouldered. Because he was still young, other chieftains aided him in the government. He was merry and friendly in his speech, playful, and had a youthful disposition. He was popular among the people."[101]

Erling Skakke: "was a powerful and resourceful man, an excellent general in times of disturbance, a good and capable ruler. He was considered rather cruel and hard. The chief reason for that was that he gave but few of his enemies permission to stay in the country, even though they asked for leniency; and because of that many flocked to bands when such arose against him. Erling was a tall and brawny man, somewhat short-necked, with a long face and sharp features. He had a light complexion and became very gray haired. He carried his head a bit on one side."[102]

Magnus Erlingsson: As an adult Magnus dressed with much finery. He "was of an easy-going disposition and gay, very cheerful, and a great lover of women."[103]

---

[99] S. Håkon the Broadshouldered, chap. 15; ÍFH III:365; Hollander, 782.

[100] S. Håkon the Broadshouldered, chap. 14; ÍFH III:364; Hollander, 781.

[101] S. Magnus Erlingsson, chap. 8; ÍFH III:384; Hollander 796–97.

[102] Hence his cognomen Skakke, which means "Wry-necked," S. Magnus Erlingsson, chap. 37; ÍFH III:412; Hollander, 816, note 1.

[103] S. Magnus Erlingsson, chap. 37; ÍFH III:412; Hollander, 816.

Summary

There were sometimes tensions between Erling and Gregorius, as when King Inge preferred Erling's advice to that of Gregorius, or when their kinsmen fought each other.[104] Of the two, Erling turned out to be the more competent supporter of King Inge, forcing Håkon the Broadshouldered to flee from a battle, in which Gregorius had done less than well. After King Inge's fall, Håkon the Broadshouldered subjected the whole country to his rule and held meetings with his followers in Saint Hallvard's Church to discuss the government. Erling's wife Kristin bribed a priest to let one of her men hide in the church in order to discover Håkon's plans and then sent a message to her husband, reporting what she had found out and warning him never to trust Håkon and his men.[105] When Erling had this report, he summoned all chieftains who had been King Inge's friends to discuss whom to take as their king (instead of Håkon). Erling's and Kristin's five-year-old son Magnus was suggested and was chosen king with his father as leader. Needing support from Denmark, Erling went to King Valdemar, who was his mother-in-law's cousin.[106] Valdemar promised to help Magnus regain Norway on condition that he himself obtain the whole of Viken as far as Rygjarbit (now the border between Agder and Telemark).

On his return to Norway, Erling immediately sought to undermine Håkon's position, first having his bailiff in Bergen killed, then sending a burning ship towards Tønsberg, where Håkon mobilized, so that the town-dwellers had to ask for peace and Håkon's army was dissolved. Erling took over all Håkon's ships and subjugated the whole of Viken and several districts north of it. Håkon returned to Trøndelag and prepared to attack Erling the following spring, but Erling prohibited all ships sailing north in order to keep Håkon ignorant of his plans. Erling was thus able to take Håkon by surprise, and in the battle between them (at Møre), chaos soon broke out on Håkon's ship. During the fight, Håkon and many of his men fell. Erling and Magnus then went to Nidaros, where Magnus was chosen king.[107] Snorri points out, however, that they did not stay there very long, since they did not trust the *bœndr* of the district.

The opposition to Erling and Magnus was by no means over. Sigurd, another son of king Sigurd Haraldsson and thus a brother of Håkon the Broadshouldered, was chosen king by the Opplanders. He was supported by Earl Sigurd Reyr, who had many retainers but only little land, so when he ran out of money, he appropriated properties illegally. In Viken, Erling and Magnus were very popular, and at the assemblies regularly held there by Erling, the misdeeds of Earl Sigurd's people were often discussed; in the end, there was a unanimous

---

104 See above under Gregorius Dagsson.
105 S. Håkon the Broadshouldered, chap. 19; ÍFH III:369; Hollander, 786.
106 S. Magnus Erlingsson, chap. 2; ÍFH III:375; Hollander, 90–91.
107 S. Magnus Erlingsson, chap. 8; ÍHF III:383; Hollander, 796.

decision to condemn the earl and all his retainers. Snorri disapproves, calling this an "unheard of decision."[108] There were those in Earl Sigurd's troop who wanted to make peace with Erling, but they changed their minds on hearing that Erling was not going to pardon anyone who had committed grave misdeeds against him. In battle with Erling, Earl Sigurd fell together with nearly sixty of his men.[109] Even so, King Sigurd and his foster-father Markus of Skog did not give up; they went south to Møre, collecting all the royal revenues wherever they came. When they reached (the island of) Hisingen, the people joined them. Erling did not fight but captured their ships and took them to Konghelle. Having lost their ships, Sigurd and Markus went to Trøndelag, where Sigurd was chosen king at the Ørething. Outside Bergen, however, both of them were taken prisoner by Erling's men; Sigurd was beheaded, Markus hanged, and their band was dispersed.

Erling then avenged himself on the people of Hisingen, forcing the *bœndr* who had joined Sigurd and Markus to pay heavy fines. He imprisoned the leaders of Markus's friends, killing many of their followers and having one of them, Frirek, bound to an anchor and thrown overboard. For this deed Erling was much hated in Trøndelag, where most powerful men were Frirek's relatives.[110] Having disposed of two rivals to the throne (Håkon and his brother Sigurd) and taken revenge on their followers, Erling went to Bergen, where he and Archbishop Øystein often met to talk. On one occasion, Erling questioned the archbishop's right to demand undebased money in payment of Church fines. Øystein, in his turn, questioned Magnus's right to be king, but after a long discussion they decided to support each other, and the archbishop agreed to crown King Magnus.

Soon after this, Valdemar sent a message to Erling, demanding Viken, which he had been promised. At the assembly in Borg (in Viken), however, the *bœndr* refused to submit to the Danes, while people in Trøndelag (where Erling was hated) agreed to welcome the Danish king, who had promised them both power and money.[111] In this situation Erling went to Nidaros, calling an assembly at Øre, where he accused the people of treason against the king and himself. He took great sums of money from many as fines and confiscated much land before returning to Bergen. Valdemar, however, insisted on having Viken and assembled a great army. Faced by stiff resistance, he had to retreat, but (despite his prohibition) the Danes pillaged extensively in Viken. Hearing of this, Erling sailed to Jutland with many vessels, and after a battle in which the Danes lost many men, Erling and his people plundered the ships and took a great booty. The hostility between Norway and Denmark lasted until Erling's wife Kristin intervened; she went to visit Valdemar, her mother's cousin, and was kindly received.

---

108 S. Magnus Erlingsson, chap.10; ÍHF III:385; Hollander, 798.
109 S. Magnus Erlingsson, chap. 14; ÍHF III:389; Hollander, 800–801.
110 S. Magnus Erlingsson, chap. 20; ÍFH III:394; Hollander, 804.
111 S. Magnus Erlingsson, chaps. 23–25; ÍFH III:399–401; Hollander, 807–9.

After many conversations with Valdemar, she urged her husband to visit the king and come to terms with him. Erling followed her advice and agreed to become Valdemar's earl with Viken as a fief under Danish rule. He remained Valdemar's earl as long as he lived.[112]

In Norway, Erling was faced with new problems; there were several rebellions, all initiated by Magnus's relatives. First Olav (a grandson of King Øystein Magnusson) gathered a troop, which many Opplanders joined, having chosen him king. In a first battle with Olav, many of Erling's men fell and Erling himself was wounded, but in a second battle he was victorious, although Olav managed to escape.[113] A second threat was Harald, reputed son of Sigurd Haraldsson and Erling's wife Kristin (!), thus half-brother of King Magnus. One of Magnus's landed men put a stop to Harald's claims, captured him, and delivered him to Erling, who had him killed. A third threat was much more serious; a man called Øystein, thought to be the son of King Øystein Haraldsson, was proclaimed king by the people in Viken. His followers were very poor and had to rob far and wide to maintain themselves. Since their clothes were worn out, they tied birchbark about their legs, hence their nickname "Birchlegs" ("Birkebeiner"). Most of them were from the Forest District and the (Göta älv) River area, and when they had procured ships, they set out along the coast, taking booty and recruiting more men. Many people joined their bands, because Erling was becoming increasingly unpopular; according to Snorri he was an able ruler but both cruel and severe, never allowing his enemies to remain in the country, even when they begged him for mercy.[114] Thus strengthened, the Birchlegs sailed north, where all people in Trøndelag submitted to Øystein and proclaimed him king. When the Birchlegs went to the Orkdalen, they numbered nearly 2,400 men, and from there they marched through Oppland, Toten, and Hadeland to Ringerike, subduing the country wherever they went.[115]

Erling and King Magnus now mobilized and prepared to fight. In the great battle at Ré, the Birchlegs were defeated; some of them fled east, but most went to Telemark, where they had their families. King Øystein also took to flight and ran into a farmhouse, begging for his life, but was killed by the owner. King Magnus himself does not seem to have taken much part in the battle; we meet him in a room at Hrafsness, warming himself by the fire.[116]

Snorri finishes this saga—and thus the whole of *Heimskringla*—with the following words:

---

[112] S. Magnus Erlingsson, chap. 30; ÍFH III:406; Hollander 812.

[113] S. Magnus Erlingsson, chaps. 31, 33, 34; ÍFH III:407–10; Hollander, 813–15. Olav fled to Denmark, where, shortly after, he fell ill and died (in 1169).

[114] S. Magnus Erlingsson, chap. 37; ÍFH III:411; Hollander, 816. In contrast to his father, King Magnus is described as easy-going, cheerful, and a great lover of women.

[115] S. Magnus Erlingsson, chap. 41; ÍFH III:414; Hollander, 818–19.

[116] S. Magnus Erlingsson, chap. 42; ÍFH III:416; Hollander, 820.

King Magnus then returned to Tønsberg, and he became very famous from this victory, because [before] everyone had said that between them Earl Erling was the shield and leader for both of them. But after King Magnus had obtained the victory over so strong and numerous a host with a smaller force of his own, everyone thought that he would surpass all [other generals] and that he would as a warrior become as much greater than the earl as he was younger.[117]

Comments

Snorri's contemporaries cannot have missed the irony in this last sentence. King Magnus was defeated by Sverre, a much greater warrior, three years after the battle at Ré, and at last he fell against Sverre in the battle at Fimreite (1184).

Nothing in Snorri's narrative contradicts his explicit characterization of Erling and Magnus, but his positive judgment of Håkon the Broadshouldered has no real basis in his story. Even though Håkon is said to have subjected the whole of Norway to his rule, Snorri has not much to tell us about him as a king. Instead, Snorri focuses on Erling Skakke and his efforts to undermine Håkon's position and claims to the throne and finally to defeat him in battle. The biggest obstacle was that Håkon was son of a king (Sigurd Haraldsson), while Erling was not, so Erling put forward Magnus, his son with Kristin, and thus a *grandson* of a king (Sigurd Jerusalemfarer). Erling also used his wife's relationship with king Valdemar and achieved Danish support to regain Norway, on condition that he promise to let Valdemar rule Viken. It appears that Erling did not intend this promise to be taken seriously, because after Håkon's fall, he refused to keep it, blaming people in Viken.

The child Magnus was chosen king with his father as leader, but the opposition to his leadership was fierce, and Erling had to yield to archbishop Øystein's demands in order to get Magnus crowned. In the hostilities between Norway and Denmark, Erling was—again—helped by his wife who achieved a reconciliation between him and Valdemar, although it meant that he had to become Valdemar's earl in Viken, a definite loss in prestige, since the Danes had not ruled any part of Norway since 1035. Erling's rule was not successful; one rebellion followed another, but Snorri finishes his history before Erling finally fell against King Sverre (in 1179).

Erling's only virtue is fortitude, and he is rich in vices: he is shrewd (rather than prudent), proud, dishonest, and cruel in dealing with his enemies.

It was the habit of Erling that, when enemies of his were brought before him, he said nothing or only a little, and that very quietly, if he was decided

---

[117] Now twenty-one to twenty-two years old. S. Magnus Erlingsson, chap. 44; ÍFH III:417; Hollander, 821.

to kill them, but would mercilessly berate those whom he meant to pardon. Erling said little to Harald, and so many feared what he might intend to do with him. So they begged King Magnus to intercede with the earl for Harald. The king did so. The earl answered, "This, your friends advised you to do. But you will not govern your kingdom in peace if you yield to counsels of mercy." Thereupon Erling had Harald taken to Northness, where he was beheaded.[118]

His son Magnus is a pale shadow compared with his father, as is shown in Chapter 3. Erling's and Magnus's rule was questioned from start to finish, and if Snorri had wanted to end his work on a high note, one wonders why Sverri's victory is not mentioned. My conclusion, therefore, is that *Heimskringla* ends as it begins: with inadequate leaders.

Conclusion

The kings

We have met twenty-four kings, but in this analysis I will omit five of them: Sigurd Slembedjakn, since he did not function as king for long; and for the same reason I will omit Harald Hardrade's son Magnus and Magnus's son Håkon, as well as Magnus Barelegs's son Olav and Sigurd's son Håkon Herdebrei. All these kings died young, and Snorri has little to tell us about them as rulers. Thus, nineteen kings remain to be considered. Of these, *only five are positively described by Snorri*: Common to them is that they *keep the old laws, listen to their advisors, and make improvements in Norway*, something that Snorri admires. Another common feature is that these good kings are said to have been popular and loved by everyone. With the exception of Harald Gille, they are all blond and described as handsome.[119]

1. Hálfdan the Black
His main role in *Heimskringla* seems to be the proper ancestor of later Norwegian kings with his power base not only in Oppland, but also in Vestfold. According to Snorri, he is praiseworthy because he graded fines according to people's birth and status. He has all virtues and no vices.

2. Håkon the Good
Having all the cardinal virtues and no vices, he is said to have restored the landowners' rights to their inherited property and to have given good laws, thus, according to Snorri an altogether successful ruler.

---

[118] S. Magnus Erlingsson, chap. 35; ÍFH III:410; Hollander, 815.
[119] Harald Gille had dark hair and eyes.

3. Olav the Gentle

He is not said to have had either virtues or vices, but he creates a problem: why is Snorri so detailed about minutiae (e.g., court habits), when so much that was useful and constructive was achieved under Olav's rule? My suggestion is that a successful king like the peaceful Olav did not fit into his—mainly—critical survey of Norwegian kings.

4. Øystein Magnusson

He has all virtues and is altogether a good king, making improvements in Norway—in contrast to his brother Sigurd Jerusalemfarer.

5. Harald Gille

He seems to have all virtues, but *one vice* led to his death: *lust*. It is interesting that Snorri seems to sympathize with this Irishman, returning to Norway to claim his right to the throne. The explanation may be that Snorri did not like Harald's nephew, King Magnus, and therefore treated Harald with sympathy. Another reason for Snorri's sympathy must be that Harald Gille was known to have *listened to his advisors*, something that Snorri values highly.

The remaining fourteen kings

Two of them, Magnus Olavsson ("the Good") and Sigurd Magnusson ("Jerusalemfarer") are described both negatively and positively. Magnus the Good turned from vices to virtues thanks to Sigvat the Skald, and Sigurd Jerusalemfarer is admired for his achievements abroad, but Snorri also shows his distrust because of the king's insanity and is critical of the king's pride, greed, and lack of judgement.

What the remaining twelve kings have in common is their lack of virtues (apart from fortitude of the wrong kind); instead, they have many vices and weaknesses. Nevertheless, most of them are described as handsome and strong, even stately. It is revealing that they are said to have been liked only by their friends/followers/relatives and to have been generous only to their friends.

Harald Fairhair

The story about him stresses Vestfold's importance as the starting point of Norwegian unification, in which Earl Håkon Grjotgardsson also plays an important role. Snorri is critical of Harald, whom he blames for taking the hereditary rights from the landowners. He belittles Harald by making his lust for a woman the incentive for his unifying efforts. Finally, Snorri emphasizes the king's troubles with his sons and his opponents, a recurrent theme in the rest of his work. Harald Fairhair is certainly not a hero in *Heimskringla*.

Eirík Bloodaxe

His fortitude is also of the wrong kind, and he has many vices. Above all, he is totally overshadowed by his wife Gunnhild and is not known as having done anything to improve conditions in Norway.

Harald Greycloak

As a leader of his brothers he is a failure and as a king, a catastrophe; Snorri contrasts him with Earl Håkon, during whose rule the country flourished.

Olav Tryggvason

Compared with him, the pagan Earl Håkon is described as a better ruler. Olav's only virtue is fortitude, but his vices are many. His evangelical methods were very cruel, and his five-year-rule of Norway ended with Norway's loss of independence.

Olav Haraldsson ("Saint Olav")

Like Olav Tryggvason, his only virtue is fortitude, but he also has many vices. His evangelical methods were as cruel as those of Olav Tryggvason, and his rule also ended with Norway's loss of independence — again.

Harald Hardrade

Again, the only virtue is fortitude, while vices prevail. Admittedly, Snorri tells us about some of his building enterprises in Nidaros and Oslo, but he is not considered a good ruler, being both greedy and cruel.

Magnus Haraldsson ("Barefoot")

His only virtue was fortitude, while vices prevail. He is known as having wasted Norwegian men and resources in useless wars.

Magnus Sigurdsson ("the Blind")

He shows no virtues, only vices, and seems altogether useless — apart from being a symbol of royal power, wherefore Sigurd Slembedjakn fetched him from the monastery.

The sons of Harald Gille

King Inge seems harmless enough, but he was totally dependent on his advisors and both physically and psychologically weak. His elder brothers, Øystein and Sigurd, did everything to get rid of him, and neither of them is known to have had any virtues, only vices.

Magnus Erlingsson

He is a pale shadow of his father, Erling Skakke, doing nothing to improve conditions in Norway.

Thus, having approved of only five kings, Snorri puts question marks on and is critical towards twelve of them. Like Saxo's *Gesta Danorum*, Snorri's *Heimskringla* is not a panegyric of kings but a "kings' mirror," dealing with politics and morality. His work is full of *exempla*, illustrating the difference between good and bad rulership. Time and again we are reminded that kings ought to listen to good counselors, and among those we meet, most attention is paid to Åsbjörn from Melhus, Torgny the Lawspeaker, and Sigvat Skald, whose speeches are quoted in the Appendix.

The magnates

Some of the magnates we meet in *Heimskringla* play very important roles, and I have concentrated on eight of them: Earl Håkon, Einar Tambarskjelve, Erling Skjalgsson, Tore the Hound, Kalv Arnesson, Finn Arnesson, Gregorius Dagsson, and Erling Skakke. With the exception of Gregorius and Erling, they all have in common their defense of traditional order in opposition to the novelties that many kings tried to introduce. Erling as well as Gregorius, however, seems to have accepted the idea of strong kingship and tried to adapt by playing according to the new rules.

Snorri describes the opposing magnates in a positive way, but seems to use a slightly different standard in measuring their qualities. As far as the four cardinal virtues are concerned, they all are strong and courageous (*fortitudo*) and have a keen sense of justice, i.e. respect for the old laws (*iustitia*), but moderation and restraint (*temperantia*) do not characterize others except Erling Skjalgsson, who is also described as wise and judicious (*prudentia*). What Snorri admires in the other magnates is, rather, their cunning and their ready wit, no doubt necessary qualities for success—and even for survival. Other qualities they have in common are their keen sense of honor and loyalty towards their kinsmen. The Christian virtues are as little represented among the magnates as among the kings, but it should be noted that Erling Skjalgsson is praised for his fair treatment of the thralls (*humanitas*), and Kalv Arnesson for helping his brothers after Stiklestad (*humanitas* and *caritas*). It should also be noted that—in contrast to several kings—none of the magnates shows any signs of the deadly sins, possibly with the exception of greed (*avaritia*).

Earl Håkon Sigurdsson (of Lade)
Snorri treats Earl Håkon with respect and admiration; he is praised for governing well and keeping the old laws. His keen interest in women is not condemned by Snorri but explained by old customs that were now quickly changing due to the introduction of Christianity. His sons, the earls Eirík and Svein, are also portrayed favorably and are praised not least for their tolerance, allowing people to decide themselves about their religion.

As pointed out earlier (in Chapter 1) Snorri's sympathetic attitude to the earls who were, after all, subordinate to Danish kings can be explained by the greater influence a distant king gave the Norwegian magnates. With strong *Norwegian* kings, however, the influence and interests of the magnates were seriously threatened, and what is common for Erling Skjalgsson, Tore the Hound, Einar Tambarskjelve, and Kalv Arnesson is their defense of the old social and political order:

Erling Skjalgsson

Erling is constant in his opposition to Olav Haraldsson, and despite short-lived reconciliations, he was the king's most dangerous enemy. Snorri describes his death almost as that of a martyr; trusting that he would be fairly dealt with when caught by the king's men, he was nevertheless killed by one of them. Erling had been unswervingly loyal to his kinsmen and is described as the ideal landowner and a great defender of old values.

Tore the Hound and Einar Tambarskjelve

Both Tore and Einar began by siding with Olav Haraldsson but changed sides and became the king's dangerous enemies. Einar managed to change sides no fewer than three times, between Norwegian and Danish kings. Although at the time he was Knud's man, he carefully avoided taking part in the battle at Stiklestad.

Though not constant in their loyalties, they are both favorably portrayed because of their loyalty to their kinsmen and defense of old rights. Both Tore and Einar are admired for their ready wit and art of survival; after Olav's death they were quick to proclaim his sanctity. Together with Kalv Arnesson Einar began to cooperate with Olav's bishop Grimkel and plan for a future without Danish rule (then exercised by Knud's son Svein and his mother Alfiva).

Kalv and Finn Arnesson

Like Einar Tambarskjelve, Kalv turned out to be well versed in practical politics: whatever his role in the killing of Olav Haraldsson, he –like Tore the Hound and Einar Tambarskjelve — was quick to accept Olav's holiness, and it was on his and Einar's initiative that Olav's young son Magnus was brought to Norway. By this move they freed Norway from Danish rule but, nevertheless, hoped to control royal power. It is with great sympathy that Snorri describes Kalv's dilemma, being torn between loyalty to his brothers and to his stepsons. His change of sides in joining Earl Håkon is made fully understandable.

Kalv's brother Finn had served both Olav Haraldsson and his son Magnus, and—to begin with—also Harald Hardrade, but loyalty to his brother made him change sides and join the Danish king (Svein Forkbeard). This is made understandable by Snorri, who emphasizes Harald Hardrade's breach of his promise to pardon Kalv and allow him to return from his exile; instead, the king drove Kalv to a certain death.

The opposing magnates

One gets the impression that Snorri wants to give more nuanced portraits of these men than of the kings, sympathizing with their double loyalties. The conflicts between them and the kings are *not* individual;[120] these magnates represent their families, whose honor they want to defend. The reason why many conflicts were so prolonged is that the families were so intertwined; their marriages created a complicated network (see table "Important families") in which ever-increasing numbers of people were engaged, fighting for their honor, status, and privileges.

Magnates supporting royal power: *Gregorius Dagsson and Erling Skakke*

The magnates presented above all opposed Norwegian royal power, but there were also those who supported it, above all, Gregorius Dagsson and Erling Skakke. They were both king Inge's men, without whom the king would have been completely helpless. Neither of them has Snorri's sympathy; as a Birchleg himself, he cannot be expected to have appreciated people who fought the Birchlegs and their predecessors. This, however, does not mean that Snorri denies their competence as advisers and able warriors. They are both praised: Gregorius for keeping his housecarls better than other landedmen; and Erling for his "excellent understanding." Snorri draws very interesting portraits of both, illustrating the contrast between them: Gregorius is eager and impulsive, while Erling is circumspect and plays a waiting game. Gregorius's eagerness—and vanity—led to his death, while Erling's qualities help him reach the highest power as father and guardian of King Magnus. His path to power is not very glorious, however: Snorri emphasizes Erling's dependence on the help of his wife, Bishop Øystein, and King Valdemar, and his ending up as Valdemar's earl in the Viken area is a real disgrace to Norway.

Kings and Magnates

In confronting the opposing magnates, some kings drew the short straw, as is time and again illustrated. In *Heimskringla* there are many examples of uncompromising magnates, and there are also many examples of strong and determined women who successfully influence their husbands and kinsmen, be they magnates or kings. In the next chapter we will focus on some of these women.

---

[120] As Sverre Bagge maintains, *Society and Politics*, 70.

CHAPTER 6
KINSHIP AND THE ROLES OF WOMEN

Among medieval authors, Snorri—like Saxo Grammaticus—is unusual in giving women so much space in his work. Not only do women frequently appear, they also play important roles, influencing the men around them, being active, and taking their own initiatives. This is a great contrast to contemporary history writing, where women seldom appear and, when they do, most often play very passive roles.[1] It is therefore surprising that someone with such expert knowledge of *Heimskringla* as Diana Whaley dismisses them in the following way: "The few [*sic*] women who appear are mainly either passive nonentities or viragos" and asks "what [in this portrayal] are the relative contributions of Snorri's thought, literary stereotypes and the actual status of women in Snorri's time or the time of the sagas?"[2] My answer is that we should, of course, be extremely careful before trying to draw conclusions from literature about women's real status at *any* time, but that it is both possible and worthwhile to examine the relationship between literary stereoptypes and authorial opinions.

Women in *Gesta Danorum* and *Heimskringla* have much in common with many women we meet in Roman histories, where they are often active, steadfast, and courageous. There is, however, an important difference between the two authors: while Saxo condemns strong-willed and independent women and only praises them where he cannot criticize their weak husbands or kinsmen, Snorri not only accepts but also often admires them and in some cases uses them as his spokeswomen. This chapter will focus on women's roles in *Heimskringla* and has the following sections:

1. Women and men in Medieval Europe
2. Polygyny in *Heimskringla*
3. Women as trophies and bridgebuilders

---

[1] Birgit Strand (now Sawyer), *Kvinnor och män i* Gesta Danorum (Ph.D. diss., Gothenburg University, 1980); Birgit Strand (now Sawyer), "Saxo's Description of Women Compared with Snorre's," *Saxo Grammaticus: A Medieval Author between Norse and Latin Cultures,* ed. K. Friis-Jensen (Copenhagen: Museum Tusculanum Press, 1981), 135–51.

[2] Diana Whaley, *Heimskringla: An Introduction* (London: University College London, 1991), 101.

4. Women who help
5. Women who incite
6. Other female activity
7. Women in *Heimskringla*

We will first deal with the different forms of heterosexual relationships in our sources.

1. Women and men in Medieval Europe

As we have seen, in *Heimskringla* kings often had several female partners, not only successively but also simultaneously. The kinds of relationship between the men and their women are very difficult—often impossible—to ascertain, since in Scandinavia as elsewhere in other parts of Europe the vocabulary is vague. In his study *All the King's Women: Polygyny and Political Culture in Europe (9th–13th c.)*,[3] Jan Rüdiger presents results from an investigation of Scandinavian and other West European sources from the High Middle Ages. His conclusion is that in most cases it is the context that enables readers to decide what was "proper marriage" and what was "concubinage," According to Rüdiger, many milieux in medieval society would not have worried about a categorical distinction that, after all, was first and foremost the concern of the clergy and (later) lawyers. In everyday practice, aristocratic or other, the different women themselves (character, looks, skills) as well as their family background, networks, and other assets, would have constituted a 'continuum' of higher- and lower-status relationships that might also shift over time.

As far as Scandinavia is concerned, Icelandic authors use words such as *nema* or *taka* ("take"), *fá* ("get") or *eiga* ("own" or "have") about all sorts of men's relationships with women.[4] The Norwegian law of Gulathing, however, distinguishes between *ambótt* ("female thrall/concubine") and *kona* ("wife"); Danish and Swedish law codes have similar distinctions (corresponding to Latin *concubina—uxor*). There is no Icelandic term for "matrimony" (*hjúnskapr*) until in a new regulation in *Grágás* (some time after 1216). Thus, at least from the thirteenth century, all medieval law codes are clear about what constitutes a proper—le-

---

[3] Jan Rüdiger, *All the King's Women: Polygyny and Political Culture in Europe (9th–13th Century* (Berlin: Akademie-Verlag) = "Habilitationsschrift," Humboldt University, Berlin, 2006. German edition forthcoming: *Der König und seine Frauen: Polygynie und politische Kultur in Europa (9.—13. Jahrhundert*, Akademie-Verlag, Berlin. English edition under preparation (Leiden: Brill).

[4] "Married" = Halvdan *fekk* Ragnhild (S. Halvdan the Black, chap. 3); Harald Hardrade *fekk* Tora (S. Harald Hardrade, chap. 33); "Wife" = han *atti* Bergljot (S. Harald Hardrade, chap. 40); "Concubine" = he (Sigurd Jerusalemfarer) *tók Borghildi frillutaki* (S. Magnus' sons, chap. 19).

gal—marriage: the man—or one of his kinsmen—has to negotiate with the woman's guardian (father, eldest brother, or other close male relative) and agree on the *mund* ("bride-price"), then on the reciprocal gifts required (dower from the man's family and dowry from the woman's). Another (implied) requirement was that the future couple were of equal social status and had a solid economic background (= a "match"); some laws explicitly forbid marriage between poor people.

The laws do not, however, actually reflect practice but try to *influence* it. We know little about the custom of marriage before the twelfth century, but, according to Rüdiger, a woman strong enough (in character, looks, ability, and of a good family) would have ruled the household and seen to it that all other women were kept in their place—without any special "marriage ceremony." But what about the offspring? If the most powerful woman's son did not meet the requirements to be a ruler, there were fair chances for the other women's claims on behalf of *their* sons and the son who won the competition was regarded as legitimate, the son of an "uxor."[5]

From this we understand that the secular idea of marriage was, above all, based on economic considerations and concerned only the landowning élite. The laws do not require the consent of either partner and say nothing about obstacles to the marriage of close relatives, which was common in order to keep landed property within the family. The Church had to fight this secular idea of marriage, requiring mutual consent and forbidding close relatives to marry. Instead, the church encouraged couples who met its requirements about consent, monogamy, and permanence (and not being closely related), declaring that they were living in a *Christian marriage.*

The Church's insistence on monogamy was not respected; many rulers and magnates continued to keep several women. A deep-rooted idea is that polygyny was typical of pagan society and that monogamy was introduced by the Church, but the fact is that we simply do not know about conditions in pagan Scandinavia,[6] while there is plenty of evidence that polygyny was common well into the fourteenth century. Ecclesiastical demands may have contributed to the disappearance of polygyny, but the most important factor was no doubt that po-

---

[5] Jan Rüdiger, "Ægteskab—fandtes det? Jon Loptssons kvinder," *Gaver, ritualer, konflikter. Et rettsantropologisk perspektiv på nordisk middelalderhistorie*, ed. Hans Jacob Orning et. al., (Oslo: Unipub. Forlag, 2010) 77–115; Jan Rüdiger: "Medieval Marriage: The Case of the Devil's Advocate," *Law and Marriage in the Middle Ages. Proceedings of the Eighth Carlsberg Academy Conference on Medieval Legal History*, ed. Ditlev Tamm et al., forthcoming.

[6] It is true that in the Icelandic Family Sagas (dealing with the period c. 850–1030), most couples seem to have been monogamous, but whether this is true or just a result of the authors' wish to idealize bygone times we do not know.

litical conditions changed; power and influence no longer required broad networks of family contacts, which were gradually replaced by royal service.

Despite semantic obstacles, Audur Magnusdóttir has managed to categorize different types of male-female relationships in medieval Iceland. In her thesis "Concubines and Wives: Politics and Cohabitation in Iceland 1120–1400"[7] she discerns three different forms of cohabitation:

1. *Contract marriage* = matrimony according to certain—strict—rules, codified in the medieval law codes;

2. *Concubinage* = a steady relationship between a man of higher status with a woman of lower status, constituted by agreement between the man and the woman's guardian without any economical transactions required.; and

3. *Companionship* ("Fylgilag") = a steady relationship between partners of the same social status without interference from their families. They were monogamous, and the partners had equal shares of the family property. This kind of relationship was common among priests.

Of these three forms, only *companionship* presupposed the consent of both the man and the woman. In order to function, mutual consent must also have been the basis of *concubinage*, while we can be less certain in cases of *marriage*, where the contracts were drawn up by the partners' families. It is noteworthy that in medieval texts the term *rape* is used *even if the woman was willing*; the violence involved in the medieval term is considered to be directed against the woman's family and the order of society. Thus, when Snorri presents the women connected with magnates and rulers in *Heimskringla*, we cannot be sure what formal status they all had. In the summaries and comments (in Chapters 4 and 5 above) I have followed the American translator Hollander, when he calls women either "wives" or "concubines," but I am aware that this does not necessarily correspond to what Snorri had in mind, even less to what might have been the reality. This is why, in this chapter, I will use the terms "married to"/"wives" for relationships between kings/magnates and women of royal/high status. This means that, according to Snorri, Harald Fairhair, Olav Tryggvason, and Harald Hardrade (Sigurdarson) were married to two or more women simultaneously, while at the same time having one or more concubines.

---

[7] Audur Magnusdóttir, *Frillor och fruar: politik och samlevnad på Island 1120–1400* (Ph.D. diss., Gothenburg University, 2001).

2. Polygyny in *Heimskringla*[8]

Jan Rüdiger has investigated the most common causes for men to have relationships with several woman serially or simultaneously. He lists examples of polygyny under five aspects, and it goes without saying that, in each exemplified case, one aim does not exclude the others:

1. *"Der generative Aspekt"*
cases where the aim is to secure *reproduction*; a rich offspring being an insurance.

2. *"Der habituale Aspekt"*
cases where the aim is to mark *one's position in society*; to keep many women gave high status.

3. *"Der agonale Aspekt"*
cases where rivalry and prestige are involved, the aim being to win the woman, and to make sure that a wide audience of peers and/or subjects know about it.

4. *"Der expressive Aspekt"*
cases where the aim is to make a political statement: to create an alliance with the woman's kin (or alternatively to force them to accept submission), to establish or reinforce local rule and/or solidarities, to offer terms or to mark domination.

5. *"Der symbolishe Aspekt"*:
the woman symbolizes a) her kin, b) her man, or c) the country, exemplified by cases where the aim is a) to damage a woman's kinsmen by taking her against their will; b) to succeed to the position/power, held by the woman's lover; or c) to exercise a ruler's right to dispose of his country, including its women. The performative act of entering into a sexual relationship is in itself considered equivalent to the assumption of power, i.e., the "hieros gamos" motive. It is rare in *Heimskringla*; Snorri rather shuns it, but according to Rüdiger, the downfall of Jarl Håkon in 995 is less of a puzzle if we allow for the view, explicit in Earl Håkons skalds, that the country is embodied in its leading women.

What is missing in Rüdiger's list of aspects is the *emotional aspect*; admittedly, love and lust are not often mentioned in our medieval texts but must often have been the cause of many male initiatives, sometimes also of female consent. We seldom hear about female initiatives, but Snorri gives at least two examples: Gunnhild urges Eirik Bloodaxe to rescue her from the two Finns who both want

---

[8] This section is based on Jan Rüdiger's unpublished manuscript "Polygynie im Hochmittelalter im europäischen Vergleich."

her; and Queen Gyda (sister of Olav Kvaran) picks out Olav Tryggvason from a crowd of men, wanting to marry him.

Snorri seldom describes how love/lust could affect men; according to Rüdiger, lust may very well be indistinguishable from power and status. In the case of Harald Fairhair's lust for Gyða, Rüdiger uses it as an example of his lust for power. Something else, however, seems to have been involved in Harald's love for Snœfriðr (daughter of Svási, a Finn), for whom he is said to have neglected his kingdom and his duties, so that people thought him bewitched. After her death he sat for three years at her bedside until persuaded to bury her. It is interesting to see that this infatuation was interpreted as the result of witchcraft. The only other example of a man's love for a woman is Olav Tryggvason, who grieved so much after his first wife' Geira's death that he left his lucrative position in Vendland and went on viking expeditions. A clear example of *lust* is when, on one of his journeys, King Inge's brother Sigurd saw a woman who sang "wondrously fine" while grinding a handmill. Snorri writes: "The king descended from his horse and went in and lay with the woman."[9]

I will not try to categorize the relationships between men and women in *Heimskringla* according to the definitions of Audur Mágnúsdóttir or Jan Rüdiger, however helpful their work has been in clarifying the complex picture of partnerships with which we are dealing. Instead, I will examine the relationships as presented by Snorri in order to see if we can discern any patterns.

3. Women as trophies and bridgebuilders

Before the establishment of a unified Norway, kings allied themselves to petty kings and important magnates from different parts of the country by marrying their daughters. Thus, by taking Ragnhild, the daughter of King Harald in Sogn, King *Halvdan the Black* could inherit Sogn after their son Harald's death. After the death of his first wife, by taking another Ragnhildr, the daughter of King Sigurðr as his wife, he gained an important ally in Ringerike.

These connections were followed up by his second son *Harald (Fairhair)*. We cannot know what status all his women had, but according to Snorri he made many successful alliances by taking women from different parts of the country. Through Åsa, daughter of Earl Håkon Grjotgardsson (Trøndelag); Svanhildr, daughter of Eysteinn, Earl in Ringerike; Áshildr, daughter of King Hringr Dagsson (also in Ringerike); and Þóra (from the island of Moster), related to Horda-Kåre, Harald gained allies and influence in wide areas. According to Snorri he left nine of his "wives" when he took Ragnhildr, the daughter of King Eiríkr in Jutland. We are not told why. In two other cases Snorri makes it clear

---

[9] S. Harald's sons, chap. 18; ÍFH III:325; Hollander, 752.

that love/lust was the driving force; Harald wanted Gyða, the daughter of King Eiríkr in Hordaland, explicitly because of her beauty and high spirits, but she was very proud and scorned Harald's lack of ambition, ruling only a couple of districts. According to Snorri, she asked the messengers to greet Harald that "she would consent to be his lawful wife only if, before that, he would, for her sake, conquer all of Norway and govern that realm as independently as did King Eirik of Sweden and King Gorm of Denmark theirs."[10] It is likely that by this episode Snorri intended to ridicule Harald for not having understood Gyda's derision but taking her condition seriously. His feelings for Snøfrid are explained as the result of witchcraft.

We do not hear that Harald Fairhair's son *Eirik Bloodaxe* had women other than Gunnhild (the daughter of a certain Ossur Tote in Hålogaland), who had learned sorcery from the two Finns, who both wanted her. She fled from them with Eirik, who married her with her father's consent. As a widow, Gunnhild proved herself to be more powerful than her husband, leading their sons for many years using her cunning—and sorcery.

Olav Tryggvason's parents, Tryggve and Astrid, also seem to have been monogamous, but Olav himself had several women: first the Vendish Princess Geira (because of mutual liking), and after her death he betrothed himself to Gyda, the daughter of a king in Ireland and widow of an English earl. She had refused the great champion Alvine, who had asked for her in marriage and turned to Olav whom she preferred. Snorri writes: "it was the custom in England that if two men contended about a matter, it should be decided by single combat." After having defeated Alvine and knocked down all his men, Olav took possession of all his property and married Gyda. [11] He married his third woman, Gudrun, daughter of Jernskeggje in Trøndelag, in order to make peace with her kin. Refusing to be his wife, she tried —but failed—to stab him during their first night together, after which she disappeared with her men.[12] Olav's fourth marriage led to his fall; the Danish king Svein Forkbeard's sister Tyre had fled from Burislav, the husband her brother had forced her to marry, came to Norway, and asked Olav Tryggvason for help. Since he "observed that she was handsome," he thought that she would be a good match. This marriage was not, however, a very wise move, since it was arranged without her brother's consent, which was one of the reasons Olav was attacked and defeated by Svein and his allies at Svolder.

Apart from his attraction to Tyre, Olav Tryggvason decided to marry her certainly due to his wish to insult her brother. This proved disastrous, and a different strategy was used by Olav Haraldsson, who tried to ally with the Swedish king Olof Eriksson by proposing to his daughter Ingegjerd. The Swedish king did not

---

10 S. Harald Fairhair, chap. 3; ÍFH I:96–97; Hollander, 61.
11 S. Olav Tryggvason, chap. 32; ÍFH I:269; Hollander, 172.
12 S. Olav Tryggvason, chap. 71; ÍFH I:318–19; Hollander, 208.

trust him, however, and gave her to the Russian ruler Jarislav instead, so Olav Haraldsson had to make do with the Swedish king's illegitimate daughter Astrid. They had no children, but, according to Snorri, the mother of Olav's son Magnus was the concubine Alvhild, a servant girl "of good family."

The strategy to combine external and internal alliances was followed by Harald Hardrade. He first married Elisabet/Ellisiv, daughter of the Russian ruler Jarislav and his Swedish wife Ingegjerd, thereby becoming related to his mother-in-law's cousin, the Danish king Svein Estridsen. In Norway he married Tora (the niece of the magnate Finn Arnesson), with whom he had the future kings Magnus and Olav ("the Gentle").

Olav the Gentle allied with Denmark by marrying Ingerith, daughter of king Svein Estridsen, and his sister Ingegjerd married King Svein's son Olav. The mother of Olav the Gentle's son, however, was not his Danish wife but his Norwegian concubine Tora.

Olav's son Magnus (Barelegs) turned to Sweden instead; after a war against the Swedish King Inge Stenkilsson, the peace negotiations included a marriage between Magnus and Inge's daughter Margret. According to Snorri she was not the mother of his children, because the three sons we hear about were born by Magnus's concubines: Øystein by a woman of low birth, Sigurd ("Jerusalemfarer") by a woman called Tora, and Olav by Sigrid, daughter of the magnate Sakse of Viken.

Magnus's son Sigurd took up the Swedish-Russian connections, marrying Malmfrid, daughter of king Mstislav of Kiev and his wife Kristin, daughter of the Swedish king Inge Stenkilsson. Sigurd and Malmfrid had a daughter, Kristin, married to the magnate Erling Skakke, but Sigurd's successor as king was his son Magnus ("the Blind"), whose mother was the concubine Borghild, daughter of the wealthy landowner Olav in the Dale.

Sigurd's son Magnus tried to ally with Denmark by marrying Kristin, sister of the Danish king Valdemar I, but this initiative misfired: since he "did not take to her" he sent her back to Denmark, which of course infuriated her family. According to Snorri, this led to Magnus's affairs "taking an unfavorable turn."[13]

King Sigurd's half-brother Harald Gille continued the Swedish connections, marrying the princess Ingerid, granddaughter of King Inge Stenkilsson, who bore his son Inge. Harald also had other sons with his concubines: with the Irish woman Bjadok he had Øystein, and with Tora, daughter of Guttorm Graybeard, a magnate in the Uppland District, he had Sigurd.

We do not hear if any of Harald Gille's sons had a wife, only that Sigurd had a son, Harald (the Broadshouldered), with a servant girl, and that Øystein had a son, Øystein Møyla, with an unknown woman. Inge seems to have had no children.

---

[13] S. Magnus the Blind & Harald Gille, chap. 1; ÍFH III:279; Hollander, 716.

Thus, the first Norwegian king known to have married outside Norway was Olav Tryggvason, and an advantage of having been married to the Vendish Geira was that her sister Astrid tried to help him escape from the battle at Svolder. We do not know, however, what advantages or support he had from his marriage to Gyda. His marriage to Svein Forkbeard's sister Tyre was not a step towards an alliance with Denmark: on the contrary, it was a provocation, intended to insult the Danish king. The only marriage alliance made with Denmark was initiated by King Olav the Gentle. According to *Heimskringla*, all the other royal marriage alliances were made between Norway and Sweden/Russia: Olav Haraldsson and Astrid; Harald Hardrade and Ellisiv (Elizabeth); Magnus Barelegs and Margret; Sigurd Jerusalemfarer and Malmfrid; and Harald Gille and Ingerid.

As we have seen, most Norwegian kings were illegitimate; apart (probably) from Harald Greycloak, Olav Tryggvason, and Olav Haraldsson, only four later kings were legitimate: Harald, Olav the Gentle, Inge, and Magnus. For three of them however, the right to the throne was not undisputable; as the son of Sigurd Syr and Åsta, Harald Hardrade could not claim descent from Harald Fairhair, only refer to his having the same mother as Olav Haraldsson. Since Olav the Gentle's mother was one of Harald Hardrade's *two* wives, even *his* right could be doubted. And Magnus Erlingsson was the son not of a king but of a king's *daughter* and her husband, the magnate Erling Skakke.

Whatever reality lies behind it, the suspicion cast on these kings' right to the throne and the emphasis on the illegitimacy of almost all the others' leads to the conclusion that Snorri is seriously questioning the Norwegian monarchy, above all, most of its representatives. In contrast to the kings, important magnates (apart from Earl Håkon and Erling Skakke) are described as monogamous.

Women could also create important networks in other kingdoms by their marriages. After the death of her first husband, Magnus Barelegs, Queen Margret (daughter of the Swedish king Inge) married the Danish king Niels and thus had important contacts in all three kingdoms, which she used for her own plans. Similarly Malmfrid, granddaughter of the Swedish king Inge and of the Russian ruler Mstislav, after the death of her first husband, Sigurd the Jerusalemfarer, married the Danish king Erik Emune. Finally, Queen Ingerid (granddaughter of the Swedish King Inge Stenkilsson) had a most impressive network: she was married four times, first to the Danish prince Henrik the Halt, then to King Harald Gille, after whose death she married the magnate Ottar Birting, a loyal supporter of her son, King Inge. After he had been killed—according to his kinsmen on King Sigurd's instigation—she married another magnate, the powerful Arne of Stårheim, later called King's Stepfather. She also had a son by Ivar Sneis, called Orm "King's Brother."[14]

---

[14] S. Harald's sons, chaps. 14–16; ÍFH III:254–56; Hollander, 750–51.

One easily gets the impression that these women were passive rather than active, but we know that many of them played important roles as wives and mothers, defending their own and their children's rights, giving advice, questioning men's decisions, supporting their family, helping sons as well as husbands in awkward situations. Unlike the authors of *Morkinskinna* and *Fagrskinna*, Snorri gives many examples.

4. Women who help

The first example of women helping their sons is Halvdan the Black's mother Åsa, who takes her son to Agthir in order to help him take over her father's kingdom. Next we meet Olav Tryggvason's mother Astrid, who rescues her son Olav from Queen Gunnhild and her sons, fleeing from Norway with him. Olav Haraldsson is also helped by his mother Åsta, who supports his claim to be the ruler in Norway. Olav Haraldsson's Swedish wife Astrid helps her step-son Magnus Olavsson (the Good) gain power in Norway, and Queen Ingerid, widow of Harald Gille, supports their son Inge, ensuring that he was chosen king at the Borgar Thing (when he was only two years old). Further, she helps Inge by inciting him to be more active in opposing his enemies, above all his half-brothers Sigurd and Øystein. Finally, Kristin, daughter of Sigurd Jerusalemfarer, married to Erling Skakke, helps her son Magnus in negotiations with her cousin Valdemar I.

Kristin is remarkable: she supports and helps not only her son, but also Gregorius, King Inge himself, and her husband Erling. When Inge's brother Øystein planned to attack Gregorius on his farm, Gregorius escaped to the Hardanger District, where he was helped and equipped by Kristin with Erling's approval. After Gregorius's death, King Inge wanted to avenge him, and suspecting that his friends would not be able to care for his body if he fell in battle, he asked his cousin Kristin to do so. After Inge's death, Kristin kept her promise.[15] When Håkon the Broadshouldered and his followers held meetings in Saint Hallvard's Church to discuss the government of the kingdom, Kristin bribed the priest in charge of the church keys to let one of her men hide in the church so that he could find out what was planned. Having heard about them, she sent a message to her husband Erling, warning him never to trust Håkon and his men.[16] Finally, when the Danish king Valdemar I reminded Erling about their agreement that he should have possession of Viken, Erling took shelter behind the *bændr* there, who flatly refused to be subjects of the Danish king.[17] This resulted in hostili-

---

[15] S. Håkon the Broadshouldered, chaps. 15, 18; ÍFH III:365–66, 368–69; Hollander, 782 and 785.

[16] S. Håkon the Broadshouldered, chap. 19; ÍFH III:369; Hollander, 786.

[17] S. Magnus Erlingsson, chaps. 23, 24; ÍFH III:399–40; Hollander, 807–8.

ties between Norway and Denmark until Kristin intervened, going to Denmark to see Valdemar. She was cordially received and provided with revenues so that she could maintain her retinue.[18] Her husband Erling followed after her and was kept as a hostage by King Valdemar, until he agreed to become an earl under the Danish king, governing Viken on his behalf.[19]

In the end, however, Kristin left Erling to join a man called Grím Rusle, with whom she went to Miklagarth and had some children. We do not know when Kristin and Erling had had their illegitimate children: together with King Sigurd Haraldsson, Kristin had a son, Harald, and Erling had four sons together with three different concubines.[20]

5. Women who incite

In *Heimskringla* we meet several women who incite men to take revenge, fight, or in other ways maintain the family honor. Two of the most significant are Tyre and Sigrid, who figure prominently in the next chapter comparing *Heimskring-la* with Saxo Grammaticus's *Gesta Danorum*. The first female inciter we hear about is the formidable Gunnhild, married to King Harald Fairhair's son Eirik (Bloodaxe).

Gunnhild

Snorri describes Gunnhild as "a very beautiful woman, shrewd and skilled in magic, friendly of speech, but full of deceit and cruelty."[21] It is clear that, as a widow, she was the real leader of the family. After Eirik's fall, she and all her (eight?) sons left Northumberland, taking with them all Eirik's ships and followers plus a great amount of treasure that he had gathered on his expeditions in England and elsewhere. They took possession of the Orkney and Shetland Islands, demanding tribute, and after King Håkon the Good's fall they sought power in Norway. Harald "Greycloak" was the most respected, but their mother Gunnhild, "Kingsmother," had great influence over them, actively partaking in the rule of the middle part of Norway, since East- and Vestfold were held by Tryggve Olavsson and Gudrød Bjørnsson and Trøndelag by Earl Sigurd. Snorri's description of Gunnhild and her incitement of her son Harald (Greycloak) is best represented by the following quotation:

---

[18] S. Magnus Erlingsson, chap. 29; ÍFH III:405; Hollander, 811.

[19] S. Magnus Erlingsson, chap. 30; ÍFH III:406; Hollander, 812.

[20] S. Magnus Erlingsson: Kristin's son; chap. 35, and Erling's children, chap. 30; ÍFH III:410, 406–7; Hollander, 815 and 812–13.

[21] S. Harald Fairhair, chap. 41; ÍFH I:149; Hollander, 94.

'What are your intentions about ruling in Trøndelag? You bear the title of kings, as have done your ancestors, but you have few troops and little land, and there are many of you to share it. Tryggve and Gudrød have sway in Viken, and they do have some claim to it because their forebears ruled there, but Earl Sigurd has the mastery in all districts of Trondheim, and I don't know what reason there exists for your letting an earl take the power over so great a territory from you. It seems strange to me that every summer you go on viking expeditions to other countries but allow an earl in your own land to take your inheritance from you. Your father's father Harald, after whom you are called, would have thought little of depriving an earl of land and life when he won all of Norway and ruled it afterwards until he grew old.'[22]

Harald Greycloak tried to defend himself for not having tried to kill Earl Sigurd, pointing out that the earl had many friends and was well liked—and shrewd but his mother just answered:

'Then we shall proceed another way with our business and go a little more slowly. Let Harald and Erling remain in North Møre this fall. I shall go with you. Then all of us together shall try and see what will come of it.'[23]

In the next section ("Other female activity") we will see more of Gunnhild, but first we must consider other women inciters. Apart from Sigrid the Haughty (see Chapter 7), there were two other Sigríds who successfully incited their menfolk: Sigrid, widow of Sigurd, the brother of Tore the Hound; and Sigrid, widow of Olve at Egge.

Sigrid, widow of Sigurd

When Sigrid's son Asbjørn ("Selsbane") had been killed by one of Olav Haralds-son's men, she urged her brother-in-law Tore Hound to avenge him. She reminded Tore that he had not kept his earlier promise to support Asbjørn:

'The fact is, Tore, that Asbjørn, my son, followed your kindly advice [i.e. not to become Olav Haraldsson's steward]. It was not granted to him to repay you for what it was worth. Now, though I am not able to do as well as he would have done, still I am minded to do what I can. Here is a gift I shall give you, and I wish it may serve you well.' It was a spear. 'Here is the spear that pierced my son Asbjørn, with his blood still on it. It will help you to remember that it came from the wound you saw on Asbjørn, your brother's son. It would be a manly deed if you parted with it in such fashion that it stood in the breast of Olav the Stout. And now I say' she continued, 'that

---

[22] S. Harald Greycloak, chap. 3; ÍFH I:204–5; Hollander, 132.
[23] S. Harald Greycloak, chap. 3; ÍFH I:205; Hollander, 133.

you will be called by everyone a vile wretch if you do not avenge Asbjørn."
With that she turned away. Tore was so enraged at her words that he could
not make answer, and so distracted was he that he did not let go of the spear
and that he did not watch out for the pier, and he would have fallen in the
water if men had not taken hold of him and supported him when he went
aboard his ship.'[24]

As we have already seen, Tore took this challenge seriously and avenged Asbjørn.

Sigrid, widow of Olve at Egge, married to Kalv Arnesson

Sigrid had two sons with Olve, and they as well as their father had been killed by
Olav Haraldsson's men. She urged her second husband, Kalv, who had hitherto
been Olav's man, to take revenge:

> She reckoned up the injuries she claimed she had received from king
> Olav—first, that he had caused her [first] husband Olve, to be killed, 'and
> now, since that,' she said, 'my two sons. And you, Kalv, were present at
> their execution and I would have least expected that of you.' Kalv replied
> that it was much against his will that Tore was executed. 'I offered money
> to reprieve him,' he said. 'But when Grjotgard was executed, I lost my own
> brother, Arnbjørn.' She said, 'It is good that you had to bear that from the
> king, because it is likely that him you will wish to avenge, even though you
> do not care to avenge the wrongs done to me. You saw, when your foster son
> Tore was killed, how little the king thought of you then.' Harangues such as
> this one she constantly made to Kalv. He often replied to her angrily; still in
> the end he gave in to her representations and promised to swear loyalty to
> Earl Håkon if the latter would increase his income. Sigrid sent word to the
> earl, informing him how it stood with Kalv. And as soon as the earl got to
> know that, he sent a message to Kalv, to the effect that he should come to
> the town in order to agree on terms. Kalv did not delay and shortly travelled
> to Nidaros where he had a good welcome from the earl, and discussed mat-
> ters with him. They agreed on all points, and in the end Kalv swore fealty
> to the earl against receiving great revenues from him.[25]

Ingerid

When Queen Ingerid (Harald Gille's widow) discovered that King Sigurd was
responsible for killing Inge's and Gregorius's housecarls, she went immediately
to King Inge, "saying to him that he would long be considered a little king if he
did not bestir himself, even if his courtiers were killed, one after the other like

---

[24] S. Saint Olav, chap. 123; ÍFH II:211–13; Hollander, 393.

[25] S. Saint Olav, chap. 183; ÍFH II:332–33; Hollander, 478.

swine." King Inge grew furious, but Gregorius agreed with the queen and persuaded him to obey her and take revenge.[26]

All these women were successful in getting their way; they and other women
were also important in playing roles other than that of incitor.

6. Other female activity

Gunnhild

Of all women portrayed in *Heimskringla*, Gunnhild is the most influential—and
dangerous. She figures in four sagas (five, if Earl Håkon's saga is counted as a
separate saga).[27] Snorri describes how in Finnmark, Harald Fairhair's son Eirik
Bloodaxe met a woman called Gunnhild, who had come there from Hålogaland
in order to learn sorcery from two Finns, said to be the wisest in Finnmark. She
warned Eirik and his men that the Finns were very dangerous and had hitherto
killed all men who approached their hut. Since she did not want to stay with
them any longer, she promised to hide Eirik and his men if they helped her kill
the Finns. Her plan was very cunning: she hid the visitors' tracks around the
hut (with ash), so when the Finns returned home, having followed the tracks
right to the hut, they lost them and could not find the intruders. The next step in
Gunnhild's plan was to take advantage of the fact that the Finns were exhausted,
not having slept for three nights; since both of them wanted to marry Gunnhild,
they had been kept awake by mutual jealousy. Gunnhild asked them both to
come and lie on each side of her, which they were glad to do. Snorri writes:

> She put an arm around the neck of both. They soon fell asleep, but she
> roused them. Then they soon fell asleep again, and so soundly that she was
> scarcely able to wake them. They fell asleep again, and now she was not able
> to wake them by any means; she even sat them up, but they kept on sleep-
> ing. Then she took two large bags and placed them over their heads, tying
> them fast under their arms. Then she made a sign to the king's men, and
> they leapt forward, killed them, and dragged them out of the hut.

After this, Eirik took Gunnhild with him, sailed to Hålogaland, and got her father's consent to marry her.[28]

As Eirik's wife, Gunnhild practiced her knowledge of sorcery; according
to Snorri people explained the sudden death of Eirik's brother Halvdan as due

---

[26] S. Harald's sons, chap. 27; ÍFH III:339–40; Hollander, 761–62.

[27] S. Harald Fairhair; Saga Håkon the Good; Saga Harald Greycloak ("Earl Håkon-
saga"); S. Olav Trygvasson.

[28] S. Harald Fairhair, chap. 32; ÍFH I:136; Hollander, 86–87.

to Gunnhild's having suborned a witch to prepare a poisoned drink for him.[29] When Eirik's brother Håkon (the Good, fostered by the English King Adalstein) returned to Norway, Eirik and his family fled to England, where King Adalstein gave Northumberland to Eirik on condition that he defended that region against other vikings and let himself, his family, and followers be baptized. Eirik agreed, but since he thought his land too small, he went on plundering expeditions, harrying in Scotland, the Hebrides, Ireland, and Wales and gained great wealth. After King Adalstein's death, however, his successor, King Edmund, wanted to get rid of Eirik, and there was a great battle between them, in which Eirik fell.[30]

After Eirik's fall, Gunnhild and her sons went to Denmark, where they were well received by Harald Gormsson, who gave them great revenues and offered to foster one of Gunnhild's sons, Harald ("Greycloak").[31] When Håkon the Good had ruled Norway for twenty years, Gunnhild and her sons came from Denmark with a big army but were defeated by Håkon. Six years later they returned and were defeated again, but when King Håkon pursued them, an arrow hit his arm, causing a lethal wound. According to Snorri, the arrow was shot by Gunnhild's page.[32]

On his deathbed, King Håkon bequeathed Norway to Gunnhild's sons, but they had a powerful rival in Sigurd, Earl in Trøndelag. Gunnhild planned to tempt his brother Grjotgard to betray him. Grjotgard was easy to persuade and promised to tell them when it would be easiest to attack Sigurd. He did so, but after Gunnhild's sons had burnt down the house where the Earl and his followers were dwelling, they had to leave Trøndelag, because people there gathered around Sigurd's son Håkon, making him their leader and Earl. Friends of both parties achieved a reconciliation, however, according to which Earl Håkon was to have the same power in Trøndelag as his father had, and Gunnhild's sons were to have the same power as King Håkon the Good. Even though the peace was confirmed with binding oaths, Earl Håkon and Gunnhild continued to scheme against each other.[33]

When Earl Håkon allied with Tryggve Olavsson (in Østfold) and Gudrød Bjørnsson (in Vestfold), Gunnhild and her sons suspected that he planned some treason against them and prepared to attack him in Trøndelag. Being warned about this, however, Earl Håkon escaped to Denmark, where, together with Harald Gormsson, he made cunning plans to get rid of Harald Greycloak and his brothers. In Norway, Gunnhild's sons killed Earl Håkon's allies, and after having heard that King Tryggve's widow Astrid was expecting his child, Gunnhild sent a messenger to Viken in order to learn how things were with

---

[29] S. Harald Fairhair, chap. 41; ÍFH I:146–47; Hollander, 94.

[30] S. Håkon the Good, chap. 4; ÍFH I:153–54; Hollander, 98–99.

[31] S. Håkon the Good, chap. 10; ÍFH I:161–62; Hollander 103–4.

[32] S. Håkon the Good, chap. 31; ÍFH I:190–91; Hollander 123.

[33] S. Harald Greycloak, chaps. 3–6; ÍFH I:204–11; Hollander, 132–36.

mother and child. When it was reported that Astrid and her son Olav were stay-ing with her father, Gunnhild immediately sent armed men to get hold of the child. Her attempt failed, however, because Astrid's father had been warned and had already sent her and her son to Svitjod. Gunnhild did not give up but sent her men with costly gifts to the Swedish king Eirik, asking him to let them take Olav with them back to Gunnhild. This attempt also failed, and after Harald Greycloak had been killed in battle, Gunnhild and her sons fled from Norway to the Orkney Islands. They went on trying to regain power in Norway but were defeated, first by Earl Håkon, and—after his death—by Olav Tryggvason.

Beyond *Heimskringla*, we meet Gunnhild in several other sources.[34] She is described as a formidable woman who steered her sons with an iron hand. Snorri seems fascinated—if not approving—of her, and unlike other authors he does not tell us how ignominiously she ended her eighty-year-long life; according to Theodoricus Monachus and *Ágríp*, she was drowned in a marsh in Denmark.

Tora of Rimul

Tora, the mother of Earl Håkon's son Svein, remained loyal to Håkon, doing what she could to help him escape his enemies. She hid him and his thrall in a pigsty, but in vain; the earl was killed by his thrall, who had been tempted by Olav Tryggvason's promises of reward.[35]

Bergljot

Bergljot was the daughter of Earl Håkon and Tora, daughter of Skage Skoftesson, a man of high rank. She was married to Einar Tambarskjelve and was the mother of Eindride. After her husband and son were slain by King Harald Hardrade, she went to the royal residence and heatedly urged the *bœndrs'* force to do battle. She said: "Now we feel the want of my kinsman, Håkon. The slayers of Eindride would not be rowing down the river if Håkon stood here on the banks." Then she had the remains of both Einar and Eindride attended to and interred near the Church of Saint Olav.

Bergljot's attempt to incite revenge did not succeed immediately, but ac-cording to Snorri, the fall of Einar and his son made King Harald Hardrade so strongly detested that "the only reason the king's stewards and the others did not attack him was the lack of a leader to raise the standard for the *bœndrs'* army."[36] After the slaying of Einar and his son King Harald therefore understood that he had to be reconciled with their kinsman Håkon Ivarsson and asked his steward Finn Arnesson to mediate. Håkon felt it was his duty to avenge his kinsmen,

---

[34] Theodoricus Monacus, Ágrip, *Fagrskinna, Egil's Saga,* and *Njál's Saga.*
[35] S. Olav Tryggvason, chaps. 48, 49; ÍFH I:293–98; Hollander, 190ff.
[36] S. Harald Hardrade, chap. 44; ÍFH III:126; Hollander, 611.

knowing that he had sufficient support in Nidaros to start a rebellion against the king, but Finn persuaded him to be reconciled with the king. Håkon's condition was that he marry the king's daughter Ragnhild, but at first she refused him because of his lower status.[37] Eventually Harald gave him both an earldom and his daughter,[38] but the reconciliation did not last long. Håkon helped Harald's enemy and continued to create problems for him. In that sense, Bergljot's inciting can be said to have been successful.

Gudrun

After having destroyed the pagan idols at Mære and killed Jernskjegge, the leader of the *bændr* in Trøndelag, Olav Tryggvason arranged for a meeting with Jernskjegge's kinsmen, offering them atonement. It was finally agreed that he would marry Jernskjegge's daughter Gudrun, and when the marriage was celebrated, Olav and Gudrun mounted the same bed. No sooner had the king fallen asleep, however, but she drew a knife and tried to kill him. The king wrested the knife from her, got up, and told his men what had happened, but Gudrun simply took her clothes and left the place together with her men.

Alfiva

After Olav Haraldsson's fall at Stiklestad, the Danish King Knud the Powerful commanded his son Svein and his mother Alfiva (Knud's concubine) to take over the rule of Norway. Svein and his mother introduced new laws, modeled on the Danish laws, but some were much harsher. When these laws became known, there was immediate opposition, and most people blamed Alfiva for them.[39] We have heard how the attitude to Olav Haraldsson gradually changed in his favor during Svein's and Alfiva's rule, and when more than a year had passed after Olav's death, his remains were disinterred. When Bishop Grimkjell and others remarked that Olav looked more alive than dead, Alfiva said, "Mighty little do bodies decompose when buried in sand. It would not be the case, if he had lain in earth." The bishop then cut the king's hair, stating that it had grown since he died, but Alfiva answered, "That hair would seem to me a holy relic only if fire does not burn it. We have often seen wholly preserved and undamaged the hair of persons who have lain in the ground longer than this man has." The bishop then laid Olav's hair into a blessed fire, and when he took it out of it, he could show that the hair was not burnt. Then Alfiva bade them lay the hair into fire that had *not* been blessed, but now Einar Tambarskjelve ordered her to be silent, using hard language against her. "So then, by the bishop's pronouncement, the

---

[37] S. Harald Hardrade, chaps. 45–48; ÍFH III:126–30; Hollander, 612–15.
[38] S. Harald Hardrade, chap. 50; ÍFH III:132; Hollander, 616.
[39] S. Saint Olav, chap. 239; ÍFH II:398–401; Hollander, 524ff.

consent of the king and the judgment of all the people, king Olav was declared a true saint."[40]

Since King Svein was only a child, it was his mother Alfiva who had the government of the country in her hand, and, according to Snorri, the Norwegians hated her greatly, both then and afterwards.[41] It was not until Olav Haraldsson's son Magnus had arrived in Norway that Svein and Alfiva left for Denmark. It is highly probable that Snorri has Alfiva express the doubts he himself had about Olav's sanctity.

7. Women in *Heimskringla*

We have met several women in *Heimskringla*, helping, inciting, or otherwise active. It is striking that, on the whole, women play active and important roles; to Snorri, it seems quite acceptable and natural that women can be dangerous enemies, and they are allowed to operate on the same footing with men. It should be noticed that Snorri does not seem to find anything remarkable about female independence, will power, and energy. The behavior and actions of women are mostly depicted without comments; Snorri neither condemns nor praises. Very few women have "bad" qualities attributed to them, an exception being Gunnhild, who is described as "insidious" and "heartless." As a rule, women are described as beautiful and prudent, sometimes good, eloquent, and/or generous. Admittedly, in the beginning of *Heimskringla*, some women are described as skilled in the witch's art; women seem to have a "natural" relationship to magic.

To sum up: women play important roles in *Heimskringla*; more than 150 are named, more than half of them only incidentally, but a considerable number of women still remain, to whom closer attention is given. The fact that so many women are named is due to the way the Saga presents people: their ancestry, including women, is carefully recorded. As to the characterizations of women, there are many things that remind one of the "virago-ideal" of late classical antiquity: women often have "male" qualities attributed to them. Even the early medieval ideal of a woman as her husband's counselor can be traced in Snorri, but he does not seem to share the worries about female indecency that are typical of some medieval writers. Nor do we notice much of the ascetic ideal of the Church or its explicit denigration of women. If *vita contemplativa* was more highly valued than *vita activa* in earlier medieval times, the opposite seems to be true of women in *Heimskringla*.

These women are allowed, within limits, to be active, and they are sometimes described as being equal to men. We do not meet the negative view of women that distinguishes much contemporary European literature, at least not

---

[40] S. Saint Olav, chap. 244; ÍFH II:403–5; Hollander, 528–30.
[41] S. Saint Olav, chap. 247; ÍFH II:410f.; Hollander, 534.

in the same guise. The question is whether woman as "sorceress," "inciter," or "dangerous enemy" should be connected with the clerical view of women as a menace and a danger to man. As far as Snorri is concerned, I do not think so; perhaps the woman as a sorceress is meant to be a warning, but as inciters and powerful actors, most of them obviously have Snorri's full respect. We have reason to believe that he lets the female inciters mediate his own views; both Sigrid, sister of Erling Skjalgsson, and Sigrid, sister of Tore the Hound, tell the truth about Olav Haraldsson and make their husbands take revenge. Thus, several of the female inciters in *Heimskringla* are Snorri's spokeswomen in criticism of royal violence that is often expressed in their complaints against their kinsmen's lack of enterprise in taking revenge.

A not uncommon way of implying criticism of men is to explicitly praise their women or let women tell the truth. This technique was used by Aristophanes in *Lysistrate*, where he is critical of the democratic rule in Athens and its war against Sparta. Since it was too dangerous to express his criticism explicitly, he has the *women* protest and voice his opinion. As none of his contemporaries would suspect him of campagning for the rights of women, letting reason speak through them was quite safe.[42] The same kind of technique is also used by Saxo Grammaticus, who praises women when he cannot criticize the men associated with them, thereby implying criticism of male shortcomings.[43] In *Heimskringla*, many of the female inciters act as Snorri's spokeswomen in their opposition either to the authoritarian power and violence of the king or to the indecision of their kinsmen.[44] In putting his own words in the mouths of women, Snorri (like Aristophanes and Saxo) could be quite safe, and at the same time he could illustrate women's lust for revenge, a common *topos* in Nordic medieval literature.

Snorri, as well as his contemporary Saxo, are unusual in letting us meet so many women in their histories, but they treat them very differently. While Saxo is clearly influenced by ecclesiastical ideas about the subordination of women, their weakness and moral inferiority, Snorri does not seem to share these ideas—on the contrary. It would be interesting to study his sources more closely in order to see how much they might have influenced him in his attitude to women; suffice it here to say that neither *Morkinskinna* nor *Fagrskinna* shows the same interest in female actors.

We can only speculate why Snorri shows this respect for active women; several factors have to be taken into account. His personal experience may have contributed, but the authors of many Icelandic Family Sagas also show the same

---

[42] Cf. Birgitta Kurtén-Lindberg, *Women's Lib. i Aristophanes' Athen* (Göteborg, Åström, 1987).

[43] See Birgit Strand (now Sawyer), *Kvinnor och män i* Gesta Danorum, e.g., 194.

[44] Cf. Mallika B. Tinlund Pande-Rolfsen, "Kvinner og menn i *Heimskringla*; eggersken og kongen," hovedoppgave i historie (Trondheim: NTNU 2002), especially 85.

kind of respect, and that is why it has been surmised that this attitude reflects contemporary reality. According to a widespread view, women in the North, especially in Iceland, were freer and more independent than women in the rest of Europe. There is no certain evidence for this. It is possible, however, that, especially in Iceland, many women were less controlled, since they were often left to fend for themselves during their husbands' and kinsmen's long absences at sea (fishing, trading, and/or raiding). Another factor may be the sex ratio; there is much to indicate that there was a shortage of marriageable women, particularly in Iceland, partly because magnates had several wives/concubines and partly because of female infanticide, habits common before the Church forbade both.[45] According to Carol Clover, their scarcity gave women advantages in many kinds of negotiations.[46]

Be this as it may, my purpose has been to study what roles Snorri allots to the principal characters in *Heimskringla*. The conclusion is that while most kings fall short compared with the magnates, many of the magnates fall short compared with their wives and kinswomen.

---

[45] As pointed out above (p. 114) the most important factor in the disappearance of polygyny was that power and influence did not require broad networks but were gradually replaced by royal service.

[46] Carol Clover, "The Politics of Scarcity: Notes on the Sex Ratio in Early Scandinavia," *Scandinavian Studies* 60 (1988): 147–88.

Chapter 7
Comparison between Saxo and Snorri

Snorri was a younger contemporary of Saxo Grammaticus, medieval Denmark's greatest historian. It is still an open question whether Snorri knew Saxo's *Gesta Danorum*;[1] to answer it, a comprehensive comparison of their works is needed.[2] They were both learned and well versed in oral traditions as well as literature. If, as is possible, they had met, they would not have needed an interpreter and would have had a lot to talk about. The histories of Denmark and Norway are so closely intertwined that many of the same events and people figure in both of their works, and sometimes they used the same sources. While a great deal is known about Snorri's life and career, very little is known about Saxo's. We know that he was Archbishop Absalon's clerk and close to the royal court; he dedicated his work to King Valdemar II ("Sejr" = the Victorious). He was obviously well educated and had probably studied abroad, perhaps in northern France.

The most obvious difference between them is that Saxo used Latin and Snorri the vernacular. This was partly because the literary traditions in Denmark and Iceland differed; in Saxo's time there were few Danish texts but many in Latin, while Snorri had a rich vernacular tradition to follow and develop. Another factor is that Danish historians seem to have had a greater need than Norwegians and Icelanders to assert themselves internationally, especially against the Germans. A recent commentator has pointed out that:

> Expressing past drama in the vernacular, as Snorri chose to do, entails the obvious advantage that the direct speech of the protagonists will be perceived as the very words spoken by this or that historical person — it brings them alive in an emotional way in front of the reader/listener. Saxo's choice of Latin, in contrast, disguises his Danish heroes as Roman (or biblical), thereby expressing their deeds through universal models and concepts.[3]

---

[1] A history from oldest times to 1185. Cf. *Heimskringla* also from the oldest times to 1177.

[2] A good start is the collection of comparisons printed in *Saxo & Snorre*, ed. Jon Gunnar Jørgensen et al. (Copenhagen: Museum Tusculanums Forlag, 2010).

[3] Lars Boje Mortensen, "Litterær teknik og sprogets repræsentative effekt," *Saxo & Snorre*, ed. Jon Gunnar Jørgensen et al.(Copenhagen: Museum Tusculanums Forlag,

It has often been maintained that, as narrators, Saxo is abstract and moralistic, while Snorri is concrete and impartial. Sverre Bagge contrasts "Snorri's simple, paratactic and straightforward Old Norse" with Saxo's complicated and hypotactic Latin. This is misleading, however; Snorri's style may *seem* straightforward, but his narrative is more complicated than it appears to be. Like Saxo, Snorri knew how to use ambiguity and irony, but the tensions between what he explicitly states and what he implies can be detected only by analyzing his *whole* work, not just a few examples.

A thorough examination of both *Gesta Danorum* and *Heimskringla* in their entireties reveals resemblances that have apparently not been previously recognized. In the first place, it is worth asking why, although both authors had predecessors who covered the same ground, they both describe the past again and in such monumental ways. Olrik-Ræder's edition of *Gesta Danorum* fills 550 quarto pages, and Islenzk Fornrít's *Heimskringla* has 1,235 pages. As far as we know, Snorri had no patron, while Saxo was commissioned by Archbishop Absalon. This did not prevent him from expressing his own views, however, and even criticizing his patron. Both lived in a time of rapid changes, some of which they did not welcome, above all kingship *Dei gratia* and the secular power of the Church. As well-educated and politically involved men they obviously wanted to give their *own* versions of the past, polemicizing against earlier works, in the hope of influencing contemporary and future audiences. Being close to the centers of power, they both had to be cautious in their criticism, and to escape suspicion—and survive—they elevated ambiguity to a fine art. *Gesta Danorum* and *Heimskringla* are, therefore, more than just historical works; they are also kings' mirrors and treatises on statecraft.

Far from glorifying kings, both give very unflattering portraits of many, especially those who do not listen to good advice. Both of them are critical of bishops who are too concerned with their worldly, military power, and neither seems to favor monasticism. Snorri rarely mentions monks (and never nuns), and the only monk Saxo presents is Abbot Jon, who was summoned when King Valdemar I fell ill "although [Jon was] not so competent as he himself imagined."[4] Indeed, Saxo casts suspicion on this monk for the king's sudden death.[5]

Neither Saxo nor Snorri seem convinced that kings are God's representatives on earth, nor do they appear to believe in the sanctity of kings or any kind of royal magic. In describing Valdemar I's journey through Germany, Saxo calls the women and peasants "superstitious" when they asked the king to bless their children and crops.[6] There were, however, two kings whose sanctity could not

---

2010), 129. Echoes from and references to the Bible are, however, very rare in *Gesta Danorum*.

[4] *Gesta Danorum* XV.vi.9; Olrik-Ræder, 535; Christiansen vol. II, pp. 599ff. ·

[5] Ibid.

[6] *Gesta Danorum* XIV. xxviii.13; Olrik-Ræder, 442; Christiansen, vol. II, 461–62.

be denied: the Danish Knud and the Norwegian Olav, but Saxo and Snorri both differ markedly from the hagiographic literature devoted to them.

Snorri depicts Olav Haraldsson as greedy, violent, and cruel and distances himself from the early rumors about Olav's sanctity.[7] In having Alfifa persist in her skepticism of Olav's miraculously well-preserved corpse, he can air his own doubts without risk. Who could blame *him* for what a Danish woman said? Admittedly Snorri reports miracles later wrought by Saint Olav, but he could hardly do otherwise one hundred years after Olav's cult had become the very foundation of Norwegian kingship. He went far enough in contrasting the evil of the living Olav with the good that happened after his death.

Saxo had also had to face the problem posed by a "national" royal saint. We will never know whether he had any doubts about the sanctity of King Knud, but if he did, he would not have had much chance to air them; commissioned by the archbishop, he had to present Saint Knud in a way that was approved by the Church. This he did: Knud is explicitly praised for his rule but is betrayed, first by his brother and then by his closest friend. His people revolted, and his death in 1086 is described as that of a martyr: having taken refuge in Saint Alban's Church (in Odense), he repents his sins kneeling before the altar, where he calmly meets his killers. In Saxo's time, Knud's status as a saint was as well established in Denmark as Olav's was in Norway, perhaps even more so, since Knud had been canonized by the pope (in 1101). It is significant, however, that Saxo repeatedly — and at length — tells us that there were many who did not believe in his holiness and, who, when they heard about the miracles, decided that he owed his sanctity not to his way of life or rule but to his penitence in facing death, an opinion held by many of Saxo's contemporaries. There are indications that Saxo shared this opinion, but by explicitly condemning those who thought so, he evaded criticism. Nevertheless, he manages to plant seeds of suspicion concerning Knud's sanctity in the reader's mind.

To Absalon, the glorification of Lund's great benefactor and the condemnation of doubters were matters of course. Superficially, Saxo fulfilled his patron's demand but leaves room for implicit criticism of Knud's rule. In ordering the administration of justice to be more rigorous he angered the magnates, and by enforcing the payment of tithes he provoked revolt. Saxo's view is that the time was not yet ripe for introducing this new custom, showing that Knud lacked judgment. In trusting his jealous brother Olaf and Blakke, who simulated friendship and loyalty, while plotting against him, Knud also showed fatal gullibility. We can deduce that Knud was imprudent, and that decided his fate; although aware that he no longer had the support of the magnates and the people, which he knew was the basis of royal power, he persisted with unpopular demands that eventually led to his death.

---

[7] See above, pp. 66, 127f.

Saxo and Snorri both report the episode when King Olav punishes himself for having worked on a Sunday. Unaware of what he was doing, he cut chips from a piece of wood, but when reminded what day it was, he swept all the shavings into his hand, set them on fire and burnt his palm.[8] Most probably *Passio Olavi* (ch. 19) was their common source; it is notable, however, that neither Saxo nor Snorri mentions that—according to *Passio*—God let Olav's hand remain undamaged.[9] If they did not intend to give us a proof of Olav's holiness, why did they include this episode in their works? One answer, of course, is that it was meant to illustrate the king's piety and strict observance of the laws and commandments, and that was probably one of the intended interpretations. There are, however, indications that both authors are ironic; the very harsh punishment Olav imposed on himself is totally out of proportion with the small offence he had committed (cutting chips can hardly be considered "work"), and it is revealing that in both works this is *the only example* of Olav's alleged piety and obedience to Christian teaching. Saxo's extensive praise of Olav's fear of God is also significant; his comment is much longer than the episode itself, and his description of Olav's spiritual agony is exaggerated. Snorri does not say much about Olav's self-imposed punishment; he just drily states that this showed that the king knew the law and commandments and did not want to do what he knew was wrong. Having described in detail the many wrongs that Olav had done to the Norwegian people, Snorri makes his irony obvious.

Women and men in *Gesta Danorum* and *Heimskringla*

Among medieval historians, Saxo and Snorri are unusual in having so many women play important roles, and my comparison of the authors will now turn to the question of their description, opinions, and use of women. Snorri seems to appreciate strong and active women, and there is no hint that he regarded them as inferior or morally weaker than men. Saxo, however, dislikes strong women; he often stresses how vicious, untrustworthy, and wicked most women are, and he teaches that, being inferior to men, they should be subordinate, obedient, and self-sacrificing. He can accept and even appreciate female activity, but only when is is directed to help their husbands or kinsmen. The few times he explicitly praises women serve as implied criticism of the men in their surroundings.[10] The differences and similarities in Saxo's and Snorri's opinions and treatment of

---

[8] *Gesta Danorum* X.xvi.2–3; Olrik-Raeder, 288–89; Christiansen, I:30–31; *Heimskringla* S. Saint Olav, chap. 190, Hollander, 485.

[9] Cf. Karsten Friis-Jensen, "Olav den hellige hos Saxo," *Olavslegenden og den latinske historieskrivning i 1100-tallets Norge,* ed. Inger Ekrem et al. (Copenhagen, Museum Tusculanum Press, 2000), 250–62.

[10] See also Birgit Strand (now Sawyer), *Kvinnor och män i Gesta Danorum.*

women are well illustrated by their accounts of the cause of Olav Tryggvason's final battle.

Saxo's version

The Swedish King Erik ("the Victorious") had conquered Denmark, and it was only after his death that Svein Forkbeard could recover his kingdom. A new threat came from Norway, where Olav Tryggvason was planning an attack on Svein. In order to gain Swedish support, he proposed to Erik's widow, Queen Sigrid, but Svein, who would not expose his country to an attack from two sides, devised a way to prevent their marriage. By tempting Olav with his young daughter (sister in *Heimskringla*) Tyre, Svein coaxed Olav into proposing to her instead. The menace of a coalition between Norway and Sweden was removed, and Olav was satisfied, preferring the maiden to the mature lady: he would rather wed the young girl than waste his youth in the arms of an old widow. "He soon brought to light how little he esteemed the latter, and how much he honoured the former."[11] He sent for Sigrid, pretending that he wanted to talk with her and asked her to come on board his ship. The chaste queen refused at first but later yielded. When she was going on board, Olav had some of his men dislodge the gang-plank, so that she fell headlong into the water. The Norwegians were not content with this but made fun of her immorality and profligacy. The queen nearly drowned and only just reached the shore. When she had regained her composure and understood that it had been Olav's intention to expose her wantonness, she could remain silent no longer and "uttered threats" against him.

Thus Svein Forkbeard's guile succeeded in depriving Olav of Sigrid's power, and, instead, he won her for himself, since she now hated Olav. Svein avenged her shame by refusing to give Olav his daughter Tyre, and the discord between the kings resulted in open war, in which Svein was helped by the Swedish king, Sigrid's son Olof Eriksson.

Snorri's version

Snorri explains how Sigrid, widow of Erik the Victorious, came to be known as "the Haughty." In order to stop minor kings courting her she invited two of these suitors to a feast and at night, when they were drunk, set fire to the hall in which were were sleeping with their men "and those who got out were slain."[12] She did, however, agree to marry Olav Tryggvason, but when she discovered that a large gold ring that he gave her had a copper core, she was furious and feared that he would defraud her in other ways. When they met at Konungahella to discuss their marriage, Olav demanded that she be baptized and accept the true

---

11 *Gesta Danorum* X.xii.2; Olrik-Ræder, 283; Christiansen, I:22.
12 S. Olav Tryggvason chap. 43; ÍFH I:287f.; Hollander185f.

faith. She replied, "I do not mean to abandon the faith that I have had and my kinsmen before me. Nor shall I object to your belief in the god you prefer." Olav was very angry and answered hastily, "Why should I want to marry you dog of a heathen?" slapping her face with his glove, whereupon he arose, and so did she, saying, "This may well be your death!"[13] With that they parted, and, instead, she married Svein Forkbeard, whose wife, Gunnhild, daughter of the Vendish king Burislav, had died.

Earlier, Svein had forced his unwilling sister Tyre to marry Burislav, but she soon escaped from him and made her way to Norway, appealing to Olav Tryggvason for help. Olav married her, and she soon began pressing him to recover the large properties that she had lost in Vendland. His friends advised him not to. When Olav tried to console her with a gift of an exceptionally large stalk of angelica, she struck it away saying:

> 'Larger gifts bestowed Harald Gormsson, and was less afraid to leave his country and redeem his possessions than you are; and that was shown when he came here to Norway and laid waste most of this land and took possession of all revenues from it; but you don't dare to proceed through the Danish realm for fear of King Svein, my brother.'[14]

Her goading was successful, and Olav declared "Never shall I stand in fear of King Svein, your brother; and if ever we meet he shall have to give way."[15] He assembled a large fleet and sailed to Vendland where Burislav agreed to his request. In Denmark, Sigrid frequently incited Svein to do battle with Olav, who had not only insulted her but also married Tyre without Svein's permission.[16] Her goading was successful; when Olav sailed back to Norway he was confronted and defeated by a large fleet led by Svein Forkbeard with Swedish and Norwegian support.

Comparison

In *Gesta Danorum* and *Heimskringla* we have very different pictures of Sigrid and Tyre. Common features are Olav Tryggvason's proposal to Sigrid and her acceptance. In both the agreement is broken, Olav insults Sigrid, she threatens him and instead marries Svein Forkbeard. Tyre's role contributes to the enmity between Svein and Olav, but the friendship between Svein and the Swedish king Olof increases. The differences, however, are more numerous.

While Saxo contrasts the older Sigrid with the younger Tyre, Snorri contrasts Sigrid's paganism with Olav's Christian faith and contrasts her tolerance,

---

13 S. Olav Tryggvason chap. 61; ÍFH I:310; Hollander 200f.
14 S. Olav Tryggvason chap. 92; ÍFH I:343; Hollander 225f.
15 S. Olav Tryggvason chap. 92; ÍFH I:343; Hollander 225f.
16 S. Olav Tryggvason chap. 91–92; ÍFH I:341–3; Hollander 224–26, 228f.

independence, and dignity with Olav's unconditional demand, imperiousness, and lack of self-control. In *Gesta Danorum*, Olav acts as a political imbecile when he, contrary to his original plan, not only refused to marry the powerful queen, but also rudely insults her. He shows himself to be a dishonest brute, and his manners are described as typical of the barbarian Norwegians. According to Saxo, Svein Forkbeard plays the leading part: fearing an attack from two sides, he marries Sigrid and uses Tyre as bait to prevent a union of Norway and Sweden.

According to Snorri, we are dealing with *three* leading actors: Olav Tryggvason, Sigrid, and Tyre. Both women are described as independent, strong-minded, and influential. Sigrid's cognomen "the Haughty" is explained, and she shows her strength in several ways, not least in persuading her husband Svein to attack Olav Tryggvason. In *Heimskringla*, Tyre is no mere bait that is withdrawn but on her own initiative flees from her husband and marries Olav Tryggvason. Like Sigrid, she shares the responsibility for Olav's fall; it is the demand for her possessions in Vendland which impels him to war and brings him to Svolder (Öresund in Saxo) to face the allied kings, Svein and Olof Eriksson. While Saxo only mentions Tyre once, Snorri paints a colorful portrait of a woman with a strong will who shows initiative and energy.

The women who in Saxo are tools for King Svein have important roles in Snorri. The brain behind the intrigue that leads to Olav's catastrophe in Saxo is Svein Forkbeard, whereas in Snorri it is Sigrid. It is obvious that Saxo's and Snorri's different versions are based on their contrasting opinions not only of the women but also of the men involved.

Saxo does not mention Sigrid's surname ("the Haughty"), nor do we meet a woman who would deserve it! He frequently says that she is powerful, but nowhere does he give us that impression. She is exposed to an extraordinarily debasing treatment, which Saxo describes exhaustively: she is persuaded to go on board Olav's ship, the gang-plank is snatched away, and she falls headlong into the water. In this undignified situation she is jeered at for her debauchery and subjected to ridicule. The description of her reaction underlines how ridiculous she appears. Saxo emphasizes how she is taunted and repeats words such as "shame" and "dishonor." He stresses her degradation twice by contrasting her high status with disgrace: such an "elevated queen" has been exposed to "the worst disgrace" and the "majestic and elevated queen" had been brought into a "disgracing" situation and "ridiculed."[17] Notwithstanding the fact that Saxo does not cherish any great opinion of the Norwegians, he must still be responsible for the detailed description of the infamies to which Sigrid is exposed. It is with ill-concealed delight that Saxo lets her fall.

In Snorri, however, we meet a proud, independent, and self-confident woman. He makes these qualities very evident: tired of proposals from minor kings,

---

[17] *Gesta Danorum* X.xii. 2; Olrik-Ræder, 283; Christiansen, 23–24.

Sigrid drastically makes an example. She takes Olav Tryggvason's offer kindly but is always on her guard against disrespect and becomes incensed when she discovers that the gold ring he sent her is a fake, interpreting this as an indication of his treacherous character. Proudly she rejects his marriage conditions, and no less proudly she replies to his insult: "This may well be your death!" Because of her powerful position she is desired by Svein Forkbeard, and her power is increased by her eloquence: by finding the proper words she incites Svein to fight against her enemy Olav. Snorri gives us abundant evidence of a woman who indeed deserves the surname "the Haughty."

Even in other respects, Saxo and Snorri treat Sigrid in very different ways: while Snorri only briefly (in one sentence) mentions Olav's insult, Saxo bases his whole story on it. In the insult scene, Snorri lets Sigrid have the last word and thereby a certain rehabilitation thanks to her reply: "This may well be thy death!" In Saxo, however, Sigrid's threat is completely devoid of the force and gravity it exerts in Snorri. Saxo's wording "she uttered threats of all sorts," hardly implies something calamitous. On the whole, Sigrid is allowed to speak for herself in Snorri (thanks to his use of direct speech), while, in Saxo, her words are not even quoted.

The different impressions we get of Sigrid in Saxo and in Snorri are partly due to differences in their narrative techniques. Snorri does not analyze mental conditions; neither does he give moralizing reflections. Saxo, in contrast, always commits himself by giving free vent to his own reactions, emotional as well as rational. Where Saxo uses indirect speech, Snorri uses direct: where Saxo tells us what happens or has happened, Snorri lets actions speak. By quoting Sigrid *verbatim*, Snorri convinces the reader of her authority. The insult makes her grow in Snorri, but makes her shrink pitifully in Saxo. Finally, it should be emphasized that Snorri does not, even with one word, comment upon either Olav's or Sigrid's reaction, whereas Saxo repeatedly points out the ignominy and shame of the situation.

These two contrasting descriptions and roles of Sigrid and Tyre can only to a small extent be traced to older sources. The explanation for why they are both treated so differently must be sought elsewhere. The part played by women and the way in which they are described reveal the authors' opinions not only of the women but sometimes also of the *men* around them.

King Svein and King Olav

In their stories of what led to Olav Tryggvason's fall, the authors of course focus on different kings, Saxo on Svein and Snorri on Olav. Following different traditions, they give different explanations for the war between them. According to the older tradition (represented in Adam, *Ágrip*, and *Historia Norwegiae*), Olav is the attacker, incited by his wife Tyre, but when in the younger tradition the role of attacker has been transferred to Svein, a new inciter appears, namely, Sigrid.[18] Saxo follows the older tradition, Snorri the younger, but in their description of the kings and the women involved they mix and alter both.

Saxo ignores Tyre's goading, reducing her to a passive role, and he belittles and ridicules Sigrid. Instead, the focus is on the king and his cunning, but this does not mean that Saxo regards him as a hero. On the contrary, in *Gesta Danorum* Svein is denigrated, repeatedly punished by God, and taken prisoner three times. His "slave nature" is underlined by his dependence on women; he was ransomed from his last imprisonment by the Danish women, who are said to have sacrificed all their jewelry to that purpose. Likewise, he needed women to outmaneuver Olav: Sigrid, in order to have her son King Olof and the Swedes as allies, and Tyre as a bait to stop Olav's marriage with the queen. Knowing Saxo's general opinion of women, Svein's dependence on them does certainly not shed lustre over his rule.

In contrast to Saxo, Snorri gives us fascinating portraits of both Tyre and Sigrid, making their actions the very cause of Olav's fall. In this they function as scapegoats, a common *topos* in medieval literature, where women are often depicted as the root of all evil, a topos well known to the audience of *Heimskringla*. The question is, however, whether Snorri regarded Olav's fall as an evil; like Svein in *Gesta Danorum*, Olav is anything but a hero in Snorri's history, where his inglorious end could be regarded as well deserved. His uncontrolled violence has earned him many enemies, and, directed against Sigrid, it seals his fate. Marrying Tyre without her brother's consent was imprudent, and in being persuaded (against the advice of his friends) by her to claim the property she owned in another country, close to Denmark, he showed himself foolish and so was doomed to fail.

Thus, in both Saxo's and Snorri's versions, the role of women is decisive and serves to illustrate the shortcomings of the kings, the main difference being that Snorri treats the women as strong, determined, and important.

This comparison between Saxo and Snorri shows that, despite totally different styles and other differences, they had much in common. Further comparative studies will certainly cast more light over the question of the relationship between *Gesta Danorum* and *Heimskringla*.

---

[18] Lauritz Weibull, *Nordisk historia; forskningar och undersökningar*, vol. 1 (Lund, Natur och Kultur, 1948), 320.

Chapter 8
Concluding Remarks

Like many of his predecessors, Snorri did not write contemporary history but ended his work in 1177. It is symptomatic that many historians did not deal with their own times; if one wanted to question or criticize current conditions, the past was a safer arena than the present, because it made it possible to transfer (and disguise) contemporary conflicts without directly challenging existing rulers. It is noteworthy that most Scandinavian historians avoided their own time; Theodoricus, writing in the 1180s, finished his history c. 50 years earlier, and Saxo Grammaticus, who worked until c. 1220, finished his in 1185. The transfer to the past of contemporary criticism was not difficult to unmask; so, for example, Saxo's commissioner, Archbishop Absalon in Denmark, seems to have been angered by his clerk, since, in his will, he only left Saxo with a reminder about some books he had been lent, presumably because of his dissatisfaction with the end product (*Gesta Danorum*) that Saxo had presented. During the 1340s, Saxo's work was abbreviated in *Compendium Saxonis*, and Absalon would certainly have become even more dissatisfied with that work; not only does its compiler cast suspicion on him but has him totally overshadowed by Valdemar I. The criticism of the monarchy that Saxo had expressed was simply not suitable in the time of King Valdemar "Atterdag."[1] Two centuries later Johannes Magnus's Swedish History provoked Gustav Vasa's anger, since he recognized in it caricatures of himself and immediately—through his "propaganda-writer" Peder Swart, answered with his own picture of his rule. It is thus plausible that—likewise—King Håkon Håkonsson recognized Snorri's criticism against both him and his predecessors when he decided to eliminate this influential critic of the royal regime.

Since Snorri was probably working on *Heimskringla* from c. 1220 until the beginning of the 1230s, the most immediate social and political developments must have left their mark in his history, and it is understandable if it was with growing unease that he followed the young Håkon Håkonsson's path to power and allied

---

[1] Birgit Sawyer, review of Anders Leegard Knudsen, *Saxostudier og rigshistorie på Valdemar Atterdags tid* (København, publisher, 1994) (Norwegian) *Historisk Tidsskrift* 74 (1995), 120–22.

himself instead with the more experienced Earl Skule, a worthy defender of old traditions. There are, indeed, several similarities between the events in Norway from 1217 until the early 1230s and Snorri's description of the period 1162–77.

Skule and Håkon were both candidates for the throne in 1217, but the choice of the regional assemblies had been the thirteen-year-old Håkon, who was an illegitimate son of King Håkon (King Sverri's son). Skule, who was legitimate but not of the royal family, had from the beginning been supported by the Church, but he soon gave up his claim to the throne when it appeared that the old rule about kings' sons' right of priority was deeply anchored. Instead, Skule agreed to continue as earl, of one-third of Norway and its tributary lands. The church did not submit to be disregarded in the question of royal succession, however, and therefore summoned Håkon to a "national" meeting in Bergen (in 1218) to decide about his birth. At this meeting Håkon's mother had to undergo an ordeal in order to prove that Håkon was really the son of a king. The fortunate result of the ordeal strengthened not only Håkon's position but also that of the Church, since, as a result, the monarchy was made dependent on the authority of the Church. At the same time, the national Church assembly could maintain its superiority over the regional assemblies (which had accepted Håkon as king the year before). In 1223, Håkon's right to the throne was finally and unanimously acknowledged by the law-speakers of the country. This final decision in the question of royal succession was a defeat for Earl Skule, and after this, relations between him and King Håkon grew tense, in spite of the renewal of their contract sharing Norway and Håkon's marriage to Skule's daughter (in 1225). Skule visited King Valdemar I in Denmark and received from him half Halland as his fief, a step in Skule's own strategy. During the 1230s his relationship with Håkon deteriorated further, and in November 1239 Skule took a king's title at Øyrathing (in Trøndelag).

A parallel to these events is found in *Heimskringla*. After King Inge's death in 1161, Erling Skakke continued his fight against (Inge's nephew) Håkon Herdebrei, pretender to the throne. His legitimate son (with Kristin, daughter of King Sigurd Jerusalemfarer) Magnus was taken king, despite the fact that he was not a king's son. The pretender Håkon Herdebrei was—like Håkon Håkonsson—illegitimate but the son of a king, and we here witness the same conflict as in the rivalry between the legitimate Skule and the illegitimate Håkon Håkonsson. Erling was stressing the fact that Magnus was a king's grandson, and by promising the archbishop the right to receive Church fines, paid in proper silver, he and Øystein began to cooperate, with the result that Magnus Erlingsson was crowned, the first coronation in Norwegian history. This cooperation also meant that Magnus's monarchy received the sanction of God and the Church, and thereby the Church strengthened its authority as co-establisher of the new monarchy. In connection with the coronation, King Magnus issued a letter of privileges to the archbishopric, including (among other things) the introduction of tithes. In *Heimskringla* the negotiations between Erling and archbishop Øystein appears as a log-rolling, bringing our thoughts to the events in 1218 and 1223.

What is *Heimskringla* about?

What occupies most of the kings in *Heimskringla* is their struggle for power, the removal of brothers and other kinsmen, revenge, harsh punishments, confiscations, and threats from both external and internal enemies; thus the most violent and warlike kings get the most attention. Explicitly and implicitly, Snorri expresses his dislike of the way in which most of them exercise their power; only five kings seem to have his sympathy: Håkon the Good, Magnus the Good, Øystein Magnusson, Harald Gille, and Olav. Snorri's main sympathies lie with many magnates—Icelandic as well as Norwegian: throughout his work they illustrate more virtues and fewer vices than the kings. Even pagan leaders often appear as wiser and more reasonable than the missionary kings, Olav Tryggvason and Olav Haraldsson.

And what is *Heimskringla* NOT about?

Snorri does not write much about the *Church*; we look in vain for information about Archbishop Øystein's regulating Icelandic affairs. We do not hear about the establishment of the bishoprics, and only very briefly about the creation of the archbishopric of Nidarós. Further, we do not hear about the important influence of the Church on literacy, international organization, written law, or common ideology.

Towns are mentioned in *Heimskringla*, but their importance for the economic, social, and political development of the kingdom is never stressed, nor do we hear much about competition between Icelandic and Norwegian merchants, an issue that concerned Snorri.

There are other important issues missing in *Heimskringla*, but here I will focus on Snorri's treatment of what modern historians call the "*Civil wars*" (1130– c. 1217/40) in Norway. In his history we do not get a clear picture of the Scandinavian context of these wars; they are presented as internal struggles for power. They were not only that, however; the pretenders for the Norwegian throne all had allies in Sweden and/or Denmark, where there were "civil wars" at the same time[2] in which rulers of both Poland and Russia were involved.

Of course one cannot draw firm conclusions from what is *missing* in a historical text; suffice it here to point out that Snorri avoids important issues such as

---

[2] Birgit Sawyer, "The 'Civil Wars' revisited," (Norwegian) *Historisk Tidsskrift* 82 (2003): 43–73.

the role of the Church, the towns, and the complicated background of the "Civil Wars."

The tendency in *Heimskringla*

According to Halvdan Koht, *Heimskringla* is about the struggle between royal power and aristocracy, and according to Gudmund Sandvik, Snorri is describing a *development* from rivalry between several chieftancies and a monarchy via a transitional period where the monarchy has been accepted but the possession of the royal power is disputed—to a stage when the landed men, led by the magnates, control the royal power. According to Sverre Bagge, however, Snorri gives a *static* picture of society and describes only struggles between individuals, not between royal power and aristocracy.

My own interpretation of *Heimskringla* is that in the first half of the work, Snorri describes the struggle *against* royal power, and in the second half of it the struggle *for* it. Sverre Bagge's interpretation of *Heimskringla* as a description of struggles between individuals does not necessarily lead to the conclusion that this corresponds to reality; my own conclusion is that Snorri chose this description in order to deny the exceptional position that the kings claimed for themselves.

It should also be stressed that most of the conflicts were not between *individual* magnates and kings[3] but between *their families and adherents*. In order to reconcile conflicts either between these families and kings, or between different families—or even between branches of the same family—women were used as "bridge-builders" (see Appendix 3 "Genealogies of important magnate families").

Thus, women were often pawns in the political game, but that does not mean that they were passive; many of them were intent on defending their own and their children's rights. Admittedly most violent actions were undertaken by men, but long before that stage, complicated strategies had been pursued and many decisions had been made in which women often played important roles.

Snorri presents many highly competent magnates, both friends and enemies of kings. There is, however, yet another group of men that has not been dealt with in this study, namely, the skalds. In a mainly oral culture, the skalds were very important, especially to the rulers. The Norse skalds were the main recorders of both past and present; their profession was to preserve memorable events in poetry,[4] to provide propaganda, and to praise in their panegyrics as well as

---

[3] Cf. Sverre Bagge, *Society and Politics in Snorri Sturluson's* Heimskringla (Berkeley and Los Angeles: University of California Press, 1991), 72.

[4] At Stiklestad, Olav Haraldsson is said to have ordered three skalds to enter the shield wall in front of him, so that they could compose verses about the battle from first-hand knowledge.

to blame in their satires. Their poetry is—and was—often difficult to understand. It has been shown that Snorri himself sometimes misunderstood metaphors (*kenningar*),[5] and it is highly likely that many of the skalds' contemporary listeners did so too. Roberta Frank describes the Norse court skald as "a dangerous being, a manipulator of the deep structure of language."[6] The skalds' mastery of expression made ambiguities possible, leaving it open to the audience to interpret their verses. The poem (*flokkr*) that Sigvat the Skald composed to warn King Magnus Olavsson, however, was very straightforward and is also called "The Outspoken Verses" (*Bersoglisvísur*). In order to prevent a revolt by the *bændr*, Sigvat told King Magnus to reconcile himself with them. Here follows the last verse:

> This they ever think on:
> thou, king, takest from them
> farmlands that their fathers
> farmed: they rise against thee!
> Robbery recks it the yeoman,
> routed from his freehold
> by high-handed rulings
> of henchmen, at thy bidding.[7]

The king took the warning seriously, changed his rule, and took counsel "with the wisest men," thus earning his surname "the Good."

As an eminent skald himself (and author of The Younger Edda, a treatise on skaldic poetry) he no doubt admired Sigvat, not only for his poetry[8] but also for his career (court poet, ambassador, and finally marshal) and his political influence. We know that Snorri aspired to a similar career and influence but failed.

The division into chapters[9]

Heimskringla is not a collection of "kings' sagas"; in modern editions, only few of the sagas form natural entities, focused on a king, above all that of Saint Olav and (perhaps) that of Harald Fairhair. Most of the other sagas focus as much—or even more—on other people; in the Saga of Olav Tryggvason, Earl Håkon, together with the earls Eirík and Svein play significant roles, as do Erling

---

5 See, e.g., Roberta Frank, "Skaldic poetry," *Old Norse-Icelandic Literature: A Critical Guide*, ed. Carol J. Clover and John Lindow (Ithaca & London: Cornell University Press, 1985), 157–96.

6 Ibid., 181.

7 S. Magnus the Good, chap. 16; ÍFH III:30; Hollander, 554.

8 Among other poems, *Vikeningavísur, Nesjavísur,* and *Austrfararvísur.*

9 For a discussion of this, see Diana Whaley, *Heimskringla: An Introduction* (London: University College London, 1991), 57–62.

Skjalgsson and Einar Tambarskjelve in Saint Olav's Saga, and Erling Skakke and Gregorius Dagsson in other sagas. This, together with the fact that one and the same king is sometimes described in two or more sagas,[10] makes it likely that the division into sagas and their titles were not done by Snorri. Whoever was responsible for the result followed a very old tradition, using rulers (cf. the Romans, using consuls when dating events) as an organizing principle. In all likelihood, Snorri himself did not intend a series of royal biographies, each focusing on a single monarch, but—like the author of *Morkinskinna*—wrote texts of episodic character, weaving in different stories (*Þættir*). Interwined with other stories we have long and interesting stories about some of the kings'opponents, e.g., Earl Håkon, Sigurd Slembedjakn, Erling Skjalgsson, and Einar Tambarskjelve. A fascinating portrait is drawn of Gunnhild "Kingsmother" (Eirik Bloodaxe's widow) in no fewer than five sagas, and there are many more portraits of important individuals, not least Icelandic heroes, confronting the kings.

Snorri's target groups

To judge by *Heimskringla*, Snorri does not focus on the relations between Iceland and Norway as much as on the relationships between magnates (Icelandic as well as Norwegian) and the central power (king and Church). Of course this does not exclude the fact that he promotes the qualities and deeds of his fellow countrymen, but that is never done at the cost of Norwegian magnates only of the Norwegian kings.[11] As a whole, however, *Heimskringla* ought to have satisfied both a Norwegian and an Icelandic audience. It is further probable that Snorri addressed himself to two different categories of readers or listeners; while a less educated group would probably have been satisfied with all the exciting stories, the more educated would certainly have read between the lines and grasped the implicit messages. Admittedly, the saga authors expected to be both read and recited, and it is possible that many of the qualities of the text, hidden meanings and irony, might have been lost in oral performances,[12] but they cannot have escaped the audience who had time and ability to scrutinize the whole written work.

Snorri had many predecessors in the art of ambiguity, and it was thanks to his mastery of this that he was able to express his own opinions, at the same time

---

[10] We meet Magnus the Blind in three sagas, Harald Gille in two, and Håkon the Broadshouldered in three.

[11] As Sveinbjörn Rafnsson has pointed out, Snorri was a sworn Birchleg, and both *Heimskringla* and *Fagrskinna* express attitudes that support the policies of the Birchlegs in the 1220s and 1230s (private correspondence with S. Rafnsson).

[12] Even if some meanings could be expressed by, e.g., pauses, facial expressions, gestures, and intonation.

as he could meet several different interests and tastes—and, not least, be entertaining. The fact that, during the nineteenth century, readers of *Heimskringla* interpreted the contents as a glorification/elevation of medieval Norwegian kings tells us more about the need for a native royal tradition and an era of glory than about the real message of Snorri's history, which, in fact, is the contrary. If we read *Heimskringla* with other spectacles than those used by the fathers of "Norwegian nation-building," we notice the balancing act that Snorri managed, between loyalty towards Norway and criticism of the expansion of the Norwegian central power. With his *Ynglingasaga* he rejects Danish claims on Viken and right to royal power in Norway at the same time as he ridicules the origin of the Norwegian kings. In the same saga he anticipates much of what happens later both in Swedish and Norwegian history, where lust for power, drunkennness, murder inside the family, and the cunning influence of women dominate, at the same time as he has women represent his own opposition to royal violence and male cowardice. At the end he depicts Erling Skakke and his son Magnus, which leads our thoughts towards Earl Skule and King Håkon Håkonsson, portraits that are also ambiguous; like Skule, Erling is driven by lust for power, while, during their youth, both Magnus and Håkon are totally in the hands of their counselors. Snorri walked a difficult tight-rope, and it is exactly his mastery of this art that has opened the way to so many different interpretations of his history.

Against the background of contemporary developments, his position, status, political double-dealing, and defence of his own power, it is hardly surprising that Snorri wanted to present his views in a work of history, giving his own version of the past and simultaneously criticizing his own time.[13] In *Heimsksringla* he opposes strong royal and archiepiscopal power (bishops and priests play only a minor—and not very flattering—role in *Heimskringla*). Not only criticizing representatives of central power, he openly praises local chieftains and important magnates, both Icelandic and Norwegian. Thus, my answer to the question of why Snorri described society and politics the way he did is that he opposed the idea that the king, as God's representative, was essentially different from other magnates.

Whether or not my hypothesis about Snorri's purpose with *Heimskringla* is accepted, the question of why the work was copied *c.* 1260 remains. The coronation of Håkon Håkonsson in 1247 meant that the Church had accepted hereditary kingship within Håkon's family, based on the principle of legitimate birth. In 1260 a new law of succession was issued, based on the principles of automatic hereditary succession, legitimacy, and primogeniture. Totally new was

---

[13] Cf. Theodore Andersson's view that *Heimskringla* should be seen "not so much as an isolated monument as a rejoinder in an ongoing political discussion"; Theodore M. Andersson, "The Politics of Snorri Sturluson," *Journal of English and Germanic Philology,* 1994): 78.

the fact that this law was promulgated by the king, who thus appears as the real law-giver. The use of "we" in the law did not—as earlier—refer to the king together with the leaders of the law courts but to the king in majestic plural. This was the situation in which *Kringla* was copied, and there is no reason to doubt that the copier shared Snorri´s opposition to a strong central government. In the nineteenth and early twentieth centuries, however, the wish to build a strong nation under a Norwegian king was decisive for the interpretation of *Heimskringla*, which was above all regarded as a success story, elevating the kings of Norway´s independent past.

There are historians who claim that they trust Snorri more than his modern interpreters;[14] what they must mean is that they trust *their own* interpretation of Snorri.

---

[14] E.g. Kåre Lunden, Review of *Aschehougs Norgeshistorie*, vol. 2 in *Collegium Medievale* 8 (1995/92): 191.

APPENDIX 1

List of Norwegian kings (before 1177)

Names in Hollander	Norwegian names	Years of rule[1]
1. Hálfdan the Black	Halvdan Svarte[2]	
2. Harald Fairhair	Harald Hårfagre	? –932
3. Eirík Bloodyaxe	Eirik Blodøks	930–34
4. Hákon the Good	Håkon den gode	934–61
5. The Sons of Eirík	Erikssønnene[3]	961–65/70,[4]
led by: Harald Graycloak	Harald Gråfell	
6. Óláf Tryggvason	Olav Tryggvason	995–99/1000
7. Óláf Haraldsson/Saint Óláf	Olav den hellige	1015–28[5]
8. Magnús the Good	Magnus den gode	1035–47[6]
9. Harald Sigurtharson (Hardruler)	Harald Hårdråde	1046–66
10. Óláf the Gentle	Olav Kyrre	1066/68–93[7]
11. Magnús Barelegs	Magnus Berrføtt	1093–03
12–14. The Sons of Magnús:	Magnussønnene:	
Óláf	Olav	1103–15
Eystein	Øystein	1103–23
Sigurth	Sigurd	1103–30
15. Magnús the Blind	Magnus Blinde	1130–35[8]

---

[1] None of the chronicles/sagas give dates.

[2] The Norwegian names are from the edition by Holtsmark & Seip 2003.

[3] After the saga about the sons of Eirík, the edition by Holtsmark & Seip has a separate saga about Earl Hákon = "Håkon jarl."

[4] Between 965/70 and 995, Earl Hákon ruled in Norway.

[5] Between 999 and 1000, the Danish king Svein Forkbeard had power in Norway, and in 1028 his son Knud the Powerful took over. After Saint Óláf's death at Stiklastathir (1030), Knud made his son Svein Álfifason king of Norway (which he remained until 1035).

[6] Between 1046 and 1047, Magnús the Good shared power with Harald Hardruler.

[7] The first two years, Óláf the Gentle shared the royal power with his brother Magnús who died in 1068

[8] Magnús and Harald Gilli shared power from 1130 to 1135, when Harald defeated Magnús, had him blinded, and put into a monastery. Magnús died in 1139.

16. + Harald Gilli	+ Harald Gille	1130–36[9]
17–19. The Sons of Harald:	Haraldssønnene:	
Sigurth	Sigurd	1136–55
Eystein	Øystein	1142–57
Ingi	Inge	1136–61
20. Hákon the Broadshouldered	Håkon Herdebrei	1161–62
21. Magnús Erlingsson	Magnus Erlingsson	1161–77[10]

In chapters 4 and 5 we meet all of them, and in chapter 3 we meet also the earlier kings, the "Ynglings."

---

[9] An alleged son of Magnús Barelegs, Sigurth Slembidiákn was king 1135–39.

[10] Magnús Erlingsson lost against Sverri, the leader of the Birchlegs in 1177 but lived until 1184.

Appendix 2
Royal Genealogies

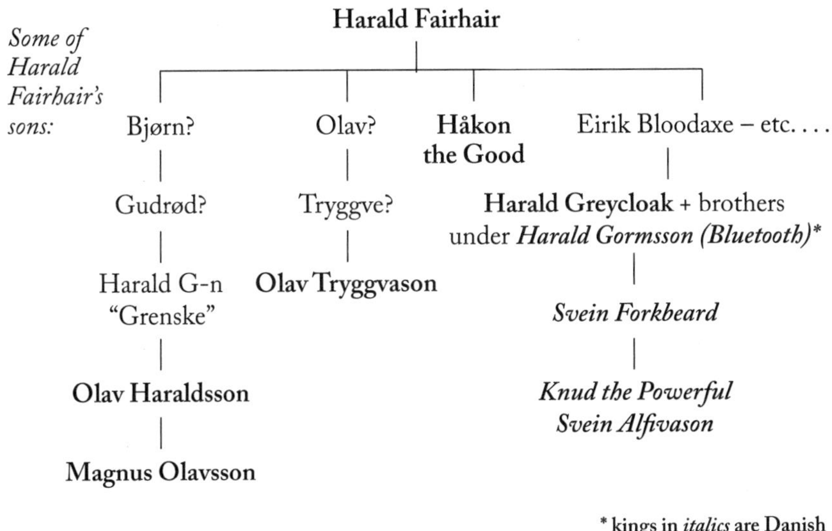

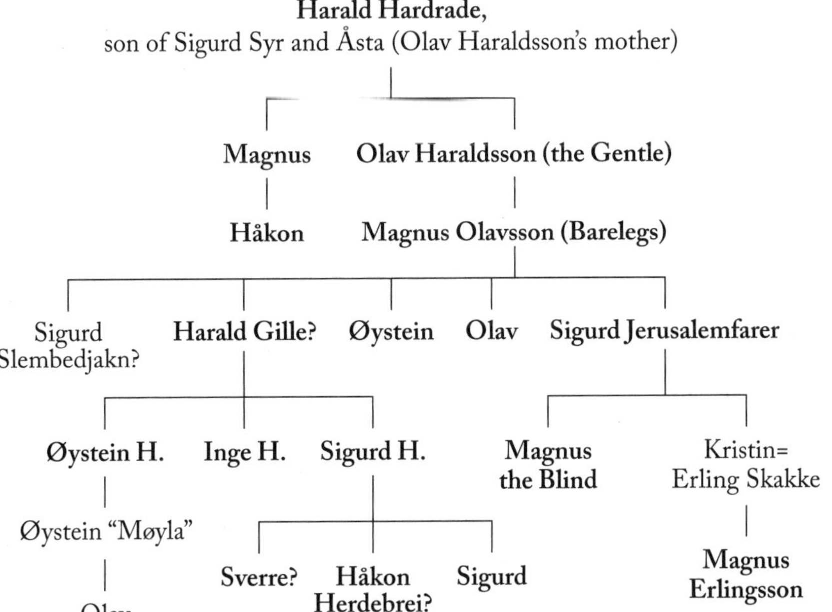

Appendix 3
Genealogies of Important Magnate Families

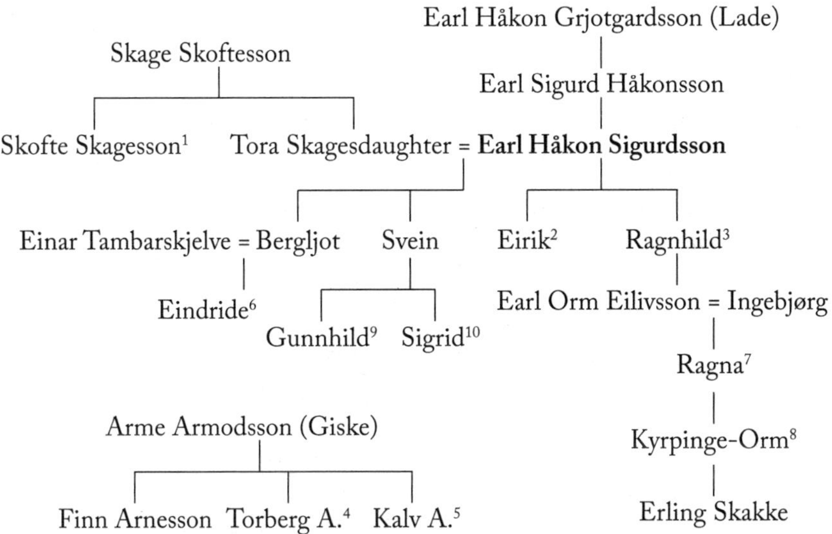

¹ Married to Earl Håkon's illigitimate daughter Ragnhild
² Mother unknown
³ Mother unknown
⁴ Married to Ragnhild, daughter of Erling Skjálgsson
⁵ Married to Sigrith, daughter of Thórir (Bjarkey), sister of Thórir the Hound, and widow of Ólvir
⁶ Marrid to Sigrith, Harald Hardruler's niece
⁷ Married to Svein Sveinsson
⁸ Married to Ragnhild, daughter of Sveinki Steinarsson
⁹ Married to the Danish king of Svein Ulfsson
¹⁰ Married to Áslák, son of Erling Skjálgsson

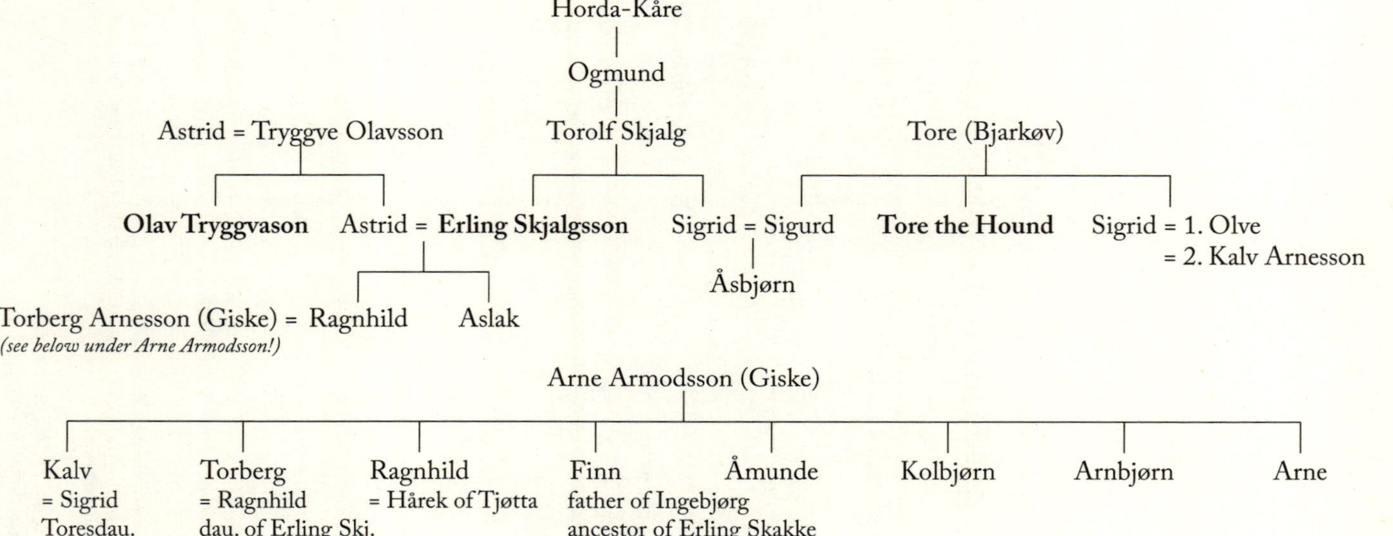

Earl Håkon's daughter Bergljot is married to Einar Thambarskjelve,
  and his niece Sigrid is married to Aslak, son of Erling Skjalgsson.
Erling Skjalgsson is married to Astrid, sister of Olav Tryggvason;
  his daughter Ragnhild is married to Torberg Arnesson, Kalv Arnesson's brother;
  his son Aslak is married to Earl Håkon's granddaughter Sigrid (daugher of Svein Håkonsson);
  his sister Sigrid is married to Sigurd Toresson (brother of Tore the Hound and Sigrid of Egge), with whom she has Asbjørn.
Tore the Hound's brother Sigurd is married to Erling Skjalgsson's sister Sigrid, and
  his own sister Sigrid is married to Olve (of Egge), later to Kalv Arnesson.

Appendix 4
Speeches

Åsbjörn from Melhus:[1]
"It was our thought, King Håkon," he said, "the time you had held our first assembly here in the Trøndelag district and we had chosen you king and received from you the title to our ancestral possessions, that very heaven had come down to earth; but now we don't know what to think, whether we have regained our liberty or whether you are going to make us thralls again with the strange proposal that we should abandon the faith our fathers have had before us, and all our forefathers, first in the time when the dead were burned, and now in the age when the dead are buried. And they were better men than we, and yet this faith has served us very well. We have put so much trust in you that we have let you have your way about all the laws and statutes of our land. Now it is our will, and all the yeomen are agreed on this, to obey the laws you have given us here at the Frostathing Assembly and to which we consented. We all want to follow you and to have you be our king so long as one of us yeomen who are at the assembly now is alive, if you, sir king, will observe moderation and ask only that of us which we can give you and which is within reason.

But if you mean to pursue this so high-handedly as to contend against us with force and compulsion, then all of us yeomen have made up our minds to desert you and choose another leader, one who will help us freely to have the faith we wish to have. Now you, sir king, shall decide on one of these alternatives before the assembly disperses."[2]

Torgny the lawspeaker:[3]
"Different is now the disposition of the Swedish kings from what it was before." [here Torgny praises earlier kings for having been easy to deal with and to approach with advice.] But the king whom we now have lets no one presume to talk to him except about what he himself wants done; and on that alone he is intent, but lets lands tributary to him defect from him through his lack of energy and

---

[1] See Chapter 4 above, p. 47.
[2] S. Håkon the Good, chap. 15; Hollander, 109.
[3] See Chapter 4 above, p. 65.

enterprise. He has the ambition to keep the dominion of Norway in his power which no other Swedish king ever coveted before, and that causes trouble to many. Now it is the will of us yeomen that you make peace with Olav the Stout, the king of Norway, and give him your daughter Ingigerd in marriage. Now if you intend to regain those lands in the east which your kinsmen and forbears have possessed there, then we shall all follow your leadership to do so. But if you will not do as we say, we shall set upon you and kill you, and not tolerate from you lawlessness and hostility. That is what our forbears did: at the Múlathing they plunged five kings into a well because they were swelled up with the same arrogance as you show against us. Say now right quickly what you decide to do."[4]

Bishop Sigurd:[5] *(freely after Laing)*
"Here are now assembled a great many men, so that probably there will never be opportunity in this poor country of seeing so great a native army. It would be desirable if this strength and multitude could be a protection, for it will all be needed, if this Olav does not give over bringing war and strife upon you. From his very earliest youth he has been accustomed to plunder and kill: for which purposes he drove widely around through all countries, until he turned at last against this, where he began to show hostilities against the men who were the best and most powerful, and even against king Knud, whom all are bound to serve according to their ability, and in whose tributary lands he set himself down. He did the same to Olof the Swedish king. He drove the earls Svein and Håkon away from their heritages; and was even most tyrannical towards his own connections, as he drove all the kings out of the Opplands, although, indeed, it was but just reward for having been false to their oaths of fealty to king Knud, and having followed this king Olav in all the folly he could invent. Thus their friendship ended according to their deserts, by this king mutilating some of them, taking their kingdoms himself, and ruining every man in the country who had an honourable name. You know yourselves how he has treated the landed-men, of whom many of the worthiest have been murdered, and many obliged to fly from their country, and how he has roamed far and wide through the land with robber bands, burning and plundering houses, and killing people. Who is the man among us here of any consideration who has not some great injury from him to avenge? Now he has come here with a foreign troop, consisting mostly of forest-men, vagabonds, and such marauders. Do you think he will now be more merciful to you, when he is roaming about with such a bad crew, after committing devastations which all who followed him dissuaded him from? Therefore it is now my advice, that you remember king Knud's words when he told you, if king Olav attempted to return to the country you should defend the liberty king Knud had promised you, and should oppose and drive away such a vile pack. Now the only thing to be done

---

[4] S. Saint Olav, chap. 80; Hollander, 320–21.
[5] See Chapter 4 above, p. 66.

is to advance against them, and cast forth these malefactors to the wolves and eagles, leaving their corpses on the spot they cover, unless you drag them aside to out-of-the-way corners in the woods or rocks. No man would be so imprudent as to remove them to churches, for they are all robbers and evil-doers."[6]

Sigvat skald:[7]
Sternly stressed it Sigvat:
"Strive not with the Sognings,
embattled 'gainst thee and bitter!"
But I shall fight if need be.
Seize we our swords then, and
sadly do as he orders,
if but thereby, king, we
bate the hateful discord.

Håkon fell at Fitjar:
folk named him the Good, and
held most high and loved him,
halt who called on outlaws;
folk e'er and aye remember
Æthelstan's foster son: they
keep his laws right loyally,
loath e'er to forget him.

Right were rich and poor to
rally round the Olavs:
these kings gave their crops and
cattle the peace they needed:
both Harald's heir and Tryggve's
hardy son strove e'er to
heed and uphold the even-
handed laws made by them.

Beware lest wroth thou wax at
warnings, frankly uttered
by men of wisdom, mainly
meant for thine own honor.
But they lie, worse laws thy

---

[6] S. Saint Olav, chap. 218; Samuel Laing, "Saint Olaf's Saga," *Heimskringla I: The Olaf Sagas*, vol 2, (London, J. M. Dent & Sons, 1964), 366f. Cf. Hollander, 505–7, misprinted.

[7] See Chapter 5 above, p. 76.

lieges have now, say they,
prince, than which were promised,
previously at Ulf Sound.

Whoever eggs thee, atheling,
eager for battle—oft thy
blade with blood is red—to
break thy promise given?
Constant a king should e'er be,
keeping his pledges. Nowise
folk-warder, befits thee
false to be and mainsworn.

Whoever eggs thee, atheling,
to axe the yeomen's cattle?
Unheard for hero is't to
harry in his country.
To youthful king such cursed
counsel never was given:
weary of sack thy warriors,
ween I, wrathful the yeomen.

Guard thee 'gainst the groundless
gossip of folk which borne is
hitherward—one's hand should,
hanger-of-thieves, move slowly.
A faithful friend is he who,
feeder-of-greedy ravens,
gives thee goodly warning:
the gorge of yeomen has risen!

Warning take thou, warlord—
wise is't to stave off danger—
hoary men of whom I
heard are set against thee;
'tis parlous, prince, if franklins
put their heads together,
suddenly grow silent,
sinking noses cloakward.

This they ever think on:
thou, king, takest from them
farmlands that their fathers

farmed: they rise against thee!
Robbery recks it the yeoman,
routed from his freehold
by high-handed rulings
of henchmen, at thy bidding.[8]

---

[8] S. Magnus the Good, chap. 16; Hollander, 552–54.

References

Sources

Editions used here:

Aggesen, Sven. *A short history of the kings of Denmark*. In *The Works of Sven Aggesen, Twelfth-Century Danish Historian*, translated by Eric Christiansen (Viking Society for Northern Research). London: University College London, 1992, 48–74.

Ágrip af Nóregskonungasogum, ed. M. J. Driscoll. (Viking Society for Northern Research) London: University College London, 1995.

Fagrskinna, a Catalogue of the Kings of Norway, a translation with introduction and notes by Alison Finlay. Leiden & Boston: Brill, 2004.

Heimskringla, translated by Samuel Laing:
The Olaf Sagas (two volumes). London: J.M. Dent & Sons, 1914; revised ed. 1964, *The Norse King Sagas*. London: J.M. Dent & Sons, 1930.

Heimskringla; History of the Kings of Norway. translated by Lee M. Hollander, Austin: University of Texas Press, 1964.

Heimskringla, I-III, Íslenzk fornrit, ed. Bjarni Adalbjarnarson. Reykjavík: Hið Íslenzka Fornritarfélag, 2002.

Historia Norwegiae, translated by Devra Kunin. London: University College London, 2001.

Morkinskinna; the Earliest Chronicle of the Norwegian Kings (1030–1157), translated with introduction by Theodore M. Andersson and Kari Ellen Gade. Ithaca & London: Cornell University Press, 2000.

Saxonis Gesta Danorum I, ed. J. Olrik & H. Ræder. Hauniæ: Levin & Munksgaard, 1931.

Saxo Grammaticus, *History of the Danes*, translated by Peter Fisher. Cambridge: D.S. Brewer & Rowman and Littlefield, 1979.

———. *Danorum Regum Heroumque Historia* I-III, translated by Eric Christiansen. Oxford: British Archaeological Reports (B.A.R.), International Series 84, volumes I–III Oxford, 1980–81.

Snorrason, Oddr. *The Saga of Olaf Tryggvason*, translated by Theodore M. Andersson, Ithaca & London: Cornell University Press, 2003.

Snorre Sturlassons Konungasagor, translated by Emil Olson (three volumes). Lund: C.W.K. Gleerups Förlag, 1919, 1922, 1926.

Snorres Kongesagaer. Oslo: Gyldendal norsk forlag, 1942.

———, translated by Anne Holtsmark and Didrik Arup Seip. Oslo: Gyldendal norsk forlag, Oslo 1979.

Snorri Sturluson Edda. new complete translation by Anthony Faulkes. London & Melbourne: Everyman's Classic Library, 1987.

Theodoricus Monachus, *The Ancient History of the Norwegian Kings* (Viking Society for Northern Research). London: University College of London, 1998.

Other references:

Adalbjarnarson, Bjarni. Íslenzk fornrit 26 (1941) and Íslenzk Fornrit 28 (1951).

Andersson, Theodore M. "The Politics of Snorri Sturluson." *Journal of English and Germanic Philology* 93, 1994, 55–78.

———. "The King of Iceland." *Speculum* 74 (1999), 923–934.

———. *The Growth of the Medieval Icelandic Sagas (1180–1280)*. Ithaca & London: Cornell University Press, 2006.

Bolin, Sture. *Om Nordens äldsta historieskrivning*. Lund: Lunds universitets årsskrift, 1931.

Boulhosa Pires, Patricia. *Icelanders and the Kings of Norway: Medieval Sagas and Legal Texts*. Leiden & Boston: Brill, 2005.

The Cambridge History of Scandinavia, vol. I: Prehistory to 1520, ed. Knut Helle. Cambridge: Cambridge University Press, 2003.

Clover, Carol J. "Icelandic Family Sagas." In *Old Norse-Icelandic Literature; a Critical Guide*, ed. Carol J. Clover & John Lindow. Ithaca & London: Cornell University Presss, 1985.

———. "The Politics of Scarcity: Notes on the Sex Ratio in Early Scandinavia," *Scandinavian Studies* 60 (1988), 147–88.

Damsgaard Olsen, Thorkil. "Kongekrøniker og kongesagaer." In *Norrøn Fortællekunst; kapitler af den norsk-islandske middelalderlitteraturs historie*, ed. H. Bekker-Nielsen *et al*. København: Akademisk Forlag, 1965, 42–71.

Danielsson, Tommy. *Sagorna om Norges kungar; från Magnús godi till Magnús Erlingsson*. Uppsala: Gidlunds Förlag, 2002.

Frank, Roberta. "Skaldic poetry." In *Old Norse-Icelandic Literature: A Critical Guide*, ed. Carol J. Clover and John Lindow. Ithaca & London: Cornell University Press, 1985, 157–96.

Goffart, Walter. *The Narrators of Barbarian History*. Princeton, N.J.: Princeton University Press, 1988.

Hallberg, Peter. "Eddic Poetry." In *Medieval Scandinavia; an Encyclopedia*, ed. Philip Pulsiano. New York & London: Garland, 1993, 149–52.

Helle, Knut. "Towards nationally organised systems of government." In *The Cambridge History of Scandinavia, vol. I: Prehistory to 1520*, ed. Knut Helle. Cambridge: Cambridge University Press, 2003, 345–52.

Indrebø, Gustav. *Fagerskinna*. [Avhandlinger fra universitetets historiske seminar 4] Kristiania: Grøndahl, 1917.

Ísaksson, Sigurjón Páll, "Höfundur Morkinskinnu og Fagrskinnu," *Gripla* 23 (2012), 235–83.

Jakobsson, Ármann. "En plats i en ny värld. Bilden av riddarsamhället i Morkinskinna," *Scripta Islandica; Isländska Sällskapets Årsbok* 59 (2008), 27–46.

Jakobsson, Sverrir. "Erindringen om en mægtig Personlighed." (Norwegian) *Historisk Tidsskrift* 81 (2002), 213–30.

Johannesson, Kurt. *Saxo Grammaticus; komposition och världsbild i* Gesta Danorum. (Lychnosbibliotek) Stockholm: Almqvist & Wiksell, 1978.

Jørgensen, Jon Gunnar. *Ynglingasaga etter Kringla*. Ph.D. diss., University of Oslo: Unipub forlag, 2000.

KHL IX = *Kulturhistorisk leksikon for nordisk middelalder* IX. København: Rosenkilde & Bagger, 1964.

Koht, Halvdan. "Sagaenes opfatning av vår gamle historie," In *Innhogg og utsyn*. Kristiania: Aschehoug & Co., 1921.

———. "Hendingsgang og tidrekning i kongstida til Magnus Erlingsson 1161–1177." (Norwegian) *Historisk Tidsskrift* 40 (1960–61), 232–59.

Konrad Maurer. *Über die Ausdrücke altnordische, altnorwegische und isländische Sprache*. München: Verlag der k. Akademie, 1867.

Krag, Claus. *Ynglingatal og Ynglingesaga; en studie i historiske kilder*. Oslo: Universitetsforlaget, 1991.

———. *Norges historie fram til 1319*. Oslo: Universitetsforlaget, 2000.

———. "The early unification of Norway." In *The Cambridge History of Scandinavia, vol. I: Prehistory to 1520*, ed. Knut Helle. Cambridge: Cambridge University Press, 2003, 184–201.

———. "Rikssamlingshistorien og Ynglingerekken." (Norwegian) *Historisk Tidsskrift* 91 (2012), 159–89.

Kurtén-Lindberg, Birgitta. *Women's Lib. i Aristophanes' Athen*. Göteborg: Åström, 1987.

Lie, Hallvard. *Studier i Heimskringlas stil*. Skrifter utgitt av Det norske vitenskapsakademi i Oslo, II. Historisk-filosofisk klasse 1936 no. 5, Oslo 1937.

Louis-Jensen, Jonna. *Senter for høyere studier; informasjonsblad nr. 2*, 2002, 6–7.

———. "Heimskringla—et værk af Snorri Sturluson?." In *Con Amore*, ed. M. Chesnutt & F. Grammel. København: C.A. Reitzel, 2006, 217–32.

Lunden, Kåre. "Review of *Aschehougs Norgeshistorie*, vol. 2." *Collegium Medievale* vol. 8 (1995/2), 181–91.

Lönnroth, Lars. "Tesen om de två kulturerna." *Scripta Islandica* 15 (1964), 1–97.

———. "Rhetorical Persuasion in the Sagas." *Scandinavian Studies* 42 (1970).

Maurer, Konrad. *Über die Ausdrücke altnordische, altnorwegishe und isländische Sprache*. München: Verlag der K. Akademie, 1867.

Magnúsdóttir, Audur. *Frillor och fruar; politik och samlevnad på Island 1120–1400*. Ph.D. diss. University of Göteborg, 2001.

Monclair, Hanne. "Snorre som historiker," in *Dagbladet* 27/11 (2003).

Mortensen, Lars Boje. "Litterær teknik og sprogets repræsentative effekt." In *Saxo & Snorre,* ed. Jon Gunnar Jørgensen, Karsten Friis-Jensen og Else Mundal. København: Museum Tusculanums Forlag, 2010, 113–29.

Munch, P. A. *Det Norske Folks Historie.* Christiania: Chr. Tønsbergs Forlag, 1852–1863.

Müller, P. E. *Om Kilderne til Snorres Heimskringla og disses Troværdighed.* København: Det Kongelige Danske Videnskabernes Selskabs philosophiske og historiske Afhandlinger, 1824.

NIYR, Norges innskrifter med de yngre runer, ed. M. Olsen. Oslo 1941–50.

Rafnsson. Sveinbjörn. *Af fornum lögum og sögum: fjórar ritgerðir um forníslenska sögu,* Reykjavík: Ritsafn Sagnfrædistofnunar 42, 2011.

Rüdiger, Jan. "Habilitationsschrift," Humboldt University, Berlin, 2006. German edition forthcoming: *Der König und seine Frauen; Polygynie und politische Kultur in Europa (9. - 13. Jahrhundert,* Akademie-Verlag, Berlin. English edition under preparation, Leiden: Brill.

———. "Ægteskab – fandtes det? Jon Loptssons kvinder." In *Gaver, ritualer, konflikter. Et rettsantropologisk perspektiv på nordisk middelalderhistorie,* ed, Hans Jacob Orning, Kim Esmark & Lars Hermanson. Oslo: Unipub, 2010, 77–115.

———. "Medieval Marriage: the Case of the Devil's Advocate." In *Law and Marriage in the Middle Ages. Proceedings of the Eighth Carlsberg Academy Conference on Medieval Legal History,* ed. Ditlev Tamm, Helle Vogt, and Helle Sigh. Copenhagen 2012: DJØF Publishing, 87–113.

———. "Polygynie im Hochmittelalter im europäischen Vergleich," unpublished manuscript.

Sawyer, Birgit. "Valdemar, Absalon and Saxo. Historiography and politics in medieval Denmark." *Revue Belge de Philologie et d'Histoire,* LXIII (1985), 685–705.

———. "Samhällsbeskrivningen i Heimskringla." (Norwegian) *Historisk Tidsskrift* 72 (1993), 205–215.

———. Review of Anders Leegard Knudsen, *Saxostudier og rigshistorie på Valdemar Atterdags tid,* København 1994, (Norwegian) *Historisk Tidsskrift* 74 (1995), 120–22.

———. "Släkt, vänner och makt." *Krigføring i middelalderen; strategi, ideologi og organisasjon ca 1100–1400,* ed. Knut Peter Lyche Arstad. Oslo: Forsvarsmuseet, 2003, 74–109.

———. "The 'Civil Wars' revisited." (Norwegian) *Historisk Tidsskrift* 82 (2003), 43–73.

———. "Snorri Sturluson's two horses." *"Vi skall alla vara välkomna!" Nordiska studier tillägnade Kristinn Jóhannesson.* Göteborg: Meijerbergs institut för svensk etymologisk forskning, 2008, 37–53.

————. "Snorre Sturlason som balanskonstnär." *Collegium Medievale* 23 (2010), 33–57.

———— and Peter Sawyer. "Adam and the Eve of Scandinavian History." In *The Perception of the Past in Twelfth-Century Europe,* ed. Paul Magdalino. London & Rio Grande: Hambledon Press, 1992, 37–51.

————. *Medieval Scandinavia; from Conversion to Reformation circa 800–1500.* Minneapolis: University of Minnesota Press, 1993.

————. "The Making of the Scandinavian Kingdoms." In *Die Suche nach den Ursprüngen; von der Bedeutung des frühen Mittelalters,* ed. Walter Pohl. Wien: Verlag der Österreichischen Akademie der Wissenschaften, 2004, 261–70.

Sawyer, Peter. "The Background of Ynglingasaga." In *Kongsmenn og krossmenn; festskrift til Grethe Authén Blom,* ed. Steinar Supphellen. Trondheim: Tapir, 1992, 271–75.

Sigurdsson, Gísli. *The Medieval Icelandic Saga and Oral Tradition; a discourse on method.* Cambridge, Massachusetts: The Milman Parry Collection of Oral Literature, 2004.

Snorri Sturluson Edda: new complete translation by Anthony Faulkes. London & Melbourne: Dent, 1987.

Storm, Gustav. *Snorre Sturlassons Historieskrivning.* København, 1873.

Steblin-Kamensky, Michail. *The Saga Mind.* Odense: Odense University Press, 1973.

Strand (now Sawyer), Birgit. *Kvinnor och män i Gesta Danorum.* Ph.D., diss., University of Göteborg, 1980.

————. "Saxo's description of women compared with Snorre's." In *Saxo Grammaticus: a Medieval Author between Norse and Latin Cultures,* ed. K. Friis-Jensen. Copenhagen: Museum Tusculanum Press, 1981, 135–67.

Thorsteinsson, Björn *Island.* København: Politikken Forlag, 1985.

Tinlund Pande-Rolfsen, Mallika. "Kvinner og menn i *Heimskringla*; eggersken og kongen." Hovedoppgave i historie, NTNU, Trondheim 2002.

Weibull, Lauritz. *Nordisk historia; forskningar och undersökningar,* vol. 1. Lund: Natur och Kultur, 1948 (reprint of *Kritiska undersökningar i Nordens historia omkring år 1000. Lund: Lybecker,* 1911).

Whaley, Diana Edwards. *Heimskringla; an Introduction.* London: University College London, 1991.

————. "Heimskringla." In *Medieval Scandinavia: an Encyclopedia,* ed. Philip Pulsiano, New York & London: Garland, 1993, 276–79.

————. "Snorri Sturluson." In *Medieval Scandinavia; an Encyclopedia,* ed. Phillip Pulsiano. New York & London: Garland, 1993, 602–3.

Wood, Ian. "Christians and Pagans in ninth-century Scandinavia." In *The Christianization of Scandinavia,* ed. Birgit & Peter Sawyer, and Ian Wood. Alingsås: Viktoria Bokförlag, 1987, 36–67.

————. *The Merovingian Kingdoms 450–751.* London & New York: Longman, 1994.

Personal Names

Íslenzk Fornrit	Hollander	Modern forms[1]
Aðalráðr	Æthelred	Adalråd
Aðalsteinn	Æthelstan	Adalstein
Aðils	Athils	Adils
Agni	Agni	Agne
Álfhildr	Álfhild	Alvhild
Álfifa	Álfifa	Alfiva
Álfr	Álf	Alv
Áli	Áli	Åle
Allógiá	Allógiá	Allogia
Álof	Álof	Ålov
Alrekr	Alrek	Alrek
Arí	Ári	Are
Árni	Árni	Arne
Ása	Ása	Åsa
Ásbjörn	Ásbjorn	Asbjørn
Áshildr	Áshild	Åshild
Áslákr Fitjaskalli	Áslák Fittjaskalle	Aslak
Ástriðr	Ástrith	Astrid
Auði	Authi	Aude
Aun	Aun	Aun
Bera	Bera	Bera
Björn	Bjorn	Bjørn
Blót-Sveinn	Blótsvein	Blotsven
Búrisláfr	Búrizlaf	Burislav
Dómaldi	Dómaldi	Domalde
Dómarr	Dómar	Domar
Drífa	Drifa	Driva

---

[1] Mostly Norwegian equivalents.

Íslenzk Fornrit	Hollander	Modern forms[1]
Drótt	Drótt	Drott
Dyggví	Dyggvi	Dyggve
Egill	Egil	Egil
Einarr þambarskelfir	Einar Thambarskelfir	Einar Tambarskjelve
Eiríkr	Eirík	Eirik/Erik
Eiríkr	Eirík Bloodyaxe	Eirik Bloodaxe
Emundr	Emund	Emund
Erlingr skakki	Erling Skakki	Erling Skakke
Erlingr Skjálgsson	Erling Skjálgsson	Erling Skjalgsson
Eysteinn	Eystein	Øystein
Fjölnir	Fjolnir	Fjolne
Fólkviðr	Fólkvith	Folkvid
Freyja	Freya	Frøya
Freyr	Frey	Frøy
Friðleifr	Frithleif	Fridleiv
Froði	Fróthi	Frode
Frosti	Frosti	Froste
Gauthildr	Gauthild	Gauthild
Gautviðr	Gautvith	Gautvid
Geigaðr	Geigath	Geigad
Gilli	Gilli	Gille
Gísl	Gísl	Gisl
Grégóriús	Grégóriús	Gregorius
Grimkell	Grimkel	Grimkjell
Grjótgarðr	Grjótgarth	Grjotgard
Guðlaugr	Guthlaug	(Gudlaug)
Guðrøðr	Guthröth	Gudrød
Gyða	Gytha	Gyda
Gýlaugr	Gylaug	Gylaug
Hagbarðr	Hagbarth	Hagbard
Haki	Haki	Hake
Hákon	Hákon	Håkon
Hálfdan	Hálfdan	Halvdan
Haraldr Gormsson	Harald Gormsson	Harald Gormsson
Haraldr gráfeldr	Harald Greycloak	Harald Gråfell/Graycloak
Haraldr inn harðráði	Harald Sigurtharson	Harald Hardråde/Hardruler
Haraldr inn hárfagri	Harald Fairhair	Harald Hårfagre/Fairhair

Íslenzk Fornrit	Hollander	Modern forms[1]
Hárekr ór Þjóttu	Hárek of Thjótta	Hårek fra Tjøtta
Hildigunnr	Hildigunn	Hildegunn
Hildr	Hildir	Hild
Hjörvarðr	Hjorvarth	Hjorvard
Hringr	Hring	Ring
Hrólfr kraki	Hrólf Kraki	Rolv Krake
Hrœrekr	Hrœrek	Rørek
Hulð	Huld	Huld
Hulviðr	Hulvith	. Hulvid
Högni	Hogni	Hogne
Ingi	Ingi	Inge
Ingigerðr	Ingigerth	Ingegjerd
Ingjaldr	Ingjald	Ingjald
Ívarr inn viðfaðmi	Ívar the Widefathomer	Ivar Vidfamne/Widefathomer
Jörundr	Jorund	Jørund
Kálfr	Kálf	Kalv
Klerkón	Klerkón	Klerkon
Knútr	Knút	Knud
Knútr inn ríki	Knút the Powerful	Knud den mektige/ the powerful
Magnús	Magnús	Magnus
Magnús berfœttr	Magnús Barelegs	Magnus
Markús	Markús	Markus
Morstrstöng	Morstrotong	Mosterstong
Óðinn	Óthin	Odin
Óláfr	Óláf	Olav or Olof
Óttarr	Óttar	Ottar
Ragnhildr	Ragnhild	Ragnhild
Rögnvaldr	Rognvald	Ragnvald
Sigríðr	Sigrith	Sigrid
Sigrøðr	Sigröth	Sigrød
Sigurðr	Sigurth	Sigurd
Sigvatr	Sighvat	Sigvat
Skaði	Skathi	Skade
Skagi	Skagi	Skage
Skjolf	Skjálf	Skjålv
Skjöldr	Skjold	Skjold

Íslenzk Fornrit	Hollander	Modern forms[1]
Snœfriðr	Snœfrith	Snøfrid
Solveig	Sólveig	Solveig
Svási	Svási	Svåse
Sveigðir	Sveigthir	Sveigde
Sölva	Solva	Solva
Sölvi	Solvi	Solve
Þangbrandr	Thangbrand	Tangbrand
Þjóðólfr	Thjótólf	Tjodolv
Þóra	Thóra	Tora
Þorgnýr	Thorgny	Torgny
Þórir	Thórir	Tor/e
Þorleifr	Thorleif	Torleiv
Þormóðr	Thormóth	Tormod
Þyri	Thyri	Tyre
Tryggvi	Tryggvi	Tryggve
Tunni	Tunni	Tunne
Vanlandi	Vanlandi	Vanlande
Visburr	Visbur	Visbur
Yngvarr, Yngvi	Yngvar, Yngvi	Ingvar, Yngve
Öndurr	Ondur	Ondur
Önundr	Onund	Anund

PLACENAMES

Íslenzk Fornrit	Hollander	Modern forms[1]
Agðir	Agthir	Agder
Álfheimar	Álfheim	Alvheim
Austrlönd	Østlandet	Østlandet
Danavirki	Danevirke	Danevirke
Estland	Esthonia	Estland
Firðir	Fjord District	Fjordane
Fýrisvellir	Fyrisvellir	Fyrisvollene/Fyrisvallarna
Garðaríki	Gartharíki	Gardarike/Gårdarike
Gaulardalr	Gaular Dale	Gauldalen
Gautelfr	Gaut Elf River	Göta älv
Gautland	Gautland	Götaland
	Geirstathir	Geirstad
Guðbrandsdalir	Guthbrands Dale	Gudbrandsdalen
Haðaland	Hathaland	Hadeland
Hálogaland	Hálogaland	Hålogaland
Heiðmörk	Heithmork	Hedmark
Helsingjaland	Helsingjaland	Helsingland/Hälsingland
Hlaðir	Hlathir	Lade
Hólmgarðr	Hólmgarth	Holmgard/Holmgård
Hringaríki	Hringaríki	Ringerike
Hringunes	Hringuness	Ringnes
Hörðaland	Horthaland	Hordaland
Inney	Inner Eyin	Inderøya
Jamtaland	Jamtaland	Jemtland/Jämtland
Meðalhús	Methalhús	Melhus
Mœrr	Mœr	Møre
Naumdœlir	Nauma Dale	Namdalen

---

[1] Given in Norwegian and Swedish respectively.

Íslenzk Fornrit	Hollander	Modern forms[1]
Niðarhólmr	Nitharhólm	Nidarholm
Niðaróss	Nitharós	Nidaros
Njarðey	Njarthey	Nærøy
Næríki	Næríki	Närke
Orkadalr	Orka Valley	Orkdalen
Ranríki	Ranríki	Ranrike
Raumaríki	Raumaríki	Romerike
Raumdœlir	Raums Dale	Romsdal
Raumelfr	Raum Elf	Raumelv
Rogaland	Rogaland	Rogaland
Skáney	Skáney	Skåne
Sóleyjar	Sóleyar	Solør
Sparbyggjafylki	Sparbyggya District	Sparbyggja (fylke)
Stíklarstaðir	Stiklarstathir	Stiklestad
Strindafylki	Strinda District	Strindafylke
Svíþjðóð	Svithiód	Svitjod
Svölð(r)	Svólth	Svolder
Upplönd	Uppland	Uppland
Vágar	Vági	Vågen
Vendill	Vendil	Vendel
Veradalr	Vera Dale	Verdalen
Vermaland	Vermaland	Värmland
Vestra Gautland	West Gautland	Västergötland/West Götaland
Vík	Vík	Viken
Vingulmörk	Vingulmork	Vingulmark
Þelamörk	Thelamork	Telemark
Þjótta	Thjótta	Tjøtta
Þótn	Thótn	Toten